SOUTH KOREA'S WILD RIDE

Rozman, Terry, and Jo analyze the geopolitical shifts in South Korea's policies toward its neighbors and allies over the course of the Park Geun-hye and Moon Jae-in administrations into the early years of the Yoon Suk-yeol administration.

2013 to 2022 was a tumultuous decade in South Korean politics and especially in its foreign policy. Through two changes of its own presidency, as well as the rise and fall of the Trump administration in the United States, South Korea's politicians and diplomats have pursued different attempts at bridge-building with North Korea, before arriving at a more cautious and defensive position. The authors track the different attempts by Park and Moon to pursue increasingly optimistic attempts at reconciliation, and how they were thwarted by excessive idealism, domestic divisions, and broader great power rivalries—notably including Russia, China, and Japan.

An essential guide to understanding the trajectory of South Korean foreign policy, for students of Korean politics as well as scholars and policy practitioners.

Gilbert Rozman is Emeritus Musgrave Professor of Sociology at Princeton University, USA and Editor-in-Chief of the Asan Forum, South Korea.

Sue Mi Terry is Director of the Asia Program at the Woodrow Wilson Center for Scholars, Washington DC, USA.

Eun A Jo is a doctoral candidate at Cornell University and a fellow at the Institute for Security and Conflict Studies at George Washington University, USA.

SOUTH KOREA'S WILD RIDE

The Big Shifts in Foreign Policy from 2013 to 2022

Gilbert Rozman, Sue Mi Terry, and Eun A Jo

LONDON AND NEW YORK

Designed cover image: © Getty Images

First published 2024
by Routledge
4 Park Square, Milton Park, Abingdon, Oxon OX14 4RN

and by Routledge
605 Third Avenue, New York, NY 10158

Routledge is an imprint of the Taylor & Francis Group, an informa business

© 2024 Gilbert Rozman, Sue Mi Terry, and Eun A Jo

The right of Gilbert Rozman, Sue Mi Terry, and Eun A Jo to be identified as authors of this work has been asserted in accordance with sections 77 and 78 of the Copyright, Designs and Patents Act 1988.

All rights reserved. No part of this book may be reprinted or reproduced or utilised in any form or by any electronic, mechanical, or other means, now known or hereafter invented, including photocopying and recording, or in any information storage or retrieval system, without permission in writing from the publishers.

Trademark notice: Product or corporate names may be trademarks or registered trademarks, and are used only for identification and explanation without intent to infringe.

British Library Cataloguing-in-Publication Data
A catalogue record for this book is available from the British Library

ISBN: 9781032496405 (hbk)
ISBN: 9781032496399 (pbk)
ISBN: 9781003394792 (ebk)

DOI: 10.4324/9781003394792

Typeset in Times New Roman
by Deanta Global Publishing Services, Chennai, India

CONTENTS

Acknowledgments   *vii*

   Introduction   1

PART I
South Korea in the Hot Seat, 2013–2015

  1 A Trustpolitik Approach to Denuclearization and Unification   15
     Sue Mi Terry

  2 Managing Four Great Powers   28
     Gilbert Rozman

  3 Remaking of Conservative Narratives   42
     Eun A Jo

PART II
South Korea's High Stakes Diplomacy, 2016–2019

  4 Great Hopes, Shattered Dreams   56
     Sue Mi Terry

  5 Gambling on Great Power Relations   69
     Gilbert Rozman

6 Return of Progressive Narratives 90
   Eun A Jo

PART III
South Korea Sobers up, 2020–2022

7 Shift to the New Missile Age: 2020–2022 111
   Sue Mi Terry

8 Edging toward Bipolarity: South Korea's Regional
   Reorientation, 2020–2022 128
   Gilbert Rozman

9 Battling Partisan Narratives 155
   Eun A Jo

Index *175*

ACKNOWLEDGMENTS

As co-authors, we had the benefit of the bi-monthly "Country Report: South Korea," posted by The Asan Forum since 2013. It summarized and interpreted articles, leaving a detailed record of the clashing narratives from conservatives and progressives and of the issues at the center of media attention in each of the past ten years. We are grateful to the various authors who assembled the report, including at one stage Eun A Jo, and to James Kim of the Asan Institute, who oversaw their work. Our chapters appeared in The Asan Forum at six-month intervals until the beginning of 2023, from which they have been removed for publication of this book.

Gilbert Rozman, Sue Mi Terry, and Eun A Jo
March 2023

INTRODUCTION

The Republic of Korea stands at the intersection of great powers contending over the geopolitical architecture of Northeast Asia and beyond. It is not a passive bystander but an active force, eying ways to deter North Korean belligerence, striving to manage great power competition, and even shifting abruptly between conservative and progressive approaches to regional dynamics. From 2013 to 2022, three South Korean presidents left their distinct mark on international relations, not shying away from bold initiatives. The upshot was that no country created more of a stir about its potential to alter the regional trajectory than South Korea. Unlike the past image of it as a shrimp perched among four whales (great powers) and a shark (North Korea), it had chosen to flail in many directions, while each of the five others had shown an appetite for putting it high on their desired menu for the region. It stood at the fulcrum of regional dynamics and envisioned itself as the key to vital transformation. Over the course of a decade, Seoul led its region on a "wild ride."

Over this period, leaders and observers alike wondered about Seoul's shifting strategy. Would it steer the great powers toward a new regional architecture, as Park Geun-hye proposed? Would it tilt toward China, as many Japanese feared? Would its bold outreach to North Korea have a transformative impact, as Moon Jae-in anticipated? Would it undermine the US alliance strategy by cutting critical ties with Japan, as many Americans worried? The narrative kept changing, but the one constancy was a country located at the frontline of regional transformation.

For a decade, South Korea played the role of the swing state in the Indo-Pacific region. It was a role its leaders had edged toward in the 1990s, following normalization of relations with China and Russia. In 2003–08, Roh Moo-hyun had prematurely sought to make Seoul the "balancer" in Northeast Asia, but conditions were

DOI: 10.4324/9781003394792-1

not ripe. US dominance remained supreme, China was still inclined to bide its time, and the impression prevailed of North Korea as a collective challenge for five countries striving together for denuclearization. In the 2010s, Seoul found scant room to maneuver. Helpless to flex its muscles regionally under Lee Myung-bak (2008–2013), it aspired to a transformative role, first under the conservative president Park Geun-hye (2013–17), then under the progressive president Moon Jae-in (2017–22). Park and Moon took wildly different approaches to foreign policy, but the external environment overwhelmed both of their efforts. In the span of less than eight months in 2022, Yoon Suk-yeol steered foreign policy on a different track, largely accepting the reality of deepening bipolarization and North Korea's unwavering nuclear ambitions without renewing Seoul's quest to become a driver of change. Seoul was settling into a steadier course, even if the external environment had become more turbulent than anything seen since the end of the Cold War.

A series of concepts emboldened South Korea over a decade. There was the claim that it had the inside track because the central question before the region was diplomacy with North Korea. Seoul defined the challenge essentially as *reunification*, albeit recognizing an extended process. Then there was the notion that *middle powers* such as South Korea could play a significant role in regional politics. Many South Koreans felt that Seoul was displacing Japan as the "*poster boy*" combining economic dynamism, democratic vitality, and cultural appeal. Finally, a "*Goldilocks*" image had taken hold of Sino-US competition as severe enough to open space for third parties to maneuver but not so severe as to force taking sides. All of these assumptions, however questionable, raised hopes of Seoul enhancing its influence.

South Korean progressives exceeded conservatives in their expectations to play a pivotal role in Northeast Asia, given their greater optimism for diplomacy with North Korea and reluctance to rely so heavily on the United States. China catered to such thinking, insisting that Seoul already had committed itself to "balance" between Washington and Beijing, whether as a result of Park's "honeymoon" with President Xi Jinping or Moon's agreement to the "three no's" in his strategic policy in response to China's pressure over Terminal High Altitude Area Defense (THAAD)—a commitment that Seoul would not deploy any additional THAAD batteries, not integrate with the US missile defense system and not join a trilateral US-South Korea-Japan military alliance. Japan, for its part, feared that South Korea had chosen to tilt toward China. Thus, the notion that Seoul had been swinging away from the US camp had gained considerable currency in the years before 2022, even if its policy remained largely centered on Washington.

While a great deal has been written about the course of South Korean diplomacy during this critical decade, there has been insufficient attention paid to its changing overall strategy. Over a decade, we trace the dynamics of the Republic of Korea (ROK)-US-North Korean triangle, observe how great power dynamics impacted Seoul, and contrast the thinking of conservatives and progressives. This book looks at South Korean foreign policy through three distinct prisms: (1) a focus on the core triangle with the United States and North Korea; (2) an analysis of regional relations with China, Japan, and Russia; and (3) the divergent interpretations of foreign policy imperatives in conservative and progressive media.

This book divides the decade of 2013 to 2022 into three distinct periods. The authors do not separate, as is customary, the presidential tenures of Park Geun-hye, Moon Jae-in, and Yoon Suk-yeol as the key chronological guideposts. Instead, the focus is put on the switch from 2015 to 2016, when Park was continuing her abortive time in office, and on 2019 to 2020 when Moon was obliged to recalibrate after the breakdown of his obsessive pursuit of a breakthrough with North Korea. These transitions proved to be watershed developments for Seoul. New directions were set in 2013, 2017, and 2022 by incoming presidents. However, the impasses reached in 2015–2016 and 2019–2020 left the prior presidential strategies dead in the water. The critical transitions resulted largely from external developments. The North Korean nuclear test of January 2016 and the Hanoi Summit of February 2019 were key turning points that exposed the reality of great power relations. In both cases, the responses of great powers had a determining role in what Seoul decided to do.

The first period we cover—2013–2015—was transformative for three reasons: (1) it exposed the fallacies in Seoul's assumptions about the future of Northeast Asia more than any other period; (2) it brought to the fore assertive leaders in four countries whose policies would be consequential for Seoul; and (3) it transformed four bilateral relationships of great salience for Seoul: the Sino-US, Japan-US, Sino-Russian, and Russo-US relationships. Seoul stood at the intersection of these regional transformations. It was threatened by the exponential growth in North Korean military power, it was put in the crosshairs of China and Russia's ambitions to drive a wedge in US alliances, and it was targeted for recruitment by the US to join a policy of countering China's expansionist foreign policy.

The period from 2016 to 2019 saw the tottering end of Park Geun-hye's abortive tenure and the blustery start of Moon Jae-in's unprecedentedly bold presidency. It was a consequential era, but by late 2019 unshakable realities had taken center stage. Seoul could not escape its harsh, regional environment, and wishful thinking about what it could accomplish faced severe limits.

South Korea's foreign policy from 2020 to 2022 tilted increasingly toward the United States and its framework for regional and global affairs, as North Korea's threat grew more ominous. China also posed a growing challenge, leaving Seoul wary of stepping across a line inviting retaliation. Russia was moving into a hostile camp, but sending weapons to Ukraine appeared too risky, given Russian ties to North Korea. The clout of the *chaebol* left politicians wary of making some tough decisions about economic security, such as moving supply chains out of China. Political divisions and indecision at the top resulted in a degree of hesitation greater than in other US allies, especially Japan, which was America's foremost strategic partner in East Asia.

Where the following chapters cover 3–4-year periods, this introduction looks at the entire decade. The conclusion offers some broader interpretations for this decade of regional transformation. We start with the narrow ROK-US-DPRK triangle, turn next to the broader great power context, and conclude with the progressive-conservative divide, viewed across the decade as a whole.

Navigating the ROK-US-North Korea Triangle, 2013–2022

The different priorities of progressive and conservative presidents in both Seoul and Washington, along with changes in Beijing and in the broader international system all impacted the ROK-US-North Korean triangle during this period. The one constant was North Korea's determination to build its nuclear and missile forces and exhibit provocative behavior.

Five distinct periods can be discerned in Seoul's management of the triangle with Washington and Pyongyang over the decade 2013–2022. The first three years of Park Geun-hye's tenure were a time of conservative idealism. In contrast to periods of progressive rule, there was unwavering closeness to the United States and conditional outreach to North Korea. Yet, in common with the progressive eras, hopes were high for some kind of a breakthrough with the North. Park launched what she labeled *trustpolitik* to defuse tensions with North Korea, but, unlike her successor, she calculated that trust had to be built with China first, on the premise that the road to Pyongyang runs through Beijing. She further distinguished her approach by insisting that only a strong alliance with Washington would serve her diplomacy with both Pyongyang and Beijing. Park insisted that unification would be a "jackpot" and that Seoul was uniquely positioned to draw all countries active on the peninsula into a regional, cooperative architecture. Yet Kim Jong-un responded with acrimony, accusations, and threats. Efforts to gain alignment with Xi Jinping were unsuccessful too, in spite of numerous meetings and momentary optimism. His supposed favoritism toward Seoul largely stemmed from deep frustration with Pyongyang and was not indicative of a larger shift in China's North Korea policy. By the end of 2015, the Korean public was weary of Park's approach. Having strained relations with the United States, she needed to make adjustments in her remaining time.

The final year of Park's abortive tenure saw her abandon hope for change in North Korea and China. In 2016 Park abruptly altered her North Korea policy by adopting tougher measures, deploying the THAAD missile defense system and closing the joint Kaesong Industrial Complex. Under attack as her impeachment advanced, Park could not take the diplomatic initiative. When Moon Jae-in took office in 2017, he too was stymied for a time by Kim Jong-un's rocket barrage, Xi Jinping's demand that THAAD be withdrawn, and Trump's "fire and fury" rhetoric. Only at the end of the year was another phase of diplomacy coming into view, beginning with the "three no's" pledge to Xi and proceeding with Moon's overtures to Kim Jong-un at the opening of the Winter Olympics in South Korea.

The years 2018–2019 witnessed the peak of triangular ROK-US-North Korean diplomacy. The frantic season of summitry began in earnest in the spring of 2018: two summits between Trump and Kim, three inter-Korean summits between Moon and Kim, and a number of summits between Kim and other leaders, most notably with Xi and Putin. Yet, while the frenetic summitry of 2018–2019 defused the "fire and fury" crisis of 2017, it did not yield a denuclearization deal. The Moon administration would oversee the greatest decline of tensions on the peninsula since the end of the Korean War, but the rapprochement would not last. Indeed, there is reason to believe it had proceeded on false pretenses. North Korea's participation in the Pyeongchang Winter Olympics was followed by a March high-level South Korean delegation to Pyongyang, which then rushed to Washington claiming that Kim was willing to negotiate denuclearization and that he wished to meet with Trump. It remains an open question what exactly was discussed in Pyongyang. It is possible, or even probable, that the South Koreans liberally edited Kim's actual words about his willingness to give up nuclear weapons. As for Kim asking to meet with Trump, National Security Advisor John Bolton wrote that the Trump-Kim summit in Singapore was a "diplomatic fandango" which was "South Korea's creation," rather than a serious strategy on Pyongyang's part or Washington's. He even noted that it was a South Korean official who had suggested to Kim that he make the invitation to Trump. Moon was in the driver's seat of rapprochement during this period, but the ratcheting up of US-China confrontation relieved much of the pressure on Pyongyang as Beijing lost interest in cooperating with Washington. While sanctions remained in place, it became clear that the United States would not launch a preemptive strike on North Korea, further relaxing pressure on Kim. The Hanoi Summit between Trump and Kim ended shortly after it began. Expectations that diplomacy with the North could succeed were dashed. Hanoi spelled the end of Moon's illusion that he was in the driver's seat. Kim turned to China and Russia. Moon was left isolated—scorned by Kim Jong-un, pressured by Trump—and dealing with a public increasingly skeptical of his peace offensive.

The fourth period lingered into 2022, as Moon sought, against all odds, to revive diplomacy with Kim Jong-un, proposing an "end of war" declaration. Moon clung to the hope that he could make an improbable breakthrough with the North and was willing to be at odds with Washington if it meant making even incremental progress on inter-Korea relations. Kim rejected the Trump administration's insistence that any improvement of inter-Korean relations should take place in tandem with the pace of denuclearization. The Kim regime, meanwhile, made clear that it was not interested in Moon's attempt to preserve the Korean détente and began to dramatically escalate tensions. On June 16, 2000, the North blew up the "useless" inter-Korean liaison office located at Kaesong—a four-story office building that had cost the Moon administration $70 million to build and that served as a de facto embassy and communications channel. This was part of an escalating pressure campaign by the North intended to push Moon to split Seoul from Washington and ease sanctions. In a 2021 summit with Moon, President Biden emphasized that the US still supports inter-Korean engagement and that it was exploring diplomatic options for North Korea with South Korea and Japan. After Biden reaffirmed the 2018 Panmunjom Declaration and the Singapore Joint Statement, Moon held on until the very end to the hope that diplomacy could achieve denuclearization and peace on the peninsula.

The final period in this tumultuous decade saw Yoon Suk-yeol take office focused on enhancing deterrence. If Moon saw himself as a peacemaker, Yoon prioritized the alliance with the US, but his tougher stance did not pay dividends, either. Preoccupied with the Russian invasion of Ukraine and China's growing intransigence—and aware that it was nearly impossible to make any progress—Biden failed to come up with an effective North Korea policy. That left Biden and Yoon discussing with Prime Minister Kishida how to bolster extended deterrence. The Ukraine war raised the specter of North Korean aggression to a new level; it may have prompted the Kim regime to consider a new "first-use" nuclear doctrine, in addition to the development and operational deployment of tactical nuclear weapons, by taking a page straight out of Vladimir Putin's playbook. Kim likely took note of Putin's nuclear saber-rattling to deter NATO and the United States from direct involvement in the war and imagined that the United States also could be forced to back off on the Korean Peninsula with nuclear threats. Following the invasion of Ukraine, the international environment became even more favorable for North Korea, and China and Russia became less likely than ever to cooperate with the United States and its allies in strengthening sanctions on North Korea.

For the Seoul-Washington-Pyongyang triangle, the period 2020–2022 proved to be a watershed. Ever since the Sunshine Policy, Seoul had envisioned some breakthrough with Pyongyang capable of transforming this triangular setting. To do so was perceived as vital to peace and stability, to leverage in great power maneuvering, and to national identity as a middle power with potential to rise further. In 2020, following the breakdown of diplomacy, these hopes were left on life support. By 2022 they were relegated to history by the North's behavior and the deteriorating global environment.

Maneuvering among Great Powers over a Decade

Situated at the juncture of China, Russia, and Japan, the Korean Peninsula has therefore become of consummate interest to the United States, which remains intent on preventing any power from gaining dominance over Northeast Asia. During the Cold War, there was no room for maneuver in Seoul, given the strict division into two opposing camps and the continued, strong support of Beijing and Moscow for Pyongyang. Tethered to anti-communism, Seoul stuck closely to Washington, with its only other great power diplomacy of note consisting of cautious contacts with Tokyo, often under duress from its ally—and largely for economic needs, not geopolitical calculations.

Already at the beginning of the 1990s, three goals, which would define the entirety of the next three decades, had become paramount: solidifying democratization; seeking reunification or, at least, peaceful coexistence with North Korea; and diplomatic rebalancing to successfully manage four great powers intent on exerting influence on the peninsula. These goals were tested starting in 2013, and the results were a blow to the hubris that had taken root.

Seoul's ideal configuration for cooperation with the four great powers never wavered: (1) close alliance but also considerable autonomy from the United States that remained heavily invested in regional security; (2) strong economic partnership with China which was relegated to a secondary role on the peninsula; (3) a peripheral role for Russia able to benefit economically from peninsular transformation but not positioned to intercede strategically; and (4) a supportive role for Japan as a trading partner without a strong voice on peninsular affairs. Progressives put less emphasis on the US role, catered to China more actively, showed greater concern about keeping Russia on board, and were more insistent on treating Japan as a pariah.

Rallying the great powers behind a ROK diplomatic strategy for North Korea was a recurrent aim. Park Geun-hye made this her centerpiece in 2013–2015, and Moon Jae-in kept it as a supplement to his triangular approach to North Korea and the United States. Yet, the regional approach broke down by the start of 2016 and again by the start of 2020. When Pyongyang turned provocative with scant regard for diplomacy in the final years of Park and Moon's tenures, Seoul turned to Washington to address the resulting impasse.

Park's early years were characterized by approaches to the four powers active in Northeast Asia. South Korean thinking presumed that their country was an "autonomous ally" of the United States, not seeking separation but empowered to pursue its own diplomacy. It then conceived of its role with China as a "trust-building suitor," capable, as no other country was, of steering that country's diplomacy in Northeast Asia. With Japan, South Korea had chosen to be a "historical avenger," putting reconciling with its past before addressing shared security concerns. Russia was not neglected. South Korea envisioned itself as a "Eurasian liaison," despite problems from 2014 sanctions in response to Russian aggression in Ukraine. All of these expectations rested on a special, trusting relationship as the "gateway compatriot" to North Korea. Finally, as the essential building block in Seoul's diplomacy, it conceived of itself as the sole possible "regional architect."

In common with administrations led by progressives, Park hoped for a transformation of Northeast Asia into some type of new regional architecture, assuming Seoul could bridge Sino-US differences by building trust. The years 2013–2015 were remarkable for the mix of initiatives taken by Seoul to steer regional relations across Northeast Asia while holding tight to the alliance with the United States. It clung to aspirations for an autonomous, leading role in the way regional architecture, including the reorientation of North Korea, unfolded. Ambitions, however, clashed with South Korea's deepening marginalization owing to the actions of other countries.

Xi Jinping launched one initiative after another, Vladimir Putin pursued a "Turn to the East," Abe Shinzo proclaimed a "proactive" regional policy, and Barack Obama moved forward with his "rebalance to Asia." Somehow, Park insisted that these moves made it easier to press her own initiatives: a "honeymoon" with Xi, "Eurasian diplomacy" with Putin, strong pushback against Abe that garnered support at home and in China, and a tighter alliance with Obama. Added to the mix was not only *trustpolitik* with North Korea intent on rallying the four great powers behind her but also a "Northeast Asia Peace and Cooperation Initiative" (NAPCI) with a bold agenda to transform a sizable region. Hopes were kept alive that Seoul could corral the various powers into a joint strategy, overcoming the serious obstacles affecting their bilateral relationships.

The period 2013–2015 exposed the fallacies in Seoul's assumptions about the future of Northeast Asia, brought to the fore assertive leaders whose policies would be consequential for Seoul, and transformed bilateral relationships of great salience for Seoul: the Sino-US, Japan-US, Sino-Russian, and Russo-US relationships. Seoul stood at the intersection of regional transformation: on the front line of North Korea's exponential growth in threat capacity, in the crosshairs of China and Russia's ambitions to drive a wedge in US alliances, and next in line for the US agenda to join with Japan in forging a wide-ranging coalition.

South Korean wooing of China and Russia was rooted in the expected impact on North Korea, while its slighting of Japan was, on the contrary, premised on its likely marginality in policy toward the North. In 2013–15 Park strengthened bilateral ties with Beijing in large part to attain increased pressure on the Kim regime and acquiescence to her unification proposal, but despite numerous meetings with Xi, Park's extensive efforts to gain alignment with China on North Korea policy were unsuccessful. *Trustpolitik* was based on the premise that the road to Pyongyang went through Beijing. China's response proved disappointing. While Xi's gesture to visit Seoul first in 2014 elevated hopes for a change in China's overall North Korea policy, enthusiasm turned to disappointment when China remained opposed to including an explicit statement on the denuclearization of North Korea in the summit joint statement. What Park did not grasp was that Beijing's changed attitude stemmed from deep frustration with Pyongyang and was not indicative of a big shift in North Korea policy.

Park's *trustpolitik* approach had failed by the end of 2015. The situation then resembled the beginning of her term in 2013, when the North conducted a third nuclear test just weeks before her inauguration. In 2016 she was forced to abruptly alter her North Korea policy by adopting tougher measures, including deploying the controversial THAAD missile defense system and closing the joint Kaesong Industrial Complex that had been a lucrative venture for the North and served as the key symbol of inter-Korean rapprochement. Beijing and Moscow proved that they were on North Korea's side when they showered blame on Seoul. Moon managed with Trump's support to back away from Park's reversal, appealing to Kim Jong-un with more vigor and making concessions to Xi Jinping, but his gambit faced very long odds.

Moon had to deal with a US president intent on squeezing Seoul over host-nation support and trade, the onslaught of Chinese retaliation over the THAAD deployment, the decision by Kim Jong-un to go all out in missile testing, and unhappiness from Japan over Moon's intended backtracking on the "comfort women" agreement. Yet, within a year, Moon's diplomacy facilitated a series of high-profile summits that seemed to place South Korea back in the "driver's seat." This dramatic turnabout represented a "Hail Mary" approach to salvaging the illusion that Seoul could lead the way to resolving the security dilemmas of the era.

The fantasyland invoked by Moon stood no chance of being taken seriously without the approval of another leader who lived in a world of illusions, Donald Trump. Xi's silence was bought by Moon's approval of the "three no's" at a cost to South Korean sovereignty. Putin was offered the "New Northern Policy," but bided his time in disbelief that Moon would succeed. Abe stewed without any interest in Moon's "two-track approach"—disaggregating diplomatic and historical issues in conducting bilateral relations—given the new time bomb the Korean Supreme Court threw in the way of bilateral relations over the forced labor issue. These three leaders would not come into play for Moon's diplomacy for a year until the Moon-Kim-Trump relationship had run its course.

Kim blamed Moon for the failure in Hanoi and turned to his traditional allies, meeting with Putin in April and hosting Xi Jinping in June, and then refused to include Moon in his meet-and-greet with Trump at Panmunjom four months after the Hanoi Summit. Seoul could not escape its harsh, regional environment, and wishful thinking about what it could accomplish had severe limits.

China's failure to rein in Pyongyang, despite its continued nuclear provocations, raised questions about Beijing's intentions. Was it a facilitator or a spoiler in denuclearization or the broader inter-Korean peace process? In the conservative narrative, China always will be a spoiler despite sincere efforts to engage it; in the progressive narrative, China remained the crucial facilitator for any regional security problem. The prescriptive implications for Seoul's foreign policy once again diverged, with conservatives advocating strengthened military deterrence and progressives more energetic diplomatic engagement.

Three triangles were tested in Seoul's interactions with Beijing. South Korea and China could not agree on what to say about North Korea; Beijing prioritized other goals over the denuclearization of its long-time ally. Nor did they find common language on Japan, because Beijing was determined to drive a bigger wedge between the two US allies Seoul feared that acquiescence to Chinese language would be taken badly in Washington. China's opposition to trilateralism was unmistakable, and South Korea gave ground in the vain hope that it could win support for its North Korea policy.

No matter how justifiable Park's rejection of China and her accommodation of Japan were, the Moon camp found neither to be in the interest of their regional strategy. Accusing Park of half measures, they doubled down on rapprochement with North Korea coupled with caution about alienating China or accepting Japan's role in reordering the region. Progressives put all their eggs in the North Korean basket, despite Sino-US discord, Japan-US bonding, and new North Korean threats. Three forces defied Moon's efforts: the unbridgeable gap between the US and North Korea; a growing divide between China and the US; and the intensifying regional coordination between the US and Japan. The "end of war" declaration appeal to Washington in 2021 paralleled the NAPCI appeal to Washington in 2015. Each was a last-ditch effort to overcome rising isolation with the idea that US support was the only way to put Seoul back in the diplomatic lead.

Under Park and Moon, Seoul was reluctant to join the emerging US regional agenda. In 2022, Yoon leaped ahead on regional cooperation but left some room for wavering. Alliance relations became more wide-ranging and more multi-dimensional including economic security. Yoon agreed with Biden on a values-based and regionally oriented alliance, supporting trilateralism with Japan beyond anything seen earlier. The fact that China sided with Russia on the essentials of the Ukraine war and was seen as threatening Taiwan in a more urgent manner cast a chill on Sino-ROK relations. Despite Chinese appeals to join against US protectionism, Yoon generally accepted the US economic security agenda on civil-military dual-use items.

Moon had remained cautious about joining in Biden's plans for Indo-Pacific regionalism, the Quad, or trilateralism with Japan. More polarization risked his plans. In the face of the Ukraine war and Biden's new economic security appeals, Moon slowly yielded ground, but Yoon responded more decisively. Yet, given the US inclusion of traditional security, new economic security, and human rights in calculations about trade, it proved hard to achieve alignment with Washington. US regional goals drew more support from Yoon but not full endorsement. On security, Taiwan and the South China Sea received new notice, but the language was left vague. On economic or "comprehensive" security, the language was upbeat but details needed to be clarified. And on values, Yoon took a strikingly new tone while limits remained on how vocal to be. A lot was left for clarification on digital trade, supply chain resilience, and high-tech decoupling. Washington prioritized security over the economy more than Seoul did in dealings with China. Yet, Yoon kept drawing closer to the Biden agenda.

Given the US transition toward China and regional security, Seoul's response was slow and incomplete. Park in 2013–15 defied Obama's "pivot to Asia," in contrast to Abe's strong support. Before her limited accommodation in 2016 could take hold, Moon strove in 2017–19 to capitalize on a vainglorious US president to buck the tide of the reorientation to the Indo-Pacific, again losing ground to Japan's success in redefining the new, shared direction. In 2020–21 Moon yielded slowly and grudgingly before the unfolding of a full-fledged US regional agenda, leaving Seoul increasingly isolated. Yoon went a long way in a short time to refocus on Biden's regional themes, although his call for "mutual respect" with China left details unclear.

Parsing the Conservative-Progressive Divide over a Decade

Partisan divides over South Korean policy remained persistent throughout the decade. From Park's earlier courting of Beijing to Moon's reboot of the Sunshine Policy, partisans continued to weaponize foreign policy successes and failures to their domestic political advantage. By the time Yoon took office, the narrative landscape had once again shifted back in favor of the conservatives who mobilized around an alliance-centered foreign policy agenda. Yet, the specific contours of the geostrategic realignment remained hotly debated. The futures that conservatives and progressives envisioned for South Korea's role in the Indo-Pacific appeared to diverge drastically from one another.

To capture the points of contention in South Korea, the chapters on domestic politics take stock of the trends in partisan narratives on foreign policy issues, from 2013 to 2015, 2016 to 2019, and 2020 to 2022. In each period, the chapter compares editorials from five major newspapers in South Korea, which are often considered to represent partisan perspectives: *Chosun*, *Joongang*, and *Donga* for a conservative outlook and *Kyunghyang* and *Hankyoreh* for a progressive one. Partisan narratives of key events over time reveal a general polarization of public discourse on foreign policy but also a rare and enduring consensus on select issues—such as Japanese colonial history—that continue to unify the country. Four sets of debates are covered based on South Korea's most salient foreign policy challenges: North Korea, the US, China, and Japan.

In the first period, from 2013 to 2015, partisan narratives revealed a growing rift on North Korea, a surprising agreement on China, a veiled divergence on the United States, and a sustained consensus on Japan. Though partisans shared concerns about a "personalist" turn in Pyongyang, they proposed divergent policy prescriptions, with a progressive emphasis on tension reduction and a conservative focus on deterrence. Yet, partisan narratives still struck an unexpected accord on the necessity of China in Park's *trustpolitik*; most analysts took a wait-and-see approach as they looked out for reciprocal signs from Beijing. Meanwhile, tensions mounted over the nature and scope of South Korea's commitment to the US alliance. North Korea's missile and nuclear provocations continued to raise questions about the viability of US security assurances, while a deepening "strategic partnership" with China generated contradictions in South Korea's broader foreign policy. Finally—and unlike the typical divisiveness of their narratives—partisans proved increasingly unified on Japan. Amid a stream of controversies surrounding the Yasukuni visits, "comfort women," territorial disputes, and textbook revisions, both sides pushed for a more aggressive stance. By the time Park reached a "comfort women" deal at the close of 2015, public discourse on Japan had turned so antagonistic that a backlash was inevitable.

In the second period, from 2016 to 2019, partisan narratives witnessed a series of ruptures. Park's untimely exit and Moon's "candlelight" mandate meant that on various dimensions of foreign policy, Seoul made notable reversals, departures, and advances. The botched *trustpolitik* and the succeeding "Moonshine" generated some notable headlines as images of North Korea shifted from an untamed provocateur to a long-lost brother. Though Moon's activism helped escape the specter of war, its impact on the status of disarmament, denuclearization, and diplomacy remains hotly debated. Crucially, South Korea's alliance with the United States was more tested during this period than ever, as Trump's "America First" foreign policy in many ways dissolved existing ideological commitments. The most prominent evidence in this regard were the growing calls on the fringes of the conservative party for South Korea going nuclear because they saw US nuclear guarantees as no longer reliable. More predictable, perhaps, were the developments surrounding China and Japan. By faulting Park's authoritarian politics, Moon could seek foreign policy reversals in the name of "candlelight" rehabilitation: recovering relations with China over the THAAD dispute with his "three no's" compromise and asserting the procedural illegitimacy of South Korea's agreements with Japan on history issues.

In the third period, from 2020 to 2022, partisan narratives highlighted divisive conceptions of South Korea's shifting role in the region. Having inherited the THAAD crisis, Moon had been particularly attuned to Beijing's sensitivities and eschewed a more explicit engagement with the "Free and Open Indo-Pacific" framework of the United States and Japan. The worsening feud with Japan also made the multilateral framework politically untenable for Moon, who had made a "victim-centered" approach to history issues with Japan the cornerstone of his progressive legacy. Partisan narratives continued to polarize as conservatives—emboldened by Moon's diplomatic failures—campaigned on promises of strategic clarity, based on a rehabilitated alliance relationship with the United States and partnership with Japan. Indeed, there seemed to be little partisan consensus around the specific configurations of strategic clarity under Yoon and the appropriate nature and scope of South Korea's realignment.

Partisan narratives over these periods, and the decade as a whole, revealed the changing ambitions and lingering limitations of South Korean foreign policy. On the one hand, a growing sense of confidence was unmistakable. Progressives celebrated Moon's earlier diplomatic activism and pitted his balancing act—between the United States and North Korea, as well as between the United States and China—as a sign of Seoul's increasing leverage. Meanwhile, conservatives lauded Yoon's pledges of strategic clarity as indicative of a bolder and liberated foreign policy agenda. Many expected a closer realignment of South Korean foreign policy with the Indo-Pacific framework of the United States, and with it, a diminished priority given to diplomacy with North Korea and engagement with China. This also meant more concerted efforts to reconcile with Japan, with whom strained ties over history issues had impeded cooperation. Still, what Seoul's rise meant diverged among partisans based on their perceived foreign policy imperatives. For progressives, it signified greater autonomy in general and from the United States in particular. Seeing the Korean division as a historical byproduct of great power competition, progressives sought a more central and independent role in peninsular affairs. For conservatives, however, it implied an expanded role within the US-led regional order, centered around shared values.

On the other hand, the long-standing structural impediments to a more decisive realignment remained, including North Korean security issues, South Korean economic demands, and unsettled "history problems" with Japan. These were compounded by newer developments, such as the insular turn in American trade and technology policy and growing public support for indigenous nuclear weapons in South Korea, that further complicated Seoul's realignment decisions. How Yoon would overcome such hurdles was the focus of much public discourse in 2022.

Together, the partisan debates during this decade captured South Korea's wild ride. Partisans recognized a change was afoot with the onset of a new competitive age; whether and how Seoul would adapt to the changing global and regional environment was thus a recurring theme. In this sense, though newspaper editorials trailed contemporary events as they unfolded, they rallied two competing visions for South Korea's new role in the region and beyond—between an enduring progressive ideal of a critical balancer in the region and an emerging conservative one of a "pivotal state" in the maintenance of the liberal international order. For the time being, the latter took charge.

Conclusion

There is a curious mix of fatalism concerning how little South Koreans can determine their own destiny, given the environment they face, and overoptimism that their country, and it alone, holds the key to unlocking the vice gripping Northeast Asia. Such hopefulness dates from the late 1980s, brought to the political forefront by the 1987 democracy wave, the 1988 Seoul Olympics, and the 1989 end of the Cold War. It was made possible by a tendency to view North Korea through ideals of national reunification, China and Russia less in their own right than as levers to manipulate the North, and Japan in historically deterministic ways. Having lived in the world of Cold War bipolarity for four decades, Koreans were so enamored of diplomatic diversification that they hung onto it even when conditions had turned against this possibility. Hopes had been repeatedly deflated, as in 2009–10, 2016, and 2019—when reunification proved to be a fantasy and diversification a dead end leading to isolation—yet the lessons were slow to be learned.

Driving the shift were three forces: leadership changes, geopolitical factors, and a refocus on economic security—Yoon's ascent, Sino-US and Russo-US tensions, and a US technology agenda.

While the fundamentals of international relations in Northeast Asia did not change much over the decade—the Sino-US competition, the goal of denuclearization of North Korea, the US alliances with Japan and South Korea, the growing partnership of China and Russia—the imagery of South Korea's policy shifted dramatically from year to year.

1

A TRUSTPOLITIK APPROACH TO DENUCLEARIZATION AND UNIFICATION

Sue Mi Terry

Ever since the Korean War, North Korea has posed the most menacing and intractable national security challenge to the South. Every South Korean leader has tried to reduce the danger; few had any success to show for their efforts. Yet each new president saw no alternative but to keep trying. When Park Geun-hye began her presidency on February 25, 2013, the South was at one of the lowest points with the North. After the North had conducted two previous nuclear weapons tests during her conservative predecessor Lee Myung-bak's presidency, a third test was conducted just weeks before her inauguration. The North had also carried out two fatal attacks against South Korea in 2010 that left 50 South Korean casualties: The North Korean sinking of the South Korean corvette *Cheonan* on March 26 killed 46 South Korean sailors and the North Korean shelling of South Korea's Yeonpyeong Island on November 23 caused widespread damage and killed four and injured 19 South Korean civilians. No foreign policy decision would be more important than how Park dealt with North Korea after Lee's inability to revive talks.

Following the limited success of Lee Myung-bak's approach to North Korea, Park sought to tack back to the center on North Korea policy during her campaign. Several years earlier, in a 2011 *Foreign Affairs* article, when she was still a presidential candidate, Park laid out what would be her administration's new approach to North Korea. In the article, titled "A New Kind of Korea: Building Trust Between Seoul and Pyongyang," Park laid out the theoretical and historical context of what she called *trustpolitik* between the two Koreas. More of a catchy slogan rather than a detailed policy, it nevertheless signaled a desire to build confidence and mend fences with the North. She wrote that "lack of trust has long undermined attempts at genuine reconciliation between North and South Korea," and added that, "in order to transform the Korean Peninsula from a zone

DOI: 10.4324/9781003394792-2

of conflict into a zone of trust," South Korea should adopt a policy of *trustpolitik* and an "alignment policy," which should remain constant in the face of political transitions and unexpected domestic or international events.[1]

This policy would not mean adopting a middle-of-the-road approach, she explained; *trustpolitik* and the alignment policy would entail assuming a tough line against North Korea sometimes (e.g., if North Korea launched a military strike) and a flexible policy open to negotiations at other times (if North Korea took steps toward reconciliation).[2] In the aftermath of Park's *Foreign Affairs* article, which got a fair amount of attention, policymakers and academics across the political spectrum in both Seoul and Washington pondered how this concept would be translated into actual policy should she become president.

As she campaigned throughout 2012, Park continued to move beyond the more hawkish rhetoric of her fellow conservatives and her predecessor, under whom there had been little economic or diplomatic contact between the two Koreas. While she would not engage with the North to the same extent as the Kim Dae-jung and Roh Moo-hyun administrations did, unlike Lee, Park said she would not hold engagement hostage to prior actions by Pyongyang. Rather, she promised in her campaign that she would reengage with, and build trust with, the North by first taking small steps such as resuming the aid that Lee had suspended and exchanging humanitarian assistance for family reunions. If these steps proved successful, the two Koreas could move on to more ambitious, large-scale exchanges such as lifting of the sanctions implemented in response to the sinking of *Cheonan*, an expansion of economic processing zones such as Kaesong, and larger investments by South Korean firms. Park also suggested the possibility of a summit meeting with the new North Korean leader, Kim Jong-un. This kind of rhetoric was not without risk for her since, beyond the younger generation, a significant part of her voting base was still deeply conservative, with strong anti-communist ideological beliefs.

Putting flesh on the flagship policy of *trustpolitik* and alignment proved to be a complex endeavor, however. Despite Park's rhetoric of building trust between the two Koreas, the nuclear test two weeks before her inauguration—the first under its new leader—likely was Kim Jong-un's way of reminding the public and the incoming South Korean administration—as well as the Obama administration—about the negative consequences of adopting a hardline stance toward Pyongyang. The underground nuclear test followed weeks of threats from the North to build up its nuclear capacity and carry out an "all-out action of high intensity" and two months after the North sent a log-range rocket into orbit.[3] By conducting the nuclear test just days before Park came into the office, Kim had certainly grabbed Park's attention.

Park's North Korea Policy in 2013: *Trustpolitik*, Alignment, and Focus on China

When Park came into the office, inter-Korea tensions were growing. The latest nuclear test led to further expansion and tightening of international sanctions against the North. Two United Nations Security Council resolutions in quick succession—Resolution 2087 in January, which condemned the December 2012 satellite launch, and Resolution 2094 in March in response to the February 12 nuclear test—extended sanctions to more monitoring of North Korea's cargoes, diplomats, banks, and organizations. Banned luxury items were itemized for the first time. US B-2 stealth bombers were deployed for the first time as part of Foal Eagle, a joint military drill and training exercise with South Korea in March.

Predictably, the North responded to this pressure with further provocations, which included specific threats to abrogate both the 1953 armistice treaty, which ended the Korean War, and inter-Korean non-aggression pacts, as well as launching more missiles and ordering all of its missiles and artillery units to be on the "highest alert."[4] These actions were accompanied by cyberattacks on major South Korean broadcasters and banks and cutting off its last remaining military hotlines with Seoul in late March—a link that had been useful in running the North-South joint venture, the Kaesong Industrial Complex (KIC).

The KIC, located inside North Korea just across the demilitarized zone, was launched in 2004 and largely financed by the South to increase cooperation with the North. It was one of the last remaining points of engagement between the two Koreas, in which South Korean companies could manufacture their products using North Korean labor. For the North, it was an important source of hard currency. Income from the KIC generated around $90 to $120 million a year for North Koreans employed there, and shutting it down would affect the lives of 200,000 to 300,000 North Koreans living in the area.[5] The previous time the North cut the link was in 2009, when many South Korean workers were temporarily stranded in the North. The North perversely followed through its threat and subsequently withdrew all of its 53,000 workers from the KIC and declared that it would "temporarily suspend the operations in the zone and examine the issue of whether it will allow its existence or close it," making it clear that the final decision would depend on the Park administration's attitude going forward. The North was seeking to use the KIC's future to pressure Seoul for further political concessions.

Amid escalating tensions on the Korean Peninsula, Park continued her focus on building "trust" and the "alignment policy," calling for both strengthening deterrence and staying steady against Pyongyang while reiterating that the South remained open to dialogue. Park also continued to provide humanitarian assistance to North Korea. Park's *trustpolitik* approach led to some progress when the North and South eventually reached an agreement in mid-August, which led to the reopening of Kaesong and an agreement for further joint North-South economic activity. The door also opened to institutionalizing North-South activity through the creation of a joint committee to oversee the operations of firms located in the Kaesong Industrial Zone; it would be responsible for adjudicating disputes, protecting corporate properties, and working out compensation damages to such properties. More importantly, the Kaesong agreement stated that the two Koreas would actively work to attract foreign businesses to Kaesong. The Kaesong agreement also raised the possibility of reopening inter-Korean railway traffic.

Park's *trustpolitik* policy also had a China component, which was based on the premise that the road to Pyongyang ran through Beijing, and that improved relations with China could lead to improved relations with North Korea. Eager to make headway with China, Park visited Beijing in June, her second overseas trip following her visit to Washington in May. In 2013, the total trade volume between China and South Korea reached over $270 billion, which was more than the value of South Korea-US and South Korea-Japan trade combined.[6] Nevertheless, Park's decision to travel to China before going to Japan broke with precedent, reflecting not only the importance of China as South Korea's top trading partner but seeing China as an important partner in dealing with North Korea. Her predecessor, Lee Myung-bak, for example, had stopped in Japan on his way home after visiting the US as his first overseas destination in April 2008; his first presidential trip to China came one month later.

The subsequent Beijing-Seoul summit was seen as a high point in their bilateral relations, with Xi Jinping and Park displaying strong personal rapport for one another. With her self-taught Mandarin and interest in Chinese culture and philosophy, Park enjoyed a warm welcome in Beijing. Park even delivered a public speech entirely in Mandarin, and the Chinese and South Korean media gushed, calling it "an unprecedented honeymoon" period for China and South Korea.[7] Xi and Park pledged to expand cooperation in all sectors, including in Park's "trust-building" approach in dealing with North Korea.

After six months in office, the South Korean public approved of Park's approach toward North Korea; polls showed approval over 50% of her foreign policy approach, some showing over 60% and even 70% when it came to Park's North Korea policy.[8] Such a positive reception for Park's North Korea policy was due to the fact that the Park administration appeared to maintain a firm and resolute deterrence even in the face of unrelenting provocations from the North. Park also pulled off a series of successful diplomatic achievements through summit meetings with the US and China and Russia, as well as regional and global meetings. Park continued to travel for the rest of the year, participating in APEC, ASEAN, EAS, and G20 summits, while holding ten summit meetings abroad with leaders of other countries.

Moreover, *trustpolitik* as a concept managed to gain broad support because the public saw Park's policy as one that seemed realistic and balanced with a potential to overcome the South's difficult relationship with the North. The public saw it as representing a middle way between the unreciprocated generosity of Kim Dae-jung and Roh Moo-hyun's Sunshine Policy of 1998–2007 and the subsequent hardline policy taken by Lee Myung-bak, which led to a worsening of inter-Korean relations. Key global leaders and experts, including then-United Nations Secretary General Ban Ki-moon, gave their enthusiastic endorsement, which had been reaffirmed in Park's meetings with both US President Barack Obama and Chinese President Xi Jinping.

Throughout the remainder of the year, Park reiterated that the goal of *trustpolitik* was to transform South Korea's policy toward North Korea. Whereas the policies of the past administrations had gone from one extreme to another, Park's approach was presented as a more effective and balanced combination of competing policy options. The public broadly supported the idea of pressure and dialogue, deterrence and cooperation, while separating humanitarian issues from those related to politics and security. It was a policy that promised the South to be strong when there was a need to be firm against the North yet flexible when there is a need to be more receptive. Yet Park's North Korea policy bore little fruit as 2013 came to an end beyond the reopening of KIC. Of course, the problem was that the KIC issue was only temporarily resolved. Having shut down the KIC once, there was no mechanism that insured that the North would not do it again.

In late September 2013, the North abruptly canceled planned family reunions, accusing South Korea's conservatives of a "reckless and vicious confrontational racket."[9] The North had a laundry list of grievances, including accusing the Park government of provoking the North by telling South Korean people that Pyongyang had been forced to make its recent conciliatory gestures because of Park's strong stance. The North also protested over a South Korean scandal involving a leftist politician who was accused of plotting to overthrow the Seoul government in case of a conflict with the North, calling it a "witch hunt" to crack down on people championing cooperation with the North.[10] In typical fashion, the North sought to shift the onus of resumption of the reunions back on the South, claiming that the visits were to be postponed until "a normal atmosphere is created" for constructive dialogue. It soon became evident that the family reunions were part of the North Korean *quid pro quo* for the reopening of Kaesong. Kaesong's operations had resumed, but with the family reunions in abeyance, the Park administration was left empty-handed. The North also announced that it would postpone talks on reopening tours for South Koreans at Mount Geumgang—the location where a South Korean tourist was shot by a North Korean soldier in 2008 for allegedly walking into an off-limits area.

By the time 2013 ended, the only other positive North Korea-related news occurred during Park's second meeting with Russian President Vladimir Putin in November, when she hosted him in Seoul. The two leaders agreed to increase economic cooperation, such as a Russian-led project to develop a North Korean border port as a gateway for exports at the end of the 54-kilometer Rajin-Khasan railway link from North Korea to Siberia. Optimism about improving relations with North Korea had faded. Kim closed the year by shocking the world with the brutal execution of his uncle, Jang Song-taek. Jang was the second most powerful man in North Korea, presumed mentor to Kim, and the main intermediary with China. Jang's execution fueled speculation about further strains in Beijing-Pyongyang relations.[11]

Park's North Korea Policy in 2014: Pivot to Unification

Early in 2014, it became evident that Park had added Korean unification as a central tenet of her North Korea strategy. As she sought a *trusptolitik* approach toward the North to defuse tensions and improve bilateral relations, she also made unification a tangible short-term goal, rather than a long-term, theoretical objective as her predecessors had done. In his January 1 New Year's address, Kim Jong-un announced that regarding inter-Korean relations, "new progress must be made for the unification of the motherland," in accordance with the wishes of his father and grandfather. In her January 6 news conference, Park took this opportunity to promote her vision of unification, stating that "building the foundation for an era of unification" is one of the two major tasks of her administration in 2014. Calling unification a "jackpot" (*daebak*) for Korea, she declared that the key policy task was "laying a foundation for peaceful unification." She said she would promote policies to strengthen humanitarian aid and expand civic exchanges.

Park's two-track approach involved implementing a new "Tailored Deterrence Strategy" in military exercises with the US and conducting South Korea's own missile tests, while calling for "trust-building" initiatives and pushing for unification. When she visited the former East German city of Dresden in March, she further expanded on the theme of unification while seeking to regularize family reunions and expand humanitarian aid, economic cooperation, and inter-Korean integration. In an address titled, "An Initiative for Peaceful Unification on the Korean Peninsula," she talked of the need for the Koreans to tear down barriers to unification as the Germans tore down the Berlin Wall. She talked of the two Koreas tearing down a "wall of military confrontation," "a wall of distrust," and a "socio-cultural wall" that divides the Korean Peninsula.[12]

She vowed to find concrete ways to promote these objectives, beginning with allowing regular reunions for separated families. She also reiterated wanting to expand humanitarian assistance to North Korean people, providing health care to pregnant mothers and infants, and building infrastructure in areas such as transportation and telecommunication. She talked of collaborating with the North to set up multi-farming complexes that support agriculture and forestry. She floated the idea of combining South Korean capital and technology with North Korean resources and labor.[13]

The reaction to Park calling unification a "jackpot" was mixed in South Korea. There was a clear generational and ideological divide in the public's responses. Skepticism was more pronounced among the younger generation: 47.6% of the public who were polled agreed with Park's Dresden statement and proposal, while 37.4% disagreed. 65.5% of self-identified conservatives agreed with Park while only 37.8% of those who identified themselves as progressives did; progressives younger than 40 years reacted most negatively, concerned, as they were, with the financial implications of unification.[14] 75% of respondents in their 20s were pessimistic about the personal financial implications of unification.[15]

Predictably, Park's unification proposal was met by a vitriolic response from Pyongyang, which rejected Park's Dresden Declaration, calling it "an unpardonable insult" and declaring that Seoul should stop having unrealistic dreams about unification.[16] The Kim regime sought to portray Park's unification efforts as attempts to push "unification by absorption." A statement published by the Korean Central News Agency argued that the venue of Park's speech—Dresden, Germany—testified to Park's "impure ulterior motive" since Germany is a country that was unified by absorption. The press statement went on to insist that the "Dresden Declaration" is an "anti-reunification nonsense" "overlooking the interests of the country and nation."[17]

From Kim's perspective, this reaction could be foreseen. It is hard to avoid the obvious question: Since any discussion of unification would realistically presume that the peninsula would end up a capitalist democracy, why would the Kim regime negotiate itself out of existence? The North's responses to Park's proposals were thus to continue to escalate tensions throughout the year. Although the North allowed the postponed family reunions to finally take place in February—the first since November 2010—it responded to the annual US-ROK military exercises held from February through April and Obama's visit to Seoul in April with more missile launches, along with threats to conduct a "new form" of nuclear test. The North threatened Seoul with a "nuclear disaster" while calling for Seoul to take practical steps to end "all hostile military acts." In April, the North even descended to unprecedented levels of personal insult by describing Park as a "repulsive wench" and "crafty prostitute," who had failed to marry or bear children.[18] It then lobbed off more than 500 artillery rounds offshore, landing more than 100 in South Korea's waters. In early May, new commercial satellite imagery showed that the North was expanding its main rocket-launching site and testing engines of what is believed to be its first road-mobile intercontinental ballistic missile.

Park's response was to continue her "principled and effective two-track approach" of pressure and dialogue for denuclearization, now pushing for unification, while continuing to ask China for help. Park and Xi met again on the sidelines of the Nuclear Security Summit in the Netherlands on March 23, which was followed by telephone talks a month later. On April 10, China's Premier Li Keqiang and South Korea's Prime Minister Jung Hong-won met on the sidelines of the Boao Forum for Asia in Hainan, while foreign ministers Wang Yi and Yun Byung-se held periodic telephone talks on peninsula tensions. In early July, Xi visited Seoul, marking the first time that a Chinese leader visited Seoul without having first visited Pyongyang. In contrast, in the almost three years since assuming power, Kim had yet to host Xi or visit China himself. Beijing-Pyongyang contacts had been limited to low-level visits, reflecting continued strain in the bilateral relationship. The highest-level meeting in early 2014 occurred between Xi and North Korean President Kim Yong-nam on the sidelines of the Sochi Winter Olympics.

Yet, while the unprecedented Chinese gesture to visit Seoul first elevated South Korea's hopes for a change in China's overall North Korea policy, enthusiasm quickly turned to disappointment when China remained opposed to including an explicit statement on the denuclearization of North Korea in the summit joint statement. There appeared to be a clear misperception on Park's part vis-à-vis China—despite a honeymoon period between Seoul and Beijing fostered by Park and Xi, and despite the unprecedented summits and gestures of friendship, South Korea's expanding ties with China did not ultimately signify an emerging shift in Beijing's North Korea policy.

For South Korea, China had become an important economic partner, and cultivating and deepening ties with China had become an important policy objective. But another major impetus for Park to engage with China was that she badly needed China for her North Korea policy: Park sought Chinese cooperation in resolving the nuclear standoff with North Korea and achieving unification, and Xi's chilly relations with Kim Jong-un provided an opening for warmer relations between Seoul and Beijing. But what Park did not grasp at the time was that Beijing's changed attitude largely stemmed from its deep frustration with Pyongyang and was not indicative of a larger shift in Beijing's North Korea policy. Rather, China's strategy seemed to have been to take advantage of the then relatively weak Sino-North Korean relationship to win over South Korea—without giving up its core geostrategic interest in North Korea. Thus, despite Park's efforts to secure cooperation with China on a strategy that emphasized both pressure and dialogue, tensions with the North continued unabated throughout the year, and China proved to be little help on the North Korea front.

By 2014, the North had conducted three nuclear tests and over 100 missile tests and made substantial progress in making nuclear weapons smaller and lighter. South Korea's Defense White Paper in 2014 stated that North Korea had achieved miniaturization and estimated that its nuclear bombs could be loaded onto missiles. In October, there was a brief mini-détente when the two Koreas held their highest-level talks in years; the North sent a high-caliber delegation and a team of athletes to the South to attend the Asian Games. But yet again, although the two sides agreed to more meetings later in October or November, North Korea backed off, citing activists' leaflet campaigns in South Korea. By November, North Korea threatened to conduct a fourth nuclear test after the UN Human Rights Committee referred North Korea to the International Criminal Court for human rights abuses.

Park's North Korea Policy in 2015: Doubling Down on Trustpolitik and Unification

The year 2015, which marked the 70th anniversary of the division of the Korean Peninsula and liberation from Japanese occupation, began with a bit of hope that North Korea sought to resurrect inter-Korea ties. Kim Jong-un declared in his 2015 New Year's Day speech that it was possible to "resume the suspended high-level contacts and hold sectoral talks if the South Korean authorities are sincere in their stand towards improving inter-Korean relations through dialogue."[19] Kim added that "there is no reason why we should not hold a summit meeting if the atmosphere and environment for it are created," while insisting that a prerequisite for dialogue would be ending the US-ROK combined military exercises.[20] The North Korean deputy ambassador to the United Nations also suggested that "many things were possible" if the joint military exercises were cancelled.[21]

When the joint exercises were not cancelled, any hope of improved inter-Korean relations and a diplomatic resolution dissolved. The Kim regime shifted from its temporary charm offensive and threatened to wage a "merciless, sacred war" against the US. As for the South, the North declared that it was "only too apparent that no major change or transformation could be achieved in inter-Korean relations even if we were to sit down a thousand times with such government officials."[22] Pyongyang conducted military exercises designed to attack a US aircraft carrier with Kim present. On February 6, it test-fired an anti-ship cruise missile on its newly displayed stealth fast patrol craft and, two days later, fired five missiles off the coast of Wonsan toward the East Sea.[23] When the US-ROK joint exercises commenced on March 2, the North fired two short-range ballistic missiles in protest. On March 3, Li Soo-yong, North Korea's minister of foreign affairs, expressed an intention to launch a preemptive nuclear strike against the US in an address at the UN Human Rights Council in Geneva.[24]

Park's response was to continue to carry on the previous year's unification campaign as the showpiece of her North Korea policy. She doubled down on her dual-track approach of deterrence and engagement. The government said early in the year that it was seeking to spur efforts in 2015 to bring about reunification by establishing a legal and institutional framework and holding joint economic and cultural events. Indeed, various measures were submitted to Park jointly by the ministries of unification, foreign affairs, national defense, and patriots and veteran affairs to prepare for unification.[25] Various policy ideas were promoted: setting up inter-Korean cultural institutes in both Seoul and Pyongyang, forming a joint committee to run joint cultural, arts, sports, and religious events marking the 70th anniversary of liberation, test-running a railway from Seoul to Sinuiju or Rajin via Pyongyang, building joint economic infrastructure and intensifying cooperation in people's livelihoods, environment, and culture. As Unification Minister Ryoo Kihl-jae said at a news conference, the Park government had set 2015 as the year "to usher in an era of unification, and our goal is to make substantive progress in unification preparations."[26] The Park government further vowed to intensify collaboration, partnering with the private sector and the international community to push the unification agenda.

Despite Park's calls for the North to accept her offer of "any form of dialogue" to work toward unification, North Korea's response was to continue making a series of demands, including that Seoul lift sanctions that had been in effect since May 24, 2010, following North Korean attacks on the *Cheonan* and Yeonpyong Island. It also continued to launch ballistic missiles. After testing five short-range ballistic missiles in early February, in early May it successfully launched a ballistic missile which it claimed came from a submarine. (Experts later assessed that the missile was launched from a submerged barge.)[27]

In August, a potential crisis loomed when North Korean soldiers sneaked across the DMZ and planted landmines on the South Korean side, maiming two South Korean soldiers. In response, Seoul resumed propaganda broadcasts along the DMZ, which led to an exchange of artillery fire, raising the potential for a broader military clash. Seoul and Pyongyang were able to subsequently reach a vaguely worded agreement to defuse tensions, which allowed both to claim they had achieved what they wanted.

The Park administration agreed to turn off the loudspeakers that had angered Pyongyang and promised it would not resume the broadcasts "unless an abnormal case occurs."[28] It then tried to showcase this agreement as a win for South Korea, even though the North's expression of regret fell short of full-throated apology. Park's defense minister, Kim Kwan-jin, called the North's willingness to express regret "very meaningful."[29] The Kim regime, meanwhile, agreed to suspend its "quasi-state of war" and allowed resumption of separated family reunions.[30] The North's subsequent decisions to engage in high-level talks with South Korea and send Kim Jong-un's personal girl band, Moranbong, to perform in Beijing appeared to suggest that improvement in inter-Korean relations before the end of the year might be possible. Meanwhile, Park continued to press on with her efforts to get Beijing on board with her North Korea policy. In September, Park traveled to Beijing to commemorate the 70th anniversary of the end of WWII in an event boycotted by most Western leaders. Park was criticized for attending the parade extolling Chinese military forces, particularly given that China intervened on behalf of the North in the Korean War.

Despite Park's efforts, by the end of 2015 inter-Korean relations were yet again back to where they had been at the end of 2013 and 2014, with little progress made with Pyongyang and with little help from Beijing. On November 28, North Korea tested a ballistic missile from a submarine, although the test failed. On December 8, the U.S. Department of the Treasury announced additional designations under Executive Orders 13551 and 13382, which included the State Department designating North Korea's Strategic Rocket Force for engaging in activities to build delivery vehicles capable of carrying WMDs. Over the weekend of December 12–13, North and South Korean vice-ministers met at the Kaesong joint economic venture to develop a plan to reduce military tensions and expand cooperation. The talks floundered over the inability to reach consensus on an agenda, and the North declared that "prospects of North-South relations became even bleaker."[31] At the same time, Kim abruptly canceled the scheduled performances of the Moranbong pop band, which was already in Beijing, due to "communication issues."[32] On December 21, North Korea closed the year by testing yet another ballistic missile from a submarine. The stage was now set for the North's fourth nuclear test, which would come at the beginning of a new year—on January 6, 2016.

Conclusion

President Park Geun-hye came into the presidency pledging a policy of *trustpolitik* and alignment designed to promote inter-Korean reconciliation through principled engagement while holding North Korea to account for misconduct. Foreign Minister Yun Byung-se called it "a vision" and a "philosophy" that was "neither a utopian idealism that shies away from realpolitik nor a naïve political romanticism."[33] It was presented as a reasonable and principled combination of carrots and sticks, where Seoul would stick to a consistent stance, urging Pyongyang to respect international standards and norms and abide by its promises or pay a penalty for broken promises. To advocates of this approach, Kim's decision to resume operations of the Kaesong Industrial Complex after a five-month shutdown in 2013 was a concrete example that this approach was working. Park's steadiness in the face of various fluctuations and machinations by the North, including the Kaesong shutdown and resumption, initially won her over 50 percent approval by the public.

But the public support soon faded. By the end of 2015, the public was weary of Park's approach, which did not result in any tangible progress with North Korea, and the public questioned the effectiveness of Park's "middle of the road policy." As Korea University Professor Shin-hwa Lee put it in 2014, if Park's North Korea policy "takes the safe road of not rocking the boat, she needed to face criticism, as Obama has, of being too wary and ineffectual in forging a breakthrough for rocky inter-Korean relations."[34] Doubts about Park's North Korea policy spread even within her own party. Some in her party had gone further than supporting strengthening of sanctions against the North, saying that it might be time for Seoul to consider asking the US to bring back tactical nuclear weapons, which it withdrew from the South in the early 1990s.[35]

Park made preparing to unify the two Koreas the centerpiece of her administration's approach to North Korea. As South Korean scholar Yoo Ho-yeol put it, Park envisioned three steps: (1) normalization of North-South relations through a trust process; (2) progression from "small unification" to "big unification"; and (3) realistic preparation for unification through capacity strengthening.[36] Perhaps more than any Korean President since Syngman Rhee, Park had sought to mobilize Korean public opinion and international support for her vision of a reunified Korea, emphasizing the benefits and downplaying costs. The Kim regime was not only unwilling to reciprocate Park's vision with positive actions, but it responded with acrimony, accusations, and threats. Park strengthened bilateral ties with Beijing in large part to increase pressure on the Kim regime and win acquiescence to her unification proposal, but despite numerous meetings with Xi, Park's extensive efforts to gain alignment with China on policy toward North Korea were ultimately unsuccessful too.

By the end of 2015, Park's approach had failed to deter the Kim regime from its decades-long quest to develop, expand, and refine its nuclear and missile arsenal.

Park had few options left. She could continue to try to engage an erratic regime that had gone so far as to call her a prostitute and had not agreed to discuss the possibility of nuclear disarmament in any future talks. Or she could shift to a more confrontational approach, pushing for more sanctions and embracing an American missile defense system. With little prospect of persuading Kim Jong-un or even Xi Jinping, as 2015 closed, the only question was to what degree she would abandon her attempts to engage with Pyongyang.

Park had come to office with high hopes of making progress with the North by pursuing a more balanced policy than her predecessors. While her efforts were worthwhile, they had failed. After nearly three years in office, she had little to show for her vaunted forays into *"trustpolitik."* Trust between the two sides was as low as ever—and in the process, with her aggressive outreach to China (as epitomized by her attendance at Beijing's Victory Day celebration), Park had also strained relations with the United States. Now the question she had to confront was what adjustments to make in her remaining time in office.

Notes

1. Park Geun-hye, "A New Kind of Korea: Building Trust Between Seoul and Pyongyang," *Foreign Affairs*, September/October 2011.
2. Ibid.
3. Chico Harlan, "In North Korea, Seismic Activity Detected Near Nuclear Test Site," *The Washington Post*, February 12, 2013.
4. Choe Sang-hun, "North Korea Calls Hawaii and U.S. Mainland Targets," *The New York Times*, March 26, 2013.
5. Choe Sang-hun, "Korean Factory Complex Is Shut Down by the North," *The New York Times*, April 8, 2013.
6. Trade Summary for China 2013, World Integrated Trade Solution, World Bank, https://wits.worldbank.org/CountryProfile/en/Country/CHN/Year/2013/Summarytext.
7. See for example, Ling Yuhan, "Xi, Park Share Nuke Position," *Global Times*, June 28, 2013; Ju-min Park, "South Korea's Park Set to Charm China, Show up the North," Reuters, June 23, 2013.
8. "6 Months on, Park Rides High," *Joongang Daily*, August 22, 2013. See also surveys conducted by the Asan Institute for Policy Studies, "Evaluating President Park Geun-Hye's Foreign Policy in its 1st Year," Issue Briefs, the Asan Institute for Policy Studies, February 24, 2014.
9. "North Korea Blames South, Cancels Family Reunions," CNN, September 21, 2013.
10. Choe Sang-hun, "North Korea Postpones Family Reunion Programs," *The New York Times*, September 21, 2013.
11. Zhu Feng and Nathan Beauchamp-Mustafaga, "Purge of Jang Song-Taek and its Impact on China's Policy Toward North Korea," in Gilbert Rozman, ed., *Joint US-Korea Academic Studies: Asia's Slippery Slope: Triangular Tensions, Identity Gaps Conflicting Regionalism, Diplomatic Impasse Toward North Korea* (Washington, DC: Korean Economic Institute, 2014), pp. 255–262.
12. Shin Yong-bae, "Full Text of Park's Speech on N. Korea," *The Korea Herald*, March 28, 2014.
13. Ibid.
14. "Evaluation President Park Geun-Hye's Foreign Policy in its 1st Year," Issue Brief, the Asan Institute for Policy Studies, February 24, 2014.

15 Ibid.
16 "N. Korea Blasts Park for her Proposals on North," *Yonhap News Agency*, April 1, 2014.
17 Lee Ji-sun, "North Korea Rejects Dresden Proposal," *Kyunghang Sinmun*, April 13, 2014, https://www.khan.co.kr/politics/north-korea/article/201404132155165.
18 Tania Branigan, "North Korea Labels South's President as 'Crafty Prostitute' after Obama Visit," *The Guardian*, April 27, 2014.
19 "Kim Jong Un's New Year Address," *KCNA*, January 1, 2015.
20 Ibid.
21 Hong So Yeon, "NK's UN Deputy Ambassador Urges Suspension of Military Drills," *Daily NK*, January 14, 2015.
22 "US Imperialists Will Face Doom: DPRK NDC," *KCNA*, February 4, 2015; "Propaganda Balloon Launches Again Presenting Obstacle to Inter-Korean Dialogue," *The Hankyoreh*, January 9, 2015.
23 Joseph S. Bermudez, Jr., "The Korean People's Navy Tests New Anti-ship Cruise Missile," *Military Affairs*, February 8, 2015.
24 *Donga Ilbo*, March 4, 2015, p. A06.
25 "Let's End the Era of Division and Open Up the Era of Unification," Joint Press Release Issued by the Ministry of Unification, Ministry of Foreign Affairs, Ministry of National Defense, and Ministry of Patriots and Veterans Affairs, January 19, 2015.
26 Shin Hyon-hee, "Seoul to Enact Unification Law," *The Korea Herald*, January 19, 2015.
27 Joseph S. Bermudez, Jr., "Underwater Test-Fire of Korean-Style Powerful Strategic Submarine Ballistic Missile," *38 North*, May 13, 2015.
28 Anna Fifield, "After Deal, North and South Korea Try to Work Together—But for How Long?" *The Washington Post*, August 26, 2015.
29 "North, South Korea Reach Agreement to End Standoff: North Korea Agreed to End the 'Semi' State of War it had Declared," Reuters, August 24, 2015.
30 Ibid.
31 Bruce Klingner, "Look Out for North Korean Nuclear Test as Isolation Grows," *The National Interest*, December 16, 2015.
32 Edward Wong, "North Korean Band Abruptly Leaves China, Its Concerts Canceled," *The New York Times*, December 12, 2015.
33 Yun Byung-se, "Park Geun-hye's Trustpolitik: A New Framework for South Korea's Foreign Policy," *Global Asia*, September 16, 2013.
34 Shin wha-Lee, "South Korea's Search for a New Diplomatic Strategy Toward North Korea," in Gilbert Rozman, ed., *Joint US-Korea Academic Studies: Asia's Slippery Slope: Triangular Tensions, Identity Gaps Conflicting Regionalism, Diplomatic Impasse Toward North Korea* (Washington, DC: Korean Economic Institute, 2014), p. 233.
35 See, for example, Chung Mong-joon, "Thinking the Unthinkable on the Korean Peninsula," *Issues & Insights*, Vol. 14, No. 2 (January 24, 2014). https://pacforum.org/wp-content/uploads/2014/01/issuesinsights_vol14no2.pdf
36 Ho-yeol Yoo, "South Korea's Unification Policy and Prospects," in Gilbert Rozman ed., *Joint US-Korea Academic Studies: Asia's Uncertain Future: Korea, China's Aggressiveness, and New Leadership* (Washington, DC: Korea Economic Institute of American, 2013), p. 211.

2
MANAGING FOUR GREAT POWERS

Gilbert Rozman

Succeeding another conservative, President Park Geun-hye was intent on seizing the initiative despite the difficult environment she faced as four leaders geared up for more active regional policies. Xi Jinping launched one initiative after another, Vladimir Putin pursued a "Turn to the East," Abe Shinzo proclaimed a "proactive" regional policy, and Barack Obama moved forward with his "rebalance to Asia." Park insisted that these moves made it easier to press her own initiatives: a "honeymoon" with Xi, "Eurasian diplomacy" with Putin, strong pushback against Abe that garnered support at home and with China, and a tighter alliance with Obama. Added to the mix was not only Park's *trustpolitk* with North Korea intent on rallying the four great powers behind her but also a "Northeast Asia Peace and Cooperation Initiative" (NAPCI) with a bold agenda to transform a sizable region. Over three years, hopes were kept alive that Seoul, while making overtures to and waiting for Pyongyang, could corral the key powers into a joint strategy, overcoming the serious obstacles in most of their various bilateral relationships.

In retrospect, Park's regional policies were rife with illusions and naivete. Her "history card" first with Japan alienated not only Japan but also the United States, which by late 2014 was blaming her more than Abe for standing in the way of intelligence sharing and trilateralism on security. Park's "Eurasian diplomacy" and, following Russia's ostracization in the West over Ukraine in 2014, pursuit of autonomous diplomacy with financial support for the Khasan-Rajin line from Russia to North Korea paid no dividends as Russia began cozying up to North Korea. Prioritizing a "honeymoon" with Xi Jinping, she was put in an embarrassing position in mid-2014 (when Xi visited Seoul) of having to stay silent as he made the thrust of his visit demonization of Japan and driving a big wedge between two US allies. Finally, Park's signature initiatives to win regional and

DOI: 10.4324/9781003394792-3

especially US support for *trustpolitk* floundered before North Korean resistance, ignored as Xi pursued regionalism through the Belt and Road Initiative (BRI) and Obama's "rebalance to Asia" saw no value added. By the end of 2015, Park was at an impasse; her tendency of doubling down on policies without good prospects was at a dead end.

The year 2015 saw Park make a last-ditch effort to secure Beijing's cooperation on North Korea and regional security by joining Xi Jinping on the podium in the celebration of the anniversary of victory in WWII. Meeting later that year with Putin, she sought his help in reopening talks with Pyongyang, essentially endorsing his active outreach to Kim Jong-un. US pressure was mounting against her approach to Japan and China, and she had begun to signal some change in course.

The first three years of Park Geun-hye's presidency can be remembered as conservative idealism. In contrast to progressive rule of South Korea, there was unwavering closeness with the United States and conditional outreach to North Korea. Yet, in common with the three administrations led by progressives, hopes were lifted for transformative leadership of Northeast Asia into some type of new regional architecture. While not premised on Seoul becoming a "balancer," they also assumed it could bridge Sino-US differences, this time as a "reconciler" by building trust. In this unique block of time, ending with a new policy toward Japan in late December 2015 and toward China with the Terminal High Altitude Area Defense (THAAD) decision in July 2016, Seoul's optimism confronted deepening challenges.

Park's first years were characterized by approaches to the four powers active in Northeast Asia unlike in other times. South Korean thinking presumed that the country was an "autonomous ally" of the United States, not seeking separation but empowered to pursue its own diplomacy. It conceived of its role with China as a "trust-building suitor," capable, as no other country was, of steering that country's diplomacy in Northeast Asia. With Japan, South Korea had chosen to be its "historical avenger," putting reconciliation before addressing shared security concerns. Russia was not neglected; South Korea envisioned itself as its "Eurasian liaison," despite problems from 2014 sanctions in response to its aggression in Ukraine. All of these expectations rested on a special, trusting relationship as the "gateway compatriot" to North Korea. Finally, as the final building block in Seoul's diplomacy, it conceived of itself as the sole possible "regional architect."

US-South Korean relations remained the bedrock of Seoul's foreign policy, as it perceived ties with China and Japan in a triangular context with the US. In the overviews below, mention is made of US bilateral ties, but subsequent sections treat the US only in trilateral contexts. As for Russia, it is a secondary concern to be noted in the overviews, especially when regional architecture is a preoccupation. The bulk of attention below is on thinking about China and Japan while weighing the US factor.

Overview of Park Administration Thinking in 2013

Extraordinary leadership flux in key countries fed the Park administration's confidence that it could break from Lee Myung-bak's policies and drive transformation in Northeast Asia. The key was the arrival of a young, untested leader in North Korea seen as likely to put some priority on economic growth and the shared search of regional powers for a breakthrough on the North. In 2012, the idea was spreading that a middle power had unique advantages to steer the region in the aftermath of the collapse of the Six-Party Talks, reviving the goal of galvanizing support for a North Korea-centered agenda.[1] With North-South relations in the doldrums and new concern about widening national identity gaps with both China and Japan,[2] Park's plan to fill the void by building trust, although not with Japan, appeared to offer a way forward. Lee Myung-bak had left a strong relationship with the Obama administration, which Park intended to sustain, as she saw Xi and Putin both ready to explore closer ties to Seoul and new diplomatic overtures to Pyongyang. In pursuing "Global Korea," Lee was seen as slighting regional Korea, leaving Park an opening amid deepening bilateral tensions there.[3] The key would be China, whose ties to Japan and the US were fraying and whose leadership had soured on Lee but not on Seoul.

Secure that the US regarded South Korea as the lynchpin of US policy for the Pacific, Park was confident Seoul had the capacity to carve out a new role.[4] She launched an "alignment policy" to proceed simultaneously on her "Korean Peninsular Trust Process" and NAPCI. Neither Xi nor Obama outright rejected this plan, but they had something very different in mind. In response to Obama's "rebalance to Asia," Park feared that US attention was shifting to Southeast and South Asia and it was counting more on Japan as well as Japan-South Korean trilateralism and missile defense cooperation, which would complicate South Korean-Chinese cooperation. She would strive to deflect that danger through diplomacy with Beijing as well as overtures to Pyongyang, even if Xi Jinping's regional plans saw Seoul as a means to impact ties to the US, North Korea, and Japan.[5]

Expectations in Seoul for some pathway toward regionalism—inclusive of both China and the US—were far stronger than in other capitals, especially Washington and Tokyo. They rested on assumptions widely shared by the South Korean public: relations with North Korea were likely to improve, even if it was also seen as a threat; the US and China were eager for a new approach to North Korea to avoid increasingly negative repercussions; and Seoul was in a unique position to take the initiative since it was considered relatively unthreatening to China, the US, Japan, and Russia.

Thinking on China in 2013

Given deteriorated public perceptions of China and the emergence of what Chung Jae-ho calls "China fear," Park faced a challenge in setting a new course.[6] Both Beijing's hostility toward the Lee administration—after expectations from the

Roh Moo-hyun period had been dashed—and its shift in favor of North Korea in 2009–11 had complicated Park's task.[7] Yet despite fear of a hierarchical relationship with China, new Chinese pressure, and a further Chinese shift toward North Korea, there was also fear of marginalization in a China-US confrontation. A slight majority of the public chose partner over rival as their label for China. Insisting that Seoul could have both alliance and leadership in a regional order with positive implications for North Korea, Park claimed to be able to resolve the dominant question on people's minds in this period.[8]

Park began her tenure by sending a delegation to China first and then made a visit there, the highlight of her first year, giving a strong impression that the road to Pyongyang goes through Beijing. There was talk of South Korea being uniquely situated between continental-power China and the maritime-power US and having the best relationship with China of any US ally. The summit was widely viewed as a success, substantively in the chemistry between leaders. Having called the pattern of "politics cold, economics hot" bilateral relations in Asia the "Asia paradox," Park claimed to be solving it. Some spoke of a Park-Xi "honeymoon." Others could see no sign of China prioritizing the nuclear issue (the phrase "denuclearization of the DPRK" was missing) or accepting unification led by the South. Moreover, they warned of China's habit of pressuring US allies to weaken their security links with Washington. Yet, advice on what Seoul should do often fell back on the argument that if "rebalancing" or, specifically, Seoul's role in it is seen as containing China, as it will be, the strategic value of North Korea to China will rise, impairing cooperation. Washington was blamed as much as Beijing for forcing a choice, as if that would be the worst nightmare for Seoul. Park ploughed ahead with Xi in the forefront.

In the second half of 2013 after Park's visit to Beijing, momentum was building for a China-South Korean FTA, but on security there were new strains with China after it declared an Air Defense Identification Zone (ADIZ) intruding into South Korea's zone. Seoul also had to digest the impact on Sino-DPRK relations of Kim Jong-un's execution of Jang Song-taek, the main intermediary with China. Some hoped that this along with the FTA would lead Beijing to tilt toward Seoul. Park clung to the "honeymoon" image with X Jinping, whose visit to Seoul would be the next test.

Thinking on Japan in 2013

Lee Myung-bak pulled back at the last second from an intelligence-sharing agreement with Japan and then made the first visit of a Korean leader to the disputed Dokdo island only months after turning a summit with Japan into a tirade over the "comfort women" issue following a Korean Constitutional Court ruling. As the daughter of the leader who had agreed to normalize relations in 1965, Park faced intense scrutiny over how she would handle ties to Japan. She also faced Abe's revisionist historical moves, inciting Koreans. Thus, Park put history in the forefront, as reflected in her August 2013 Liberation Day speech and as seen in her stress on the need for trust as a precondition in this relationship as well as others. Compared to coverage of repellent behavior in North Korea, China, or Russia, Japan drew the most vehement denunciations. Yet on both the left and the right, there was concern that Park's hard line toward Japan was putting national interests at risk. Politics was interfering with economics; official relations were falling behind private sector ties, trapped in what Park Cheol-hee called "mutual abandonment,"[9] arguing that Koreans do not give credit to the more than half of Japanese politicians and officials' intent on improving ties and trying to resolve history issues. It appeared that relations with China were crowding out those with Japan. Just as the US was boosting military ties to Japan, Seoul was accusing Tokyo of "military expansion." Seoul, Park Cheol-hee argued, needed to broaden its diplomatic horizons from bilateralism with Japan to the Northeast Asia region. This pinpointed the fallout from letting anti-Japanese sentiments spill over into pro-Chinese statements, shaking up trust in Seoul not only in Japan but also in the US—more serious because the US was "prioritizing Japan" in the region. The South Korean leadership was clearly warned.

Concerned with Japan's past when the US valued Japan's future, Seoul was fueling alarm it was leaning toward China while defying the US effort to counterbalance that country by fortifying the regional order. A more realistic policy required more sober thinking about the difficulties facing Seoul, given threats from North Korea and Sino-Russian relations, and the tightening bond between the US and Japan. However, supporters of Park's policy saw it as deterring an arms race in the region, recognizing that China should not be labeled an "enemy," and the right response to Abe's militaristic inclinations. Most importantly, it was the best hope for the paramount goal of keeping the door open to North Korea and Seoul's central diplomatic role.

Overview of Park Administration Thinking in 2014

In the first part of 2014 South Koreans perceived an advantageous environment for Park's foreign policy agenda. Calling reunification like "hitting a jackpot," Park's New Year's speech set the tone for mobilizing the powers since North Korea showed no interest. Saying that the current international circumstances are the most favorable since the peninsula was divided, one article focused on promoting a strategic dialogue with Beijing and Washington.[10] This was in accord with the assumption that security on the peninsula is heavily influenced by a power game between the US and China. Another assumption was that Kim Jong-un is giving priority to economic growth to stabilize his leadership. With China halting its activities after the execution of the official on whom it had relied and the US stuck in "strategic patience," Seoul can fill the void, it was thought, not only by its offers to Pyongyang but by organizing others to endorse its agenda. Whether this new urgency was due to discomfort with the status quo or misreading signals from others, the debate was well removed from media debates elsewhere.

The United States was viewed somewhat warily for its excessive patience with North Korea, tough line toward China and Russia, and soft line toward Japan, while calling on South Korea to separate history from security. Apart from some conservative angst about letting such differences impact relations, Park's policy toward China, Japan, and Russia was not much criticized. As talk spread that Kim Jong-un might visit Russia in 2015 for the May celebration of the 70th anniversary of victory in WWII, some warned that Moscow was preparing to nullify sanctions against the North, even as some saw an opportunity to implement Park's Eurasia Initiative and seize a chance for diplomacy. Russians were appealing for implementation of trilateral economic cooperation with North Korea and for Seoul to relax its conditions for resuming the Six-Party Talks, fueling the case that Seoul is key to altering Kim Jong-un's calculus in regard to engagement. Yet, the US sought a tougher line on Moscow as well as continued sanctions enforcement. When Obama visited East Asia in late April, Moscow was secondary, given three main triangular lenses: Japan, China, and North Korea.

As much as Park Geun-hye sought to build trust with North Korea, cozied up to China, and kept pressure on Japan, progressives insisted that she could pursue these objectives much better. On July 21, Moon Chung-in blamed Park for failing to make a breakthrough with Pyongyang, which would unlock the door to diplomacy with the four great powers.[11] He argued that closer ties with Beijing would follow, and Tokyo and Moscow would be dissuaded from cooperating with the North in order to pressure the South. Inter-Korean relations are not the dependent variable, as many argue, but the independent variable to reduce pressure from China and the US. Seoul must stabilize the regional order, encouraging Sino-US cooperation. The more the conflict, the worse it is for Seoul's national interests. Moon further argued that Seoul could enhance its value for Beijing by bridging its proposed norms and institutions with US alliances and designing some norms of its own.

Thinking on China in 2014

The "pivot to Asia" worried some commentators that it would reduce China's incentives to work with the US on North Korea. Indeed, it was linked to US "strategic patience" and prioritization of US-Japan-South Korean trilateralism as a barrier to Seoul's agenda for focusing on North Korea and boosting ties to China as key for that pursuit. The pivot was criticized as having an excessive focus on the US-Japan alliance, hampering other issues from being resolved. The North Korean nuclear issue had stalled, as cooperation with China was not encouraged. Both on the left and on the right, this led to frustration. Many sought to keep alive Seoul's options with Beijing. While the US was trying to counter China through the Trans-Pacific Partnership (TPP), cooperation with China was necessary to have the desired outcome, given that Southeast Asian countries had much closer economic relations with Beijing and Seoul also saw hope in its ties with Beijing. Also, US neglect of the Abe administration's revisionism in order to empower its alliance with Japan damages the US position with Beijing as well as Seoul, Korean writers argued.

Assuming that China was intent on stability, many argued that South Korea had an opening to win its cooperation concerning North Korea if the right kind of strategic vision is proposed to ease China's concerns. It must not be bypassed in reunification plans or isolated by alliance moves. Many of its concerns can be addressed: on history by keeping pressure on Japan to back away from revisionist moves; on North Korea by taking a multilateral approach eschewing regime change and working closely with China; on values by downplaying Seoul's support for US themes; on alliance military build-ups by distancing Seoul from those viewed in Beijing as directed at it; and on Japan by not boosting bilateral military ties or trilateralism with the US. Deference to China remained a major concern in Park's foreign policy and in the debate in Seoul over it. As Chinese labeled Obama's "pivot" a containment strategy and called the US-South Korean alliance the main constraint to deepening bilateral China-South Korean ties, many Koreans looked for ways to accommodate China. They calculated that differences over North Korea, history, and maritime issues were all manageable, as Seoul kept its distance from US and Japanese activities—made harder as the US-Japan alliance strengthened.

China kept complaining of a lack of mutual trust in the China-South Korean relationship, and Park insisted that she was prioritizing building that trust. Indeed, she envisioned NAPCI as the multilateral security framework to complement her bilateral wooing of Xi Jinping. If China insisted that the mistrust was exacerbated by an alliance not limited to North Korea, South Korea offered reassurance that it was not integrated into US regional strategy. Yet, China kept up its pressure, opposing US-South Korean military exercises, seeking joint condemnation of Japan's views of history, and arguing that Park needed to do more to win its trust. Park kept trying to build bilateral trust through 2015.

In mid-2014, geopolitical tensions grew more complicated. Xi Jinping became the first Chinese leader to visit Seoul before Pyongyang—taken as a positive sign in South Korea—but his messages were not so well received, especially on collaborating over the history issue. Meanwhile, US desire to locate the THAAD missile system in South Korea was unmistakable. Together, this raised the urgency of clarifying Seoul's diplomatic strategy. Yet the most conspicuous response was to assume that Seoul's strategic opportunity was growing since it was the only country with a sound relationship with the two competing great powers. China encouraged this optimism, suggesting that South Korea, not just North Korea, could be a "buffer zone" and it would gain from "balanced diplomacy." No longer, it was argued, does Beijing separate Seoul from Pyongyang. Instead, it has an overall "diplomacy toward the Korean Peninsula." Assuming that China is so upset with

North Korea's nuclear development and disrespect for China that it has turned more to South Korea, the prevailing discourse grew more optimistic about taking advantage of the deeper Sino-US rivalry. It was said that Seoul could serve as a bridge even as Sino-US relations declined over other issues.

The backlash against such rosy arguments was considerable. On North Korea, despite Xi's support for Park's Dresden Declaration, indirect as it was, he had stuck to "denuclearization of the Korean Peninsula." If some interpreted that to mean no adverse impact on China would be acceptable, the possibility was raised that China had a much bigger transformation of South Korea in mind.

Chung Jae-ho assessed China-South Korean relations after the Xi visit to Seoul, arguing that the "Seoul-in-the-China orbit" thesis is overblown despite claims since Park's June 2013 "trip for heart-to-heart building of trust" that relations have never been better.[12] Xi had scarcely changed his position from 2013 on North Korea, called again for the Six-Party Talks, and pressed without success on Japan. If a year earlier Xi was more of an unknown quantity and Sino-US relations uncertain, Park now faced growing concern about China's "assertive rise" and Sino-US divisions with Seoul caught in the middle. The letdown after the Xi visit was unmistakable although Park kept up hopes for a year.

Thinking on Japan in 2014

Believing that Abe's late 2013 visit to the Yasukuni Shrine meant that Japan would stay on course to become a "revisionist state," commentators insisted on sticking to Park's hard line and trying to get the US to keep pressuring Abe, as it did after the visit. Yet, there were warnings that Seoul not overplay its hand, given regional geopolitics, and not give the impression that it is acting in league with Beijing.

When Obama traveled through Asia in April 2014, it was clear that his priority was a stronger US-Japan alliance, posing a challenge for Koreans, who had recently viewed the US-South Korean alliance as at the forefront. Increased US pressure for Japan-South Korean reconciliation was evident, too, seen in a March trilateral summit. Yet national identity kept a tight grip on Korean consciousness, even as Obama strove to shift the focus to international security. The defensive reaction was pronounced in Korea, blaming Japan's historical conflicts with neighbors for regional instability, when Washington had its eyes on Chinese and North Korean threats. The focus was put on changing US thinking, appealing to it on such issues as recognizing that the East Sea is the name of the Sea of Japan. Requests to separate security from the history issue coincided with divergence in views of China and diplomacy toward North Korea. Yet there were also voices recognizing the dead-end nature of Seoul's policy toward Japan, which was alienating its ally. Focusing on history, it was said, played into Chinese efforts to change the subject from the US "values alliance" and alienated the US, while ceding the advantage to Japan-US relations. In light of this awareness, it was not surprising that Park on liberation day refocused on the future, saying that the 50th anniversary of normalization should be a starting point and proposing cooperation in areas other than history. Her position was starting to shift.

Overview of Park Administration Thinking in 2015

The old Cold War triangles were recalled in 2015 as Sino-Russian ties built on a breakthrough in 2014 and Russo-North Korean ties broke the ice with Pyongyang; and US-Japan ties drew closer, while US pressure mounted to enhance US-South Korean relations through trilateral ties linked to Japan. Eager to talk to Kim Jong-un, Park advanced the "Eurasia Initiative" launched in October 2013, projecting a "Silk Road Express" of transport from Busan to Europe accompanied by energy and trade networks through North Korea and Russia. Moscow was the chief target of this initiative, and its recent upsurge in diplomatic and economic ties to Pyongyang made it of more interest. It was said that rising North Korea-Russia economic cooperation could lead to trilateral economic cooperation in the framework of the Eurasia Initiative. Seoul was eager to keep Russia's support.

Although some in Seoul worried that the "rebalance to Asia" damaged Sino-US relations and, thus, complicated Seoul's diplomacy, others saw it as an "important symbolic manifestation" of the US commitment to Asian security, including the North Korean threat, and as leverage for China-South Korean relations.[13] South Korean public opinion strongly supported the alliance, and Park was refusing to take an equidistant approach to Washington and Beijing, as China had sought. Yet, pleading that Seoul's strategic dilemma was arguably more pronounced than that of any other Asian country, due to China's support for North Korea and the South's unique position between continental and maritime Asia, many strove to find a way to straddle the growing Sino-US military competition. In 2015, the THAAD decision loomed, and straddling could not be sustained, given North Korea's new missile capabilities and the urgency of keeping bipartisan support in the US for the ROK alliance.

With little prospect of persuading Kim Jong-un or even Xi Jinping, Park concentrated on selling her regional initiative to Obama. If only the US endorsed NAPCI, she would be able to approach the others more confidently. But US audiences were bewildered by the unjustified optimism behind the idea. To build trust requires grasping the thinking of the obstreperous parties and testing their interest through small steps not some grand but vague architecture. The US side did not openly oppose the initiative but responded skeptically that more proof of its feasibility was necessary. As on repeated occasions, US analysts saw Seoul badly misjudging the regional environment.

Optimistic talk of Seoul's potential as a middle power to change regional architecture conflicted with growing pessimism about what it could achieve. Optimism rested on the view that China had become a more promising partner in dealing with North Korea, given poor bilateral ties, but they were beginning to improve. Optimism also rested on a judgment that Sino-US relations were more cooperative than competitive, but by 2015 this was untenable. A third factor was ongoing confidence in strong US-South Korean relations, but even when Park and Obama in October 2015 claimed their meeting went well, there was an undercurrent of discord and a sense of a ticking time bomb that they would have to face, given divisions on North Korea, China, and Japan. Finally, if some Koreans took the launch of NAPCI as the start of an era of regionalism, in which Seoul would lead the way, optimism was in no way echoed in Washington.[14] Park's moves to reassure the US convinced some that she was succeeding, but the façade of a successful summit with Obama misread US expectations, given growing alarm about China and growing confidence in Japan-US ties, for Seoul to sign onto a regional strategy. The differences emerged in challenging China's aggressive moves, joining with Japan on regional security, and beefing up deterrence. Pessimistic arguments were rising to the surface. Park's concessions did not satisfy the US but alienated China.

Clarity was missing in thinking through five options for Seoul elucidated in one analysis: enhancing military deterrence, strengthening the US-South Korean alliance, reclaiming diplomatic ownership, resuming the Six-Party Talks, and rethinking middle-power diplomacy. Pure-balancing of China through the first two options risked entrapment in a Sino-US conflict, but light hedging in the third option had the drawback of increasing dependence on China substantially; the fourth option was a recipe for pure bandwagoning with China. The final option, specified in 2015, was to shift away from self-confident, activist diplomacy to reinforce the first two options while cautiously exploring what is possible in conditions of increasing bipolarity—what is viewed as heavy hedging versus China.[15]

Thinking on China in 2015

Although 2016 is usually flagged as the year when China-South Korean relations turned irreversibly bad, 2015 served as a precursor, as seen from South Korea. The aftermath of the Park-Xi summit of 2014 coupled with the backlash from the Park appearance with Xi at the September 2015 victory event were factors, but so were perceptions of a downturn in Sino-US relations and the need to make a choice. After Park's trip to China, Chun Yungwoo argued it was of less consequence than many had argued since the idea that Beijing will help to resolve the nuclear issue is a fantasy. Intensified pursuit of Beijing on this only increases its voice on other issues. Beijing has essentially financed the nuclear arms development by limiting UN sanctions and increasing its imports from the North. After giving the impression that South Korea is being incorporated into the Chinese regional order, Park must restore US confidence by agreeing on military measures to counter the North's threat.[16]

Critics were pouncing on Park for her foreign policy. On one side, she was accused of giving the impression of leaning toward China, alienating the US in 2015 even more than in 2014. On the other, her overtures to China were seen as failing to lead to talks with Pyongyang or signs that China will be helpful. Having raised expectations unduly, she bore the brunt of blame for obvious failure.

Park's trip to Washington in October appeared to clear suspicions that she was leaning toward China. Yet Obama had pressed for Seoul to support "freedom of navigation," as well as to shift on Japan. The debate about being pressed to pick a side only intensified. The expectation Park had nurtured about reunification as a "jackpot" and growing trust with multiple states came back to haunt her when Seoul appeared isolated and embattled. The reality that US relations matter far more than relations with China left Park alone, boxed into a corner near the end of 2015. For the sake of the US alliance relationship, she defied China and public opinion to cut a deal with Abe.

Thinking on Japan in 2015

Abe's April visit to the United States strongly impacted South Korea's debate on Japan policy. It was seen as raising the US-Japan alliance to the top of all US bilateral relationships with a trend line for decades ahead, showcased in new defense guidelines, putting pressure on Seoul to respond or be isolated. Moreover, Abe's speech to a joint session of Congress showed that he did not have to address the "comfort women" issue to satisfy the US on values. Pointing to this state visit as a turning point, Chung-min Lee predicted that it could "trigger a minor U-turn" in Korean foreign policy even as Koreans were waiting to evaluate Abe's 70th anniversary speech in August.[17] Also, writing just before the summit, Sue Mi Terry posed an agenda for three-way strategic cooperation—joint peacekeeping missions, counter-terrorism, counter-proliferation, counter-narcotics, cyberspace, humanitarian assistance, and disaster operations—suggesting that the US could act as an honest broker. Yet her call for trilateral security talks did not gain the necessary support, particularly given Park's insistent priority on history issues with Abe.[18]

Park found her foreign policy criticized by overly stressing principles without achieving progress. Neither conservatives nor progressives, however, had an answer for the unprecedented boost to US-Japan relations they were seeing, as the focus was shifting southward, not only to the Senkaku Islands, newly besieged by Chinese ships, but toward the South China Sea as well. The security consequences of South Korean tensions with Japan had become more sensitive than ever. Also, on values US-Japan resistance to dwelling on historical memory issues was isolating Seoul.

Anticipation rose over what Abe would include in the 70th anniversary statement in August. There were both nervousness that the relationship could get worse if Abe did not show restraint and a slight sense of opportunity that the ongoing stalemate could be broken, even if hopes centered on Washington more than Tokyo. A big reason for anticipating improvement was the notion that Japan's historical revisionism would be likely to so offend the US that US pressure would focus there.[19] Progressive warnings of worse to come took a different tack. They pointed to a perceptual gap between the two sides on the 1965 normalization agreement. For Seoul, it was a humiliating outcome, which must be changed, notably the omitted "comfort women" issue. Japan, however, could not abandon the 1965 framework.[20] Meanwhile, the US tilt to Japan on history was evident.[21] It was recognized that the US considered Seoul rigid, damaging ties to Japan and US interests. Talk of changing US opinion through public diplomacy revealed how out of touch some Koreans were.

A sense of isolation within the triangle only deepened with recognition that it is about China. Tokyo joined Washington in rejecting the Asian Infrastructure Investment Bank (AIIB) and preparing to join the TPP. Defense ties were tightening, along with pressure on Seoul. After Abe's April visit a qualitatively new relationship obliged Seoul to respond, many argued. Coupled with concern about rising anti-Korean attitudes in Japan, this awareness spurred calls for Park to drop her linkage of history issues to a summit with Abe. Awaiting the Abe statement, attention was turned to whether Abe would mention the four words "colonization, apology, aggression, and deep remorse." Indeed, they were included but left ambiguous in the way they were used, leaving Koreans mainly unsatisfied.

With the statement settled to apparent US satisfaction, pressure on Seoul rose precipitously. A Park-Obama summit was seen as targeted at altering Japan-South Korean ties with security in the forefront, despite Korean discomfort with Japan's expanded military role. Obama's "rebalance to Asia" had drawn Japan in and was turning to South Korea. Park Cheol-hee agreed with cooperating more, arguing that it is an asset to assure "passive peace" in case of a North Korean military provocation. The seven United Nation Commands stationed in Japan should be utilized to prevent the worst-case scenario, and the backup of Japan's Self-Defense Forces is also essential to prevent misjudgment by North Korea's leader.[22] Yet the mood was unprepared for a "final and irreversible" agreement.

Conclusion

Pre-THAAD and before the "comfort women" agreement with Japan, the first three years of the Park presidency saw a continuous search for a regional framework with Seoul at the center. It was premised on optimistic assumptions about China, pessimistic reasoning on Japan, and slow awareness of the drift of US policy. By late 2015 Park faced an impasse with the US and Japan while having little to show for her pursuit of China, North Korea, and Russia. Doubling down on her pursuit of Korea-centered regionalism did not persuade any of the countries concerned. On the surface, Park had a good summit with Obama in October 2015, but she could no longer go forward with the initiatives that guided her administration to date. She had to change course.

Why had Park misjudged the regional situation so badly? We can discern at least three factors. First, this pattern of overoptimism dates from the 1980s. The exception in 2008–10 was Lee Myung-bak. As Seoul's situation grew more dire—North Korea's rising threat capacity, the shift in China to greater assertiveness, Sino-US relations deteriorating, Russia tightening ties to China and also searching for a bond with North Korea—South Korea insisted it could do more to draw these states together under its leadership. This willful blindness could not long persist.

Second, the mirage of reunification drove policies toward China and Russia more than to North Korea. Little was known about North Korean politics, and misjudgments of China's reasoning somehow persisted after China's troubling responses to North Korea turning its back on the Six-Party Talks and then launching attacks on the South in 2010. Lee Myung-bak under this shadow veered away from overoptimism, but Koreans may have been so disheartened by the reality they faced that they—conservatives as well as progressives—backed Park's strong revival of it. More than any other factor driving this was the longing for a path to reunification, despite the divisions over the sort of transition that would require and what financial burden was needed.

Third, having lived in the world of Cold War bipolarity for four decades, South Koreans were so enamored of diplomatic diversification that they hung onto it even when conditions had turned against this possibility. Afraid of losing their voice, they pretended they did not have to change. Fearing the consequences of a revival of bipolarity, they desperately clung to their autonomy. China, Japan, and, possibly, the United States played a role in fostering this world of illusions. In the case of China, it nourished false hopes, although it also missed opportunities to sustain them as seen by 2015 and more so after. Keen on driving a wedge between Seoul and both Washington and Tokyo, Beijing played on false hopes until its duplicity was clearly exposed. In Japan's case, it aroused unnecessary alienation—more due to Abe in 2013–14 than before. If a more accommodating Japanese posture could have eased Seoul's awakening to the hard facts of regional security, that was not forthcoming. The US helped to calm Abe's revisionist language and played a critical role in enabling Park to change course, but that did not persuade Koreans.

Finally, the US strove to accommodate a succession of South Korean leaders except in 2001 when Bush offered no hope to Kim Dae-jung. Such US "strategic patience" with an ally could have been vital for avoiding any rupture, but it also likely encouraged excessive expectations. Yet it was also Washington that quietly tried to lower those expectations, as seen in 2014–15.

Notes

1 Taeho Kim, "Security Challenges and the Changing Balance on the Korean Peninsula," in Gilbert Rozman, ed., *Joint U.S.-Korea Academic Studies: Asia at a Tipping Point* (Washington: DC: Korea Economic Institute, 2012), pp. 113–126.

2 Leif-Eric Easley, "Diverging Trajectories of Trust in Northeast Asia: South Korea's Security Relations with Japan and China," in Gilbert Rozman, ed., *Joint U.S.-Korea*

Academic Studies: Asia at a Tipping Point (Washington: DC: Korea Economic Institute, 2012), pp. 149–169.
3. Park Cheol-hee, "Bilateral Competition and Cooperation under New Leadership: South Korea and Japan," in Gilbert Rozman, ed., *Joint U.S.-Korea Academic Studies: Asia's Slippery Slope* (Washington, DC: Korea Economic Institute, 2013), pp. 39–50.
4. Scott Snyder, "Bilateral Competition and Cooperation under New Leadership: South Korea and the U.S," in Gilbert Rozman, ed., *Joint U.S.-Korea Academic Studies: Asia's Slippery Slope* (Washington, DC: Korea Economic Institute, 2013), pp. 51–63.
5. Ibid.
6. Chung Jae-ho, "Leadership Changes and South Korea's China Policy," in Gilbert Rozman, ed., *Joint U.S.-Korea Academic Studies: Asia at a Tipping Point* (Washington: DC: Korea Economic Institute, 2012), pp. 5–17.
7. Gilbert Rozman, "Japan's National Identity Gaps: A Framework for Analysis of International Relations in Asia," in Gilbert Rozman, ed., *Joint U.S.-Korea Academic Studies: Asia's Slippery Slope: Triangular Tensions, Identity Gaps, Conflicting Regionalism, and Diplomatic Impasse toward North Korea* (Washington, DC: Korea Economic Institute, 2014), pp. 79-92.
8. See-won Byun, "China's National Identity and the Sino-U.S. National Identity Gap: The View from Korea," in Gilbert Rozman, ed., *Joint U.S.-Korea Academic Studies: Asia's Slippery Slope* (Washington, DC: Korea Economic Institute, 2013), pp. 97–111.
9. Park Cheol-hee, "Bilateral Competition and Cooperation under New Leadership: South Korea and Japan," in Gilbert Rozman, ed., *Joint U.S.-Korea Academic Studies: Asia's Slippery Slope* (Washington, DC: Korea Economic Institute, 2013), pp. 39–50.
10. *Chosun Ilbo*, March 2014.
11. *Joongang Ilbo*, July 21, 2015.
12. Chung Jae Ho, "A South Korean Perspective," *The Asan Forum*, September 29, 2014.
13. Chung-min Lee, "Recalibrating the Rebalance: A View from South Korea," *The Asan Forum*, April 9, 2015.
14. Shin-wha Lee, "South Korea's Middle Power Multilateral Diplomacy: Optimistic and Pessimistic Views," *The Asan Forum*, December 7, 2015.
15. Cheng-Chwee Kuik, "Introduction to the Special Forum: Decomposing and Assessing South Korea's Hedging Options," *The Asan Forum*, June 11, 2015.
16. Chun Yungwoo, *Donga Ilbo*, September 18, 2015.
17. Chung-min Lee, "A South Korean Perspective," *The Asan Forum*, May 15, 2015.
18. Sue Mi Terry, "South Korea's Triangular Relations: Japan-South Korea-U.S. Relations," in Gilbert Rozman, ed., *Joint U.S.-Korea Academic Studies: Asia's Slippery Slope*, pp. 7–21.
19. *Joongang Ilbo*, January 6, 2015.
20. *Hankyoreh*, February 12, 2015.
21. *Chosun Ilbo*, March 3, 2015.
22. Park Cheol-hee, *Joongang Ilbo*, December 16, 2015.

3
REMAKING OF CONSERVATIVE NARRATIVES

Eun A Jo

On the heels of Park Geun-hye's election—and the introduction of her *trustpolitik*—there was a sense that South Korean foreign policy was undergoing a sea change. After a dizzying back-and-forth between "Sunshine" engagement and containment by "strategic patience" vis-à-vis North Korea, Park had hoped to strike a balance: building trust by decoupling initiatives for economic cooperation and security deterrence. To this end, she courted Beijing openly and vigorously—and, for a moment, concerns about South Korea's realignment appeared genuine. Meanwhile, South Korea's relations with Japan deteriorated to new lows over the years as controversies surrounding historical revisionism periodically resurfaced: high-profile visits to the Yasukuni Shrine, the celebrations of "Takeshima Day," and textbook amendments dominated public discourse. Tepid as they were, US efforts to forge a trilateral security framework were finding little resonance in South Korea that had found renewed optimism in China and deepening distrust of Japan.

Partisan narratives during this period indicated important changes and continuities in South Korean foreign policy: (1) a growing rift on North Korea; (2) a surprising agreement on China; (3) a veiled divergence on the US; and (4) an enduring consensus on Japan. Under Park's tenure, conservative narratives were gradually evolving, away from the orthodox approaches in favor of a balancing framework that had been long championed by progressives.

North Korea

On North Korea, the partisan divide has been particularly wide and growing wider. Two topics dominated discussions of North Korea in the South during this period: (1) the stability of the North Korean regime (in the aftermath of Jang Song-taek's

DOI: 10.4324/9781003394792-4

execution); and (2) the prospects of Park Geun-hye's *trustpolitik*. While both sides found cause for concern in the immediate term—more provocations were likely—their prescriptions for policy in the longer run tended to vary widely. For the conservatives, in particular, Jang's ouster and Park's *trustpolitik* signaled an opportune moment for diplomacy with China; Beijing appeared intent on reining in Pyongyang. Meanwhile, progressives guarded against what they construed were populist impulses driving Park's policy change; to strike a meaningful balance, in their view, Park needed to offer more without conditions. Conspicuously absent in progressive analyses was a mention of China.

The sudden and public execution of Jang Song-taek on December 12, 2013, triggered renewed discussions about the possibility of regime collapse, the consequences of instability in North Korea, and China's role. An uncle of Kim Jong-un, Jang was widely deemed the second-most powerful figure in the North; he was also famed to be reform-minded and had campaigned to introduce China-like economic overhaul.[1] For this reason, many saw his overthrow as Kim's attempt to consolidate power as well as to signal his intention to resist Chinese-style reform. Beijing's displeasure at the news of Jang's ouster was evident; one observer in the *Global Times*—the Chinese Communist Party's mouthpiece—stated that Jang's fall "reveals Pyongyang's anxious desire to shake off its overdependence on China and find a way out of the deadlock with the US."[2] Though the official response was far more tepid, reinforcing that the incident is North Korea's "internal affair,"[3] an overwhelming majority of observers believed ties had been strained.[4]

Partisan narratives were divided as to whether Jang's purge indicates North Korea's internal instability or Kim's growing power. Progressive coverage of the event tended to emphasize the latter. According to *Hankyoreh* on December 4, 2013, Jang's exit signaled Kim's ability to project unity without a long-time party patron. In this view, Kim executed Jang and his followers—all from Kim's father's generation—because he finally could stand on his own.[5] At the same time, a *Kyunghyang* editorial on December 10, 2013, suggested that more aggressive actions on the international stage would emerge as Kim seeks to consolidate one-man rule.[6] It called for closer examination of the deep internal fissures in North Korean domestic politics as inter-Korean relations entered a new phase of the Kim regime.

Conservative coverage focused, instead, on the long-term consequences of the North's instability, and highlighted the extreme extent to which the Kim regime was willing to go to install fear. A *Donga* editorial on December 10, 2013, noted: "while the Kim regime may stabilize in the short run [through a series of purges], it is uncertain how long the regime can survive as a one-man dictatorship."[7] A politics of fear was a "double-edged sword," it asserted, which could sow the seeds of the regime's demise even if it could temporarily stamp out dissent. Meanwhile, both *Donga* (in a later editorial on December 14) and *Chosun* on the same day underscored the cruelty of the Kim regime.[8] *Donga* portrayed Kim's decision as "barbaric"; *Chosun* called it a sign of his "madness." While calling similarly for vigilance, the tones in these pages were far more negative: a stronger, swifter response to this "abnormal" regime was necessary.

One particular aspect on which progressive outlets had been notably silent, but which conservative coverage abounded, was the implications of Jang's ouster for China-North Korea relations. A *Segye* editorial on December 10, 2013, argued that "pro-Chinese" factions within the North were in retreat, and another editorial on December 18 noted streams of defections as evidence of mounting instability.[9] Both asserted this was an opportune moment for South Korea to tighten relations with Beijing: China is able—and may now be willing—to rein in Pyongyang and dampen the consequences of Kim's erratic behavior in Seoul's favor. This view was echoed in a *Chosun* editorial on January 3, 2014, which argued that China no longer saw North Korea as a strategic asset, but a liability.[10] The shift in this strategic environment was a boon for diplomacy. *Chosun* wrote with striking optimism: "2014 could be the first year that the United States and China could start strategic conversations about the fundamental solutions for the North Korean problem."

Against this backdrop, among the most important developments in South Korean foreign policy was the introduction of Park's *trustpolitik*—a loosely defined principle underlying a mixed—if somewhat incoherent—set of measures aimed at deterring and engaging North Korea. As a presidential candidate, Park shared the blueprints of her North Korea policy in *Foreign Affairs*: "In order to transform the Korean Peninsula from a zone of conflict into a zone of trust, South Korea should adopt a policy of *trustpolitik*, establishing mutually binding expectations based on global norms."[11] She argued that this approach will be two-pronged: on the one hand, trust must be maintained through adherence to existing agreements, and on the other, consequences for breaches of trust must remain credible. This required a concerted effort by the international community to bind North Korea to "global norms" by building the right incentive structure.[12]

In practice, this approach generated two streams of initiatives. First, the Park administration sought to mobilize international support for her "trust" agenda and deepen inter-Korean cooperation. During her summit meetings with US President Barack Obama and Chinese President Xi Jinping, Park secured—at least rhetorically—their support for the policy of *trustpolitik*.[13] With their endorsement, she adopted a series of symbolic and material gestures to engage North Korea, including normalizing the Kaesong Industrial Complex and providing humanitarian assistance via international organizations such as the UNICEF. Later, she also launched an attendant regional initiative called the Northeast Asian Peace and Cooperation Initiative (NAPCI), aimed at fostering trust and cooperation with China, Japan, and Russia, among others.[14] As a multilateral process, the NAPCI was intended to create an "infrastructure of trust"—to institutionalize dialogue and regional cooperation on shared "soft" interests, such as public health, environmental protection, and disaster relief.[15] These initial efforts, she asserted, would be followed by more ambitious attempts to cooperate on "hard" security issues.

Second, the Park administration still continued to emphasize deterrence. In the initial months of Park's inauguration, North Korea instigated a series of nuclear and missile provocations, which tested Park's commitment to trust-building.[16] In addition, it closed the Kaesong Industrial Complex—an industrial park that combines South Korean capital and North Korean labor for joint economic enterprises[17]—and unilaterally suspended plans for family reunions, which were scheduled for September 2013.[18] According to a survey by the South Korean Unification Ministry, South Korean firms in KIC suffered close to $910 million in losses during the suspension of its operation.[19] Even so, the Park administration was lauded—including by Obama—for maintaining a firm and balanced stance, in favor of pursuing *both* international pressure and diplomatic overtures.[20]

The nature, scope, and prospects of Park's *trustpolitik* became a key area of contention in partisan narratives during this period. Conservative media highlighted Park's effort to reframe unification as an economic, rather than political agenda. During her first New Year's address in 2014, she had referred to unification as a "jackpot (*daebak*)," claiming that Korea's economic future in the globalized world lies, first and foremost, in unification.[21] To this end, she had also launched a preparatory committee for reunification as part of a three-year economic innovation plan. Conservative commentators also noted the strategic imperative for South Korea to adopt a balanced approach toward North Korea and forge trust among "unlikely" parties in the region. On *Chosun Ilbo* on July 3, 2014, former deputy foreign minister Kim Sung-han argued that China was central to any resolution regarding North Korea. Yet, he underscored the distinctions in South Korea's relations with the United States, which are based on shared values and democratic principles, and with China, which reflect shared interests in economic cooperation and regional stability. Marking these distinctions, in his view, were critical for Park's *trustpolitik* and South Korea's future as a strategic balancer.

Progressive media, on the other hand, questioned the motives behind Park's approach. In a *Hankyoreh* roundtable discussion, several experts pointed out the practical limitations of Park's foreign policy concepts, ranging from domestic economic insecurities, waning public support for unification, and continued international economic sanctions on North Korea.[22] They stressed, in particular, two problems: (1) recent controversies surrounding misuse of the National Security Law and other actions by her government refute the purported spirit of her "trust-based" approach; and (2) even if by economic means, the kind of unification that Park envisions is ultimately one of absorption. Given these internal contradictions, commentators questioned the principal motives of *trustpolitik*. They pointed out the government's relative emphasis on its public relations elements, hinting at its possibly populist underpinnings, and argued that it must do more to shape the country's foreign policy agenda than just make unification a salient feature of public discourse.

United States

On the United States, debates over South Korea's defense posture and alliance—including attendant themes such as the nuclear umbrella and the operational control (OPCON) transfer—dominated discussions. These debates highlighted the pressure points in the US-South Korean alliance. As North Korea consolidated its status as a nuclear-armed state, fears of a tilting balance of power prompted calls for indigenous nuclearization; this marked an emergent identity clash among the conservatives, as some began to question the extent to which US assurances could effectively deter the North. At the same time, debates over OPCON transfer illustrated the "stickiness" of security institutions: most—including the public—feared any instability that this transfer might introduce and searched for ways to preserve the institutional entanglement. Amid a new series of provocations from the North, progressive criticisms of procedural illegitimacy largely fell flat.

On nuclear weapons, Park continued to warn about the danger of a "nuclear domino effect" in the region as she sought to galvanize international pressure against North Korean nuclear weapons program.[23] But some prominent members of the National Assembly had begun to challenge the status quo reliance on US nuclear assurances. Won Yoo-chul, then chairman of the Committee for Formulating Strategy Against North Korea's Nuclear Weapons, and Chung Mong-joon, its longest-serving member, voiced their support for indigenous nuclear capability[24]; others suggested introducing tactical nuclear weapons instead.[25] Overall, this discursive development reflected growing concerns about the credibility of US nuclear deterrence and South Korea's changing threat landscape.

Partisan narratives about nuclear weapons bifurcated as a small, but loud minority of the conservative political elite began to voice support for nuclearization. In an oft-cited *Chosun* interview on April 22, 2013, then assemblyman Chung argued that South Korea needed nuclear weapons to maintain peace with the North.[26] When asked about the US nuclear umbrella, he answered: "It's like a marriage certificate. Married people can get a divorce, can't they?" Because the US nuclear umbrella has no operational guidelines (unlike the nuclear sharing agreement the EU has with the US), South Korea needed better assurances. Chung added: "The government and the intellectuals have been irresponsible."

Progressive commentators challenged this perspective. Moon Chung-in (together with Peter Hays) argued that indigenous nuclearization in South Korea was neither feasible nor desirable.[27] They raised, in particular, three related points: (1) mutual deterrence by nuclear balance is fragile because the incentive for preemption is too high (especially when the nuclear-armed states are geographically so close), and it will undermine the deterrent effects of South Korea's existing conventional weapons; (2) South Korea will be defying its obligations as a signatory to the Non-Proliferation Treaty (NPT) regime and the Nuclear Supply Group, which will incur significant diplomatic and economic costs; and (3) the US nuclear capabilities and assurance are more credible than whatever indigenous nuclear weapon South Korea will be able to build under time constraints, and no vacuum of protection is acceptable. Underlying each of these arguments was a critical assumption that nuclearization will damage the alliance with the US—a rare emphasis in the progressive narrative.

The debate over nuclear weapons gained renewed salience in the wake of the 2015 US-Iran nuclear deal. The Joint Comprehensive Plan of Action (JCPOA) was reached between Iran and the P5+1 (China, France, Russia, United Kingdom, United States + Germany) together with the European Union, following a 20-month-long negotiation. This detailed document provides sanctions relief in return for Iran's verified compliance with nuclear-related obligations.[28] The success of this multilateral deal found resonance among many observers in South Korea, who saw it as a potential blueprint for negotiations on the North Korean nuclear problem. The similarities and differences between Iran and North Korea became the center of partisan narratives on the nuclear issue.

Progressive coverage, in particular, focused on the lessons of the negotiation process for the North Korean nuclear problem and other issues requiring international cooperation. A *Hankyoreh* editorial on July 15, 2015, for instance, portrayed the deal as an outcome of restraint and compromise.[29] It recalled the disastrous consequences of resorting to force in Iraq or maximum pressure in Greece; by comparison, what worked in the case of Iran was that the US "gave and took what it could," while respecting Iran's "exercise of sovereignty." According to *Hankyoreh*, then, the problem with the North Korean issue was twofold: a lack of "will to resolve" in the US and, relatedly, an absence of activism to foster the right conditions in South Korea. Look beyond just the US was the message.

Conservative coverage, on the other hand, differed slightly in interpretation, seeing the Iran deal as evidence of a change in US attitudes from "strategic patience." A *Joongang* editorial on July 15, 2015, found cause of optimism in three ways.[30] First, as a presidential candidate, Barack Obama had promised a "handshake with the enemies" and mentioned three countries: Cuba, Iran, and North Korea. Since the first two were now "resolved," it was time for a deal with North Korea. Second, key members of the Six-Party Talks—the US, China, and Russia—worked together to forge the Iran deal. This provided ideal operational conditions for cooperation on North Korea. Third, North Korea should find itself increasingly isolated as its partners Cuba and Iran have opted to work with—rather than against—the US. This may incentivize the North to seek a resolution of its own. For these reasons, *Joongang* argued the atmosphere was ripe for deal-making.

On the OPCON, the official discourse during this period had shifted from a "time-based" to "condition-based" transfer. The OPCON debate first appeared in 2005 when the then President Roh Moo-hyun expressed his desire for its transfer: "I have been emphasizing self-reliant defense. It is so natural and fundamental for a sovereign nation to have this."[31] In 2007, he officially proposed the transfer to the then US President George Bush, and the two agreed to execute the transfer on

April 15, 2012.[32] This, however, became postponed to December 1, 2015, under Roh's successor Lee Myung-bak, and further postponed under Park for an unspecified date in the 2020s. Rather than stipulate a particular date, Park argued that the transfer should take place when South Korea has developed sufficient, "critical" military capabilities, including notably its missile defense system.

Partisan narratives about the OPCON transfer surrounded the trade-off between its utility for improving inter-Korean relations versus potential for harming the US-South Korean alliance. For those in the progressive camp, the key motivation for the OPCON transfer was recovering autonomy to pursue peace and unification with North Korea and minimizing reliance on the US.[33] In this vein, a *Hankyoreh* editorial on July 18, 2013, condemned Park and the broader conservative forces for choosing to relinquish the country's sovereignty; the editorial also highlighted the secrecy with which the decision had been struck as evidence of its illegitimacy.[34] In a later editorial on October 1, 2013, *Hankyoreh* continued its criticism as the US began to request—presumably in return for delaying the OPCON transfer—South Korea's participation in the US-coordinated missile defense network.[35] This could not be more damaging to Park's *trustpolitik*, it argued, as such maneuvers will engender fear and suspicion.

Some conservative outlets sympathized with the view that the decision lacked procedural legitimacy. A *Joongang* editorial on July 20, 2013, for instance, criticized it on three grounds.[36] First, postponing a previously agreed-upon transfer every few years hurts South Korea's diplomatic credibility. Second, rather than forged in secrecy, a decision of this import should have first sought public consultation. Finally, the underlying reason for this repeated delay is that South Korean military does not have the requisite capability to confront the North on its own. On this last point, *Joongang* stressed that the initiative to modernize the military has been thwarted due to various logistical challenges in the past. To overcome this hurdle, the government must obtain public approval for increasing investment into capacity-building.

Still, other conservative coverage sought to justify Park's decision given its national security imperative. According to *Donga* on July 18, 2013, the details of the "conditions" for the transfer were still to be determined. Instead, it stated: "What is important—whether the OPCON transfer is executed on time or delayed somewhat—is that the United States and South Korea's allied strategic capability against the North Korean threat cannot be weakened." This seemed to suggest that, in fact, the emphasis on the specific date of the transfer is misplaced; so long as the decision provided greater national security, it was worthwhile.

China

As China's relations with North Korea soured, public discourse began to speculate about the prospects of China-South Korea cooperation. Two events, in particular, highlighted this debate: (1) Xi's visit to Seoul in 2014; and (2) Park's visit to

Beijing in 2015. Both sides were increasingly optimistic about the warming ties with Beijing, although progressives underscored some fundamental constraints posed by the intensifying US-China competition. Most notably perhaps, conservatives who had historically chided cooperation with China were—if somewhat less enthusiastically—supportive of Park's endeavor. This could signify one of two things: (1) a deepening identity clash as conservatives recalibrate how best to counter the North Korean threat; or (2) the dogmatization of partisan media as conservatives rallied in support of their conservative leader, regardless of the specific contours of her policy agenda. Either way, the surprising unity among partisan narratives on China boded well for Park's *trustpolitik*.

Xi's visit to South Korea on July 3, 2014, was seen as consequential for many reasons—Xi had not yet been to Pyongyang, and the visit had emerged in the wake of Japan's decision to revise its pacifist Constitution, presumably to counter China.[37] For this reason, Xi's visit was observed with wariness in the US, interpreting it as an attempt to drive a wedge among US allies. In advance of the visit, China's vice foreign minister Liu Zhenmin warned explicitly: "The United States and South Korea are allies, but I think South Korea will be cautious to respond to the request because South Korea, like China, wants stability and does not want to see tensions and an arms race."[38] In this manner, Xi's visit was emblematic of intensifying US-China competition, and South Korea's ambiguous role in it.

Partisan narratives split over the meaning of the visit. In general, conservative coverage provided a more nuanced critique: symbolically, the visit was consequential, though practically, some of the key details regarding the North Korean nuclear problem remained unspecified. A *Joongang* editorial on July 4, 2014, noted that the visit signified a maturing of the two countries' strategic partnership on issues ranging from trade, financial infrastructure, and environmental protection to nuclear safety; from a broad perspective, they had become "a step closer."[39] At the same time, *Joongang* emphasized: "US-South Korean alliance founded on principles of freedom and democracy is fundamentally different from China-South Korea relations based on economic gains and historical ties." The key was, thus, to ensure the two did not become a zero-sum game.

By contrast, progressive outlets were less optimistic. A *Hankyoreh* editorial on July 4, 2014, observed that no meaningful consensus was reached on two issues of import: North Korean nuclear proliferation and Japanese historical revisionism.[40] On the former, besides reiterating support for denuclearization, no specific solutions were provided; South Korea should have been the one to prepare creative options and steer the discussion, but it failed to embrace this kind of activism. Already, the US-led pressure approach, accompanied by multilateral sanctions, was losing support—even its most staunch ally Japan was loosening its grip in exchange for the return of Japanese abductees. Yet, a new course of action was nowhere to be seen. On the latter, no mention of Japan's historical revisionism was made, although both China and South Korea shared interests in correcting it. Once again, *Hankyoreh* blamed Seoul's tepid attitudes, fearing that any mention of Japan would trigger charges of geostrategic realignment (away from the trilateral framework that the US has sought in concert with Japan). Overall, progressive narratives construed Xi's visit as an illustration of the fundamental constraints in China-South Korea relations and a confirmation of the status quo positionalities.

Still, Park continued to court China, culminating in her attendance as the only US ally at the Victory Day Parade in Beijing in 2015. This decision had been highly controversial abroad.[41] Though the US State Department had officially maintained that it "respects" Seoul's decision as a "sovereign" state, many were wary about possible strains this might pose on US-South Korean relations.[42] Nonetheless, partisan narratives about Park's decision were not as polarizing as one might have surmised; both camps accepted that it was the right—albeit risky—decision. Where they differed was what Seoul should do in its immediate aftermath: progressives pushed for the resumption of talks with North Korea whereas conservatives recommended a careful debrief with the United States.

Indeed, progressive commentators welcomed Park's decision to accept Xi's invitation. A *Hankyoreh* editorial on August 27, 2015, saw Park's visit as a sign of warming ties—a rare opportunity for her to cement China's commitment to the multilateral peace process (within the Six-Party Talks framework).[43] It noted, too, that the conditions for this type of diplomatic maneuver were propitious: there was now a stable channel of communication between the two Koreas, and South Korea had successfully arranged bilateral summits with all key stakeholders. Likewise, a *Kyunghyang* editorial on September 1, 2015, urged her to adopt an active approach to diplomacy, one that guards South Korea's autonomy in the face of US-China competition.[44]

Surprisingly, conservative commentators—who have tended to prioritize the US alliance—were also sympathetic toward Park's decision. A *Chosun Ilbo* editorial on August 21, 2015, seemed to suggest it was inevitable: China is an integral part of South Korea's economic and political realities; it was thus important for South Korea to engage China diplomatically.[45] In this vein, a *Donga Ilbo* editorial on August 28, 2015, urged Park to use the opportunity to consolidate Beijing's support for her North Korea policy as well as South Korea's broader strategic role in the region.[46] A *Joongang* editorial on the same day echoed this message, emphasizing that the summit was a high-stakes event because Park chose to go in spite of US and Japanese reservations.[47] In this way, conservative coverage pressed for caution.

Some saw the conservative coverage of Park's China policy during this period as unprincipled. One analyst referenced conservative reactions to previous China-related issues, including South Korea's decision to join the China-led Asia Infrastructure and Investment Bank (AIIB) or *not* to join the US-led THAAD missile defense system.[48] In both occasions, conservative media condemned the government for pursuing a pro-China policy at the expense of alliance commitment. Yet, when Park sought to court China, criticisms by conservative commentators became muffled; instead, rosy projections about middle power diplomacy and

South Korean leverage abounded. This, the analyst argued, indicated a "dogmatization" of conservative media, adopting whichever position is politically expedient for partisan interests.

Japan

Several scandals during this period continued to plague South Korea-Japan relations. On December 26, 2013, the then Japanese Prime Minister Abe Shinzo made an official visit to the Yasukuni Shrine—a controversial site that houses Japan's war dead, including 14 convicted war criminals—to the outrage of South Korea and China. This had long been feared, as by *Chosun* on October 19, 2013, which noted the rise of historical revisionism under the Abe administration.[49] By early April 2014, other controversies abounded, as Japanese officials made incendiary remarks about the lack of coercion of wartime sex slaves—commonly called the "comfort women"—and attended the "Takeshima Day" events. Crucially, Japan also introduced new history textbooks that described the disputed islands as Japan's "sovereign territory" and claimed South Korea's occupation "unlawful." Each controversy was seen as an attempt to warp the meaning of prior apologies and deny official recognition of responsibility. Tensions were mounting fast.

Unlike most other issues where partisan narratives tended to differ in scope and emphasis, they were uniquely consensual on Japanese historical revisionism. Both sides condemned Japan for its lack of contrition—which many observers described as immature, arrogant, and dangerous—and questioned even the sincerity of its previous acts of penitence. It was only as relations improved in the latter half of 2015—culminating swiftly in the ill-reputed "comfort women" agreement on December 28—that partisan narratives began to diverge once again, with a progressive emphasis on historical rectification and a conservative focus on strategic cooperation.

Partisan narratives converged on the idea that the Yasukuni Shrine carried special connotations, which whitewash and glorify Japan's violent past. When Abe likened the Shrine to the Arlington national cemetery in an interview with *Foreign Affairs* on May 16, 2013,[50] criticisms reverberated in South Korea. A *Joongang* editorial on May 21, 2013, found the analogy entirely misguided[51]: it argued that while Arlington symbolized the unity and reconciliation of a divided country, Yasukuni worshipped those who fought in service of a militaristic empire. That one can visit Yasukuni to wish for peace was, therefore, a contradiction. A *Hankyoreh* editorial on the same day echoed this view, adding that "it was as ignorant, anti-historical speech-act as if the German chancellor paid her respects in Hitler's grave and asked how it differed from going to Arlington."[52]

Partisan narratives also voiced in unison that visits to Yasukuni Shrine constituted a provocation. This was particularly so when Abe himself made a surprise visit to the Shrine on December 26, 2013. A *Donga* editorial the next day argued that it was fundamentally at odds with Japan's claims to seeking peace and, in fact, revealed the remnants of its imperial thinking.⁵³ A *Kyunghyang* editorial on the same day similarly portrayed his visit as an "insult to history"—one that erases the image and reputation that Japan had sought to build as a peaceful country in the postwar period.⁵⁴ Notably, *Kyunghyang* speculated, too, that Abe had orchestrated the visit on populist impulses; recalling South Korea's ex-president Lee Myung-bak's visit to Dokdo on the heels of a domestic legitimacy crisis, *Kyunghyang* saw Abe's visit to the Shrine as a last-ditch effort to recover approval ratings. It warned in this regard: "Actions provoking nationalism in neighboring countries often give power to the hardliners and this in turn brings the conservatives within Japan together, leading to a vicious cycle where conflict intensifies. [...] At a time when Abe should have refrained from disturbing the situation in Northeast Asia, he chose to light a fire in the powder magazine."

Partisan narratives continued to converge as reports of Japan's new history textbooks in mid-2014 and its coverage of the disputed islands raised South Korea's ire. Both sides argued that the textbooks make reconciliation less likely in the future because they instill a misguided sense of patriotism and rationalize Japan's past wrongdoings. In this regard, a *Kyunghyang* editorial on April 4, 2014, emphasized the importance of education for learning from history and avoiding past mistakes: recent textbook revisions defied this imperative by planting the seeds of conflict over generations.⁵⁵ Likewise, a *Joongang* editorial on April 5, 2014, stressed how the islands were mischaracterized as illegally occupied by South Korea—a standpoint that will surely impart a desire for their "retrieval."⁵⁶

At the same time, conservative editorials noted the contradictory and gradual processes by which Japan had orchestrated the textbook revisionism. The aforementioned *Joongang* editorial criticized Abe's "two-face" politics; he had put on a friendly face during the trilateral summit with the US in the Hague less than two weeks ago but revealed his true attitudes when it mattered. A *Chosun* editorial on April 5, 2014, also pointed out that Japan had sought to revise its textbook a little by little since 2008 when it first explicitly acknowledged the "differences in perspectives" surrounding the territory.⁵⁷ In 2010, it had only asserted one out of five islets to be its own; now it was claiming all of them. Overall, they insinuated that Japan was purposefully carrying out historical revisionism, countering suspicion with symbolic gestures but implementing a steady process of historical forgetting.

Conclusion

A deepening rift about the implications of instability in the North Korean regime for Park's foreign policy emerged. While both sides saw internal purges and external provocations as Kim's attempt to consolidate power, they diverged on policy prescriptions. Progressives expected a strengthening of the North Korean regime as Kim eliminated factions; this, in their view, paved the way for more dialogue and compromise as a secure regime would find diversionary crises less necessary or desirable. Conservatives, meanwhile, speculated about the impending regime collapse in North Korea; they saw mounting frictions at home as evidence of a systemic flaw that would eventually result in breakdown. These varying interpretations undergirded what each side believed was the "right" balance of coercion and engagement vis-à-vis North Korea—with a progressive emphasis on tension reduction and a conservative focus on deterrence.

Still, partisan narratives struck a surprising accord on the necessity of China in Park's *trustpolitik*. Progressives supported Park's engagement with China, even as they questioned Park's motives or China's enthusiasm. More remarkably, conservatives also endorsed Park's policy despite the frictions it would generate with the US. Beijing's aloofness toward Pyongyang and the US "strategic patience" had created an auspicious opening for a more conspicuous balancing act. Though progressives identified and highlighted the inconsistencies in conservative stances vis-à-vis China as US demands for trilateralism grew, these criticisms found little traction in the midst of what appeared a genuine breakthrough in relations with China. Most took a wait-and-see approach.

Against this backdrop, tensions mounted over the nature and scope of South Korea's commitment to the US alliance. North Korea's missile and nuclear provocations continued to raise questions about the viability of US assurances, while a deepening "strategic partnership" with China generated contradictions in South Korea's broader alignment decisions. This posed a particularly daunting dilemma for the country's conservatives, whose identities had been historically conditioned by their antagonism of North Korea and, therefore, allegiance to the US. This was evident as a small but growing bloc of conservatives found "alternative" solutions to the North Korean threat—including self-nuclearization and bargaining with China—increasingly palatable. Yet, existing security institutions, such as the OPCON arrangement, provided some sense of continuity in the US–South Korean alliance. The conclusions to this debate were far from predetermined.

If partisan narratives continued to diverge on North Korea—and shape, by extension, those on the US and China—they proved unified on Japan in a unique and lasting manner. Amid a stream of controversies surrounding the Yasukuni visits, "comfort women," territorial disputes, and textbook revisions, both sides pushed for a more aggressive stance. In this regard, Park's sidelining of Abe was largely deemed appropriate if not inevitable. Any unilateral, conciliatory gestures would have triggered a strong public backlash; if there were attempts at rapprochement, they certainly could not be public. This would prove true when Park announces the "comfort women agreement" at the very close of 2015, having blindsided the country with a "final and irreversible" resolution that would resonate with few. In fact, the secrecy with which the deal had been forged will come to backfire massively a year later, when following a series of scandals, Park will be impeached for corruption.

Notes

1 Choe Sang-hun, *The New York Times*, March 12, 2016.
2 Da Zhigang, *Global Times*, January 6, 2014.
3 Mu Chunshan, *The Diplomat*, December 21, 2013.
4 Scott Snyder and See-won Byun, "Crying Uncle No More: Stark Choices for Relations," *Comparative Connections,* Vol. 15, No. 3 (2013). https://cc.pacforum.org/2014/01/crying-uncle-no-stark-choices-relations/
5 *Hankyoreh*, December 4, 2013.
6 *Kyunghyang Shinmun*, December 10, 2013.
7 *Donga Ilbo*, December 10, 2013.
8 *Donga Ilbo*, December 14, 2013; *Chosun Ilbo*, December 14, 2013.
9 *Segye Ilbo*, December 10 & 18, 2013.
10 *Chosun Ilbo*, January 3, 2014.
11 Park Geun-hye, *Foreign Affairs*, September/October 2011.
12 Yoon Byung-se, *Global Asia*, September 2013.
13 Mark Landler and David Sanger, *The New York Times*, May 7, 2013.
14 Zachary Keck, *The Diplomat*, May 9, 2013.
15 Sang-hyun Lee, "The Northeast Asia Peace and Cooperation Initiative (NAPCI): A Vision toward Sustainable Peace and Cooperation in Northeast Asia," *The Asan Forum,* December 14, 2014.
16 See Beyond Parallel: https://beyondparallel.csis.org/database-north-korean-provocations/.
17 Curtis Melvin, *38 North*, May 21, 2013.
18 Scott Snyder, *Asia Bound*, January 31, 2014.
19 Korea Chair Monitor, CSIS, June 13-June 26, 2013.
20 Mark Landler and David Sanger, *The New York Times*, May 8, 2013.
21 Park Geun-hye, *New Year's Address*, January 6, 2014.
22 *Hankyoreh*, March 12, 2014.
23 Hong Kyudok, "A South Korean Perspective on Dealing with North Korean Provocations: Challenges and Opportunities," in Gilbert Rozman, ed., *Joint US-Korea Academic Studies* (Korea Economic Institute, 2015), p. 211.
24 Chung Mong-joon, "Thinking the Unthinkable on the Korean Peninsula," *Issues & Insights,* Vol. 14, No. 2 (January 24, 2014).
25 *Chosun Ilbo*, April 28, 2014.
26 *Chosun Ilbo*, April 22, 2013.
27 Peter Hays and Moon Chung-in, "한국, 핵무장 해야 하는가?" NAPSNet Policy Forum, July 28, 2014.
28 See "JCPOA at a Glance," Arms Control Association, November 2021, https://www.armscontrol.org/factsheets/JCPOA-at-a-glance.
29 *Hankyoreh*, July 15, 2015.
30 *Joongang Ilbo,* July 15, 2015.
31 President Roh's Speech at the 57th Armed Forces Day's Ceremony, October 1, 2005.
32 Yoon Seo-yeon, "Seoul's Wartime Operational Control Transfer Debate," *Journal of International and Area Studies*, Vol. 22, No. 2 (2015), pp. 89–108, p. 89.
33 Yoon Seo-yeon, "Seoul's Wartime Operational Control Transfer Debate," *Journal of International and Area Studies*, Vol. 22, No. 2 (2015), p. 94.
34 *Hankyoreh*, July 18, 2013.
35 *Hankyoreh*, October 1, 2013.
36 *Joongang Ilbo*, July 20, 2013.
37 Jane Perlez, *The New York Times,* July 2, 2014.
38 Ibid.
39 *Joongang Ilbo*, July 4, 2014.

40 *Hankyoreh,* July 4, 2014.
41 Robert Kelly, *The Interpreter,* September 7, 2015.
42 *Hankyoreh,* September 5, 2015.
43 *Hankyoreh,* August 27, 2015.
44 *Kyunghyang Shinmun,* September 1, 2015.
45 *Chosun Ilbo,* August 21, 2015.
46 *Donga Ilbo,* August 28, 2015.
47 *Joongang Ilbo,* August 28, 2015.
48 Kim Min-ha, *Mediaus,* August 28, 2015.
49 *Chosun Ilbo,* October 19, 2013.
50 *Foreign Affairs,* May 16, 2013.
51 *Joongang Ilbo,* May 20, 2013.
52 *Hankyoreh,* May 20, 2013.
53 *Donga Ilbo,* December 27, 2013.
54 *Kyunghyang Shinmun,* December 27, 2013.
55 *Kyunghyang Shinmun,* April 4, 2014.
56 *Joonang Ilbo,* April 5, 2014.
57 *Chosun Ilbo,* April 5, 2014.

4
GREAT HOPES, SHATTERED DREAMS

Sue Mi Terry

President Park Geun-hye entered office with high hopes of making progress with the North by pursuing a more balanced, middle-of-the-road policy than her predecessors. Yet, her so-called *trustpolitik* approach had failed by the end of 2015. The situation at the end of 2015 resembled the beginning of her term in 2013, when the North conducted a third nuclear test just weeks before her inauguration. The question Park had to deal with for her remaining time in office was what course corrections she needed to make. In 2016 she was forced to abruptly alter her North Korea policy by adopting tougher measures, including deploying the controversial THAAD missile defense system and closing the joint Kaesong Industrial Complex that had been a lucrative venture for the North for over a decade. At the end of the year, she was ousted from the presidency over a corruption scandal involving her and her lifelong confidant, Choi Soon-sil. In 2017, when the new president, Moon Jae-in, came into office, he championed a policy of engagement and rapprochement with Pyongyang even as the North crossed the twin thresholds of developing a thermonuclear weapon and flight-testing intercontinental ballistic missiles (ICBM's). Meanwhile, the new US administration of President Donald Trump pursued a "maximum pressure" policy while talking of "fire and fury" and a "bloody nose" preemptive strike against the North. After a dramatic shift to summitry and diplomacy in 2018–2019—which included three unprecedented, face-to-face meetings between Kim Jong-un and Trump in Singapore, Hanoi, and the DMZ—the Moon administration would oversee the greatest decline of tensions on the peninsula since the end of the Korean War. But the rapprochement would not last.

Moon's gamble on Trump and Kim would not lead to lasting peace on the Korean Peninsula or progress toward denuclearization. Donald Trump, despite a

DOI: 10.4324/9781003394792-5

declaration that he and Kim "fell in love" with the exchange of beautiful letters, was not able to convince Kim to take steps toward giving up his nuclear arsenal. Moon's optimistic approach in the end exposed a profound misreading of both Trump and Kim. After the failure of the Hanoi Summit in February 2019, Moon was left isolated: scorned by Kim, who blamed him for the failure, and eyed warily by Trump. This chapter covers these dramatic years from 2016 to 2019, which saw both great tensions and high hopes on the Korean Peninsula. This period represented a high point in South Korean expectations that diplomacy and summitry with the North could succeed—only to have those expectations brutally dashed.

The Rocky Transition in 2016–17: THAAD Controversy, Park's Impeachment, and Trump's "Fire and Fury"

The year 2016 began on an unsettling note when, on January 6, the North carried out its fourth nuclear test. Park's immediate response was to raise South Korea's military posture, seek additional sanctions against the Kim regime from the United Nations Security Council (UNSC), and resume anti-North Korea messaging through loudspeakers at the DMZ.[1] Park also declared on January 13 that Seoul would finally consider deployment of the US Terminal High Altitude Area Defense (THAAD) missile system. The initial discussions on THAAD deployment began several years earlier on February 27, 2014, in the aftermath of a fresh round of Scud-class ballistic missile tests conducted by the North. In June of that year, the then-commander of United States Forces Korea, General Curtis Scaparrotti, revealed that he had personally made a request to Washington to deploy a THAAD system to Korea. Seoul, however, did not explicitly declare its intention to participate in the missile defense system at that time. A year later, in February 2015, Beijing formally expressed its concerns over the deployment of THAAD during a meeting between the defense ministers of China and South Korea. In the following month, the South Korean presidential office offered reassurances to Beijing with the so-called "three no's," stating that South Korea had neither requested nor consulted with the US government on the deployment of the THAAD system and that it had not made any decisions on the deployment. In fact, whenever Beijing had asked about the THAAD issue, the Park government had maintained the posture that nothing was determined and the government position continued to be "no request, no consultation, and no decision" on THAAD.[2]

That thinking changed with the North's fourth nuclear test. Xi Jinping's refusal to take a call from Park following the North's nuclear test likely reinforced her thinking that she had made the right call on THAAD. This must have been deeply disappointing for Park since she had invested considerable time and resources to improve Seoul's bilateral relations with Beijing. Seoul and Beijing had enjoyed a degree of "honeymoon" in the previous few years; Park and Xi had exchanged visits in 2014, and, in 2015, Park even observed the military parade in Beijing, where no other leader from the liberal world was in attendance.

A combination of the North's fourth nuclear test, Xi's disappointing nonresponse, and yet another satellite launch by the North on February 7, in violation of UNSC resolutions, led to a broader shift in Seoul taking a tougher stance toward the North for the remainder of Park's presidency. Following her declaration on THAAD in January, Seoul and Washington announced the establishment of a joint task force to discuss the deployment a month later. Furthermore, in an effort to impose unilateral sanctions against the Kim regime, Park declared on February 10 that Seoul would "completely shut down" the 11-year-old joint Kaesong Industrial Complex (KIC), an important symbol of inter-Korean rapprochement.[3] KIC housed at the time around 55,000 North Korean workers and churned out products ranging from watches to clothes. The joint venture was highly lucrative for the Kim regime; in 2015 alone, 124 South Korean firms operating in the complex paid North Korea around $120 million for their workers.[4] In response to Park's announcement, the North announced that it was expelling all remaining South Korean workers in the KIC and freezing all assets in the complex. It also severed inter-Korean military hotlines and restored military control over the KIC zone and warned there would be future "consequences."[5]

On July 8, the joint South Korea-US task force officially announced its decision to deploy a THAAD battery in the mountains of North Gyeongsang Province in the southeastern part of South Korea. This announcement was met with fierce resistance from local residents and other opponents who argued that, since the interception range of the THAAD system was only about 200 kilometers, it was unable to defend the capital region, where close to half of South Korea's population is concentrated. Rather than protecting Korean civilians, the system was being used to cover the US air base at Osan, the planned new US headquarters at Pyeongtaek, the South Korean military headquarters at Gyeryongdae, and nuclear power plants in the vicinity. Other critics also pointed out that the US-South Korea agreement on the deployment of the THAAD system should have required ratification by the National Assembly, so the entire process was undemocratic.[6] North Korea also predictably reacted with fury, calling it "aggressive war machinations" with a warning that the North would "take physical countermeasures to thoroughly subdue" the deployment.[7] In response to the protests, and after a brief review process, the Ministry of National Defense finally announced that the THAAD system would be deployed to a civilian golf course owned by the Lotte Group located within the same county but at a higher altitude, and that, based on the US-South Korea Status of Forces Agreement (SOFA), the deployment of the THAAD system was scheduled to be completed in the following year, in mid-2017.

Meanwhile, the North continued to conduct missile tests, including a submarine-launched ballistic missile (SLBM) on August 24, three medium-range ballistic missiles simultaneously on September 5 (which fell in waters that lie within Japan's exclusive economic zone), and its fifth nuclear test on September 9. With controversy still raging over the THAAD decision and concern growing over continued nuclear and missile testing by the North, the Park administration came to an abrupt end in a corruption scandal. Choi Soon-sil was accused of using her proximity to Park to extort massive amounts of money and wield undue influence in the administration, although she held no official government position. On December 9, the National Assembly voted overwhelmingly for Park's impeachment, 234 to 56, with only six abstentions.

As the Constitutional Court deliberated on the impeachment motion at the beginning of the new year, Prime Minister Hwang Kyo-ahn became acting president. (Park's impeachment would be formally approved on March 10, 2017.) Hwang stayed the course on Park's decision to complete deployment of THAAD. With the conclusion of a land exchange agreement on February 28 and with cooperation from Lotte Group, the deployment began to proceed rapidly in early 2017 despite Park's impeachment. By March 7, 2017, it was disclosed to the public that two launchers for THAAD missiles had been moved by transport aircraft into the Osan Air Base. (One THAAD battery is comprised of six truck-mounted launchers and a powerful radar system.)[8]

Beijing had repeatedly expressed its disapproval prior to the decision to deploy the system, and its official media joined in with intense criticism after the decision was made. Economic retaliation swiftly followed, including banning package tours to South Korea, levying penalties against the Lotte Group (Beijing closed down 74 of 99 Lotte stores in China for "fire violations"), canceling Korean artist performances, and restricting dissemination of South Korean entertainment content in China, even as South Korean officials repeatedly explained that the deployment of the THAAD system was aimed at countering nuclear and missile threats from North Korea and had nothing to do with China. These explanations fell on deaf ears. In the first half of 2017 alone, South Korean companies lost an estimated $4.3 billion as a direct result of Beijing's coercive measures.[9]

With a presidential election looming in May to fill Park's seat, candidates in the conservative ruling party generally favored the deployment, while candidates in the opposition progressive camp decried it or took a neutral stance. As a presidential candidate, Moon Jae-in criticized what he called the undemocratic and opaque decision-making processes of the THAAD agreement as well as the partial deployment in the spring.[10] The public was divided on the issue, but, in general, more people supported than opposed deployment.[11]

When Moon became president in May 2017, he embarked on an ambitious engagement policy with the North to "realize peace and prosperity on the Korean peninsula." He had three stated goals: "resolution of the North Korean nuclear issue, development of sustainable inter-Korean relations, and realization of a new economic community on the Korean peninsula."[12] Even as the North tested an ICBM on July 4, Moon remained resolute in his desire to engage the North. The day before the North flight tested an ICBM, while in Washington, Moon promised that Seoul would be in the "driver's seat."[13] A few days after the test, he outlined a vision for inter-Korean peace and economic cooperation focused on establishing a permanent peace regime on the Korean Peninsula.[14] Yet, despite these overtures, the Kim regime continued to respond to Moon's outreached hand with a clenched fist, which included the second test of an ICBM capable of hitting the continental United States on July 28.

Even while pursuing a peace initiative with the North, Moon ultimately chose to stay the existing course on THAAD. After the North's ICBM test in early July, Moon held an emergency meeting with the National Security Council and, in a reversal of his position on THAAD, announced that he would agree to allow the United States to deploy the four remaining launchers to complete the THAAD battery, albeit only "temporarily." Moon's decision triggered more demonstrations by anti-THAAD activists. On September 6–7, despite the North testing a powerful thermonuclear weapon just days before, a fierce 16-hour confrontation took place between 8,000 police and some 600 protesters in Soseong-ri as the Moon administration cleared the way for US delivery of the launchers and other equipment.[15]

The North kept pace with its testing. On September 3, the North conducted its sixth nuclear test, this time testing a powerful hydrogen bomb that could be mounted on an intercontinental missile. The bomb's explosive yield was at least five times larger than the one detonated in September 2016 and up to eight times stronger than the bomb dropped on Hiroshima in 1945.[16] In response, Trump dispatched a US Navy carrier battle group, making a high-profile show of military force near the Korean Peninsula. He also threatened to unleash "fire and fury" on the North while boasting of his "much bigger" nuclear button if the North conducted another nuclear or missile test. His aides even talked of possibly taking preemptive military action by giving the Kim regime a "bloody nose." The United States also ramped up its enforcement of sanctions by targeting North Korean shipping and blacklisting small banks based in China and Eastern Europe in a bid to cut off nearly all of Pyongyang's sources of hard currency. By the fall of 2017, to the surprise of many long-time Korean hands, even Beijing finally appeared to be taking genuine steps to enforce UN sanctions.

In the aftermath of the sixth nuclear test, Moon continued his pursuit of peace initiatives with the North. A mere three weeks after the North tested the hydrogen bomb, Moon attended the UN General Assembly and used his keynote speech to announce the Pyeongchang Peace Initiatives, under which North Korea would participate in the 2018 Winter Olympics. Moon envisioned turning the Winter Olympics into the Olympics of Peace, an opportunity to entice Kim to dialogue. Trump criticized the Moon administration for his supposed appeasement of the North. By the time the tumultuous year came to a close, North Korea had conducted more than ten missile tests in addition to its sixth nuclear test.

Summitry and Diplomacy in 2018: Maximum Engagement

Kim Jong-un began 2018 with a dramatic turn to diplomacy and a charm offensive. Just as concerns about North Korea nearing the finish line in its development of nuclear-armed ICBMs increased, Kim declared the North's nuclear program to be "complete" and used his 2018 New Year's Address to signal a move away from testing. Accepting Moon's olive branch, Kim indicated a willingness to participate in the February 2018 Winter Olympics in South Korea. Kim subsequently sent a delegation of North Korean athletes led by high-level officials including his own sister, Kim Yo-jong, who arrived in the South on February 9 for the opening ceremony, carrying a personal letter from Kim Jong-un to Moon. Diplomacy ramped up in the coming months with Moon and Kim meeting on two separate occasions and culminated in the 2018 summit between Trump and Kim in Singapore. The signing of a peace treaty between the two nations seemed likely until the collapse of the Hanoi Summit in 2019.

North Korea's participation in the Pyeongchang Winter Olympics was soon followed by a March trip of high-level South Korean officials to Pyongyang, led by Moon's National Security Adviser Chung Eui-yong and Chief of National Intelligence, Suh Hoon, the first South Korean envoys to visit Pyongyang in over a decade. The five-member South Korean delegation met with Kim Jong-un. The delegation then rushed to Washington claiming that Kim was willing to negotiate denuclearization and that he wished to meet with Trump. To date it remains an open question what exactly was discussed in Pyongyang. It's possible, or even probable, that the South Koreans liberally edited Kim's actual words about his willingness to give up nuclear weapons. As for Kim asking to meet with Trump, Trump's former National Security Advisor John Bolton wrote in his memoir that the Trump-Kim summit in Singapore was a "diplomatic fandango" which was "South Korea's creation," rather than a serious strategy on Kim's part or Washington's. He even noted that it was Chung who had suggested to Kim that he make the invitation to Trump.[17] Whatever the case, it did the trick. Moon was in the driver's seat of rapprochement during this period; on March 8, the world saw South Korean National Security Advisor Chung standing in front of the White House, announcing that Trump had, on the spur of the moment, accepted Kim's invitation for a summit. Affirming the announcement, Trump quickly tweeted, "Great progress being made but sanctions will remain until an agreement is reached. Meeting being planned!" And with that tweet, the frantic season of summitry began in earnest that spring: two summits between Trump and Kim, three inter-Korean summits between Moon and Kim, and a number of summits between Kim and other leaders, most notably Xi and Putin. Yet, while the frenetic summitry of 2018–2019 defused the "fire and fury" crisis of 2017, it did not yield a denuclearization deal.

The season of summitry began with Moon visiting Beijing on March 28, where he met with Xi Jinping in his first foreign trip since taking office. (Xi and Kim had not yet met each other at this point.) On April 21, the North announced with great fanfare that it was foregoing further nuclear and ballistic missile testing because it was a nuclear power. A summit between Moon and Kim followed a week later on April 27 in the Demilitarized Zone at Panmunjom. Moon and Kim announced a joint declaration declaring their commitment to the denuclearization of the Korean

Peninsula, the future establishment of a permanent peace regime, and the resumption of economic and political exchanges.[18]

The Korean public mood was euphoric. It finally appeared the two Koreas were close to making a breakthrough. Moon's approval ratings soared above 80%.[19] Progressive media outlets emphasized the symbolic significance of the summit, noting that Kim Jong-un was the first North Korean leader to have stepped foot in the South since the Korean War when he crossed the demarcation line.[20] Kim and Moon's conviviality also felt authentic, particularly because Kim appeared more open and self-effacing than his father. In a break with his father, Kim Jong-un conceded some of his country's deficiencies—including the decrepit state of its transit system—which helped to create a level of trust with the public in the South. Little gestures were also noticed. Moon wore a blue tie, the color of the Korean Unification Flag, to greet Kim at the demarcation line. Kim Jong-un brought with him a chef who was famous for making *naengmyeon* noodles, a Pyongyang delicacy, as well as a noodle-making machine, so the participants could enjoy freshly made authentic cold noodles from Pyongyang.[21] The two leaders marked the summit by planting a sapling from a pine tree that was originally planted in 1953, the year the Korean Armistice was signed.

Moon was "ecstatic" when he called Trump following his meeting with Kim, according to Bolton. Moon told Trump that Kim had made a commitment to "complete denuclearization," offering to close the Punggye-ri nuclear test site in May.[22] Moon said that, during their meeting, Kim even disclosed that two of the four underground tunnels at the test site were still "usable" but that they would be sealed off as well.[23] Moon reportedly asked Kim to denuclearize in one year, and Kim agreed. The two leaders left the summit agreeing to an additional summit in Pyongyang in the fall, making concrete their plans for deepening engagement. When Moon suggested that Kim visit the South someday, Kim readily consented, raising the prospect of an unprecedented inter-Korean summit in South Korea.

The opposition conservatives expressed skepticism while acknowledging the summit's effect on relieving tension on the Korean Peninsula. The conservative media coverage criticized the summit as mostly empty in substance, particularly regarding denuclearization. One of the chief concerns was over the fact that "denuclearization," a "sole objective" for which the summit was convened, has taken a back seat to other, less important matters, such as North-South cooperation. There was also concern over the ambiguity of the term "complete denuclearization of the Korean *peninsula*," particularly in comparison to the more precise wording used in prior agreements with the North. To critics, Moon seemed to have promised too much to Kim, including agreeing to designate the Northern Limit Line (NLL) a "peace zone" and to halt all hostile activities by land, sea, or air.[24]

Some also pointed out that the "peace act" in Panmunjom could lead to a premature—and potentially dangerous—jubilation and sense of relief in the South. One public opinion survey found that 65% of the respondents said they trusted the North's willingness to denuclearize, while only 28% were skeptical. A similar survey before the summit had painted a very different picture, with 78% saying they distrusted the North's peace gestures and only 15% saying they trusted the North.[25] In the post-summit euphoria, real estate prices near the border spiked, and there was talk of abolishing military conscription in the South.[26]

The Korean public's mood was similarly upbeat about the prospects of the upcoming Trump-Kim summit. Many, particularly in the progressive camp, attributed the historic summit to Moon's commitment to diplomacy.[27] Even opposition party members reluctantly commended the Moon administration for facilitating the Trump-Kim summit, while emphasizing that the ultimate objective of any talks with the North should remain complete, verifiable, and irreversible denuclearization (CVID) and that any decision to temper the US-ROK alliance—either by repealing the US nuclear umbrella or removing US forces from South Korea—must wait until CVID had been achieved.[28] The conservatives also warned of various deals that should not be acceptable to Seoul, including a deal in which Washington demanded that Pyongyang relinquish its ICBMs (which directly threatened the United States) instead of its entire nuclear force.[29]

Moon and Kim met again at the DMZ on May 26, this time on the North's side, four days after Moon met with Trump in Washington and assured Trump that there was no reason to doubt Kim's sincerity on denuclearization. This second meeting between Moon and Kim was held at Kim's request. Since the Trump-Kim meeting was scheduled to be held in Singapore in June, Kim may have sought Moon's advice over how to negotiate with Trump, while reaffirming the two Koreas' will to carry out the Panmunjom joint declaration announced in April. This meeting was followed by more inter-Korean high-level talks to discuss ways to implement the Panmunjom Declaration and reopen a joint liaison office in the KIC.

After hectic summit preparation in which Secretary of State Mike Pompeo made two trips to Pyongyang, Trump finally met Kim in Singapore on June 12–13. However, the joint US-North Korea statement published after the meeting lacked any details of how to move toward the stated goal of the denuclearization of the Korean Peninsula.[30] The Joint Statement shifted from talk of "North Korean denuclearization" to the "denuclearization of the Korean Peninsula," possibly signifying Trump's willingness to trade away US nuclear guarantees to Seoul. Trump had achieved the photo-op that he wanted but not a binding agreement with the North.[31]

Moon was undeterred. Various concessions and peace overtures continued. Two days after the Trump-Kim summit, the two Koreas held high-level military talks, agreeing to fully restore military communication lines in the East Sea and Yellow Sea. The two Koreas also agreed to hold a basketball game in Pyongyang, to make a joint entrance at the opening and closing ceremonies of the 2018 Asian Games, and to field joint teams for several events in the Asian Games. On June 19, Seoul announced jointly with Washington that it would suspend the Ulchi Freedom Guardian joint ROK-US military exercise. There appeared to be momentum for peace. On June 22, the two Koreas held the 12th Red Cross talks at Mount

Geumgang where they agreed to hold family reunions in August. They also agreed to reconnect the western Gyeongui railroad line and the eastern East Sea line, to modernize the section linking Mount Geumgang and the Tumen River, and the section linking Kaesong and Sinuiju. The Moon administration sent a delegation to Mount Geumgang to prepare for family reunions. More working-level talks followed on boosting forestry and road cooperation and resuming ship-to-ship radio communication links for the first time in a decade. By early July, Seoul began preparing for the establishment of the joint liaison office. A 101-member delegation of South Korean athletes and government officials led by Unification Minister Cho Myoung-gyon visited North Korea to participate in inter-Korean basketball games.

Momentum also continued between Washington and Pyongyang. In mid-July, the United States and North Korea held working-level talks on repatriating the remains of American soldiers killed during the Korean War, per the Singapore Declaration. On July 27, North Korea returned 55 sets of remains of American soldiers killed during the war, as described in Kim's personal letter to Trump.

More high-level talks followed during the summer and in late August, and the two Koreas held family reunions at Mount Geumgang. On September 5, Moon's special delegation, led by National Security Adviser Chung, visited the North and met with Kim, and they agreed on a date for the third inter-Korean summit. On September 14, the two Koreas opened a joint liaison office, establishing the first 24/7 inter-Korean communication channel. On September 18–20, Moon and Kim held their third summit, this time in Pyongyang. Moon made a historic speech at the stadium in Pyongyang with about 150,000 rapt North Korean citizens in attendance. Kim publicly seemed to show his willingness to denuclearize in front of his people. This period was the high point in inter-Korea relations, the very moment when it looked as if Moon's peace process could make progress. But these hopeful days would not last. Disappointment was waiting in the wings.

A March Toward Failure and the Collapse of the Hanoi Summit

By 2019, it became clear that things were not going as well as Moon hoped. The ratcheting up of US-China confrontation relieved much of the pressure on Pyongyang as Beijing lost interest in cooperating with Washington. While sanctions remained in place, it became clear that the United States would not launch a preemptive strike on North Korea, thereby further relaxing pressure on Kim. The Hanoi Summit between Trump and Kim ended shortly after it began. Kim demanded that Trump lift most of the US economic sanctions in exchange for the dismantling of the Yongbyon nuclear facility. Trump refused Kim's offer and instead demanded the "complete, verifiable, and irreversible dismantlement" of North Korea's nuclear program—a longtime US demand that is anathema to Pyongyang. At the core, the issue was that both Trump and Kim misunderstood each other and both miscalculated. Trump, thinking Kim was brought to the negotiating table primarily because of his maximum pressure policy and "fire and fury" rhetoric—rather than the North's own advances in its nuclear and missile program—thought he could entice Kim with Vietnam-style economic development. His expectation did not bear out, which was no surprise. In Vietnam's case, adopting Chinese-style economic policies was only possible because of the installation of genuinely reformist leaders who turned their focus toward liberalizing and expanding Vietnam's economy without threatening its neighbors—and that in turn only occurred after they had achieved their dream of unifying all of Vietnam under their rule. Trump had a much more difficult task with Kim—he needed to convince the North Korean leader that he should abandon the nuclear arsenal that keeps his own regime safe and open up the country while its freer, richer rival state continued to exist in the south. Put another way, the Vietnamese were magnanimous in victory, whereas Trump was asking Kim to make sacrifices in de facto defeat. Meanwhile Kim also miscalculated, thinking that Trump was so eager for a deal (and a Nobel Peace Prize) that he was willing to sign on to a bad deal. But, back in Washington, Republicans supported Trump's decision to walk away from the negotiating table without reaching an agreement with Kim, saying that "no deal is better than a bad deal."[32]

Trump walking away from Hanoi basically spelled the end of Moon's illusion that he was in the driver's seat. Kim subsequently seemed to blame Moon for the failure in Hanoi and turned to his traditional allies, China and Russia. He met with Putin in April and hosted Xi Jinping in June and then refused to include Moon in his meet-and-greet with Trump at Panmunjom four months after the Hanoi Summit.

Yet the Moon administration persisted in its peace offensive. Even after the Hanoi debacle, Moon and his advisers still sought to improve relations with the North, and some probably held onto hopes of a lasting deal. But, there was little they could do other than continue to call for a softer approach to Kim and relaxation of sanctions, more in line with Xi and Putin's positions than the US one. The Kim regime, having recovered from the uncertainty of 2017, the undue hopes of 2018, and the frustration and embarrassment of Hanoi in early 2019, returned to a hardline stance: Kim did not need more promises from Seoul but money and sanctions relief that the Moon administration could not give. UN Security Council sanctions made it all but impossible for Seoul to provide North Korea with material aid of any kind.

Increasingly desperate, the Moon administration tried to create the right optics by insisting that the North remained interested in denuclearization even though there was no evidence to support this claim. The collapse of the 2019 Hanoi Summit had put an end even to the hopes of a partial arms-control deal and firmly demonstrated that North Korean denuclearization was not going to happen, no matter what Moon's officials kept telling themselves, the public, and Washington. The Moon administration kept showering the North with various proposals for cultural exchanges and humanitarian aid while downplaying or turning a blind eye to Pyongyang's outrageous actions. Moon continued to support scrapping the annual US-ROK joint military exercises and, more controversially, enacted and continued to defend an anti-leaflet law which criminalized the distribution of anti-regime leaflets into the North, despite mounting international criticism that the legislation curtailed freedom of speech.

Conclusion

In 2017, Moon started his term of office quite cautiously, dealing with the difficult challenges of deploying THAAD and coping with the fallout, while managing US-South Korea alliance relations during the year of Trump's "maximum pressure" and "fire and fury." In 2018, Moon made a bold bet on Kim and Trump, which appeared to put Seoul in the driver's seat in a spurt of diplomacy. Yet this optimism reflected a misreading of both Kim and Trump. The euphoria continued into 2019 without any proof that diplomacy would end well. After February 2019, Moon was isolated—scorned by Kim Jong-un, pressured by Trump—and dealing with a Korean public increasingly skeptical of his peace offensive. In the end, Moon did not accomplish his goal of trying to end the threat from North Korea and bring peace to the Korean Peninsula. But no other Korean leader going back to the dark days of the Korean War has had any greater success in dealing with the intractable threat from the North. Neither the Sunshine Policy, *trustpolitik*, "maximum pressure" nor a policy of "maximum engagement" has succeeded in ending the North Korean nuclear and missile programs. By 2019, it was clear that Moon had failed. He was learning again what should have been already obvious: Until there is internal change in North Korea, there is little that South Korea or the United States can accomplish diplomatically.

Notes

1 Saetbyul Park, "President Park Assembles NSC in Response to North Korean 4th Nuclear Tests," *Gonggam*, January 11, 2016, https://gonggam.korea.kr/newsView.do?newsId=01Ic02ewDGJMP000. Also see, Hwanyong Kim, "South Korean President 'North Korean Missiles Unacceptable... Strong UN Sanctions Needed'," *VOA Korea*, February 4, 2016, https://www.voakorea.com/a/3176303.html.
2 Kyounghui Kim and Yongho Shin, "'Government's Position on THAAD Is 3NO'," *Joongang Ilbo*, March 11, 2015, https://www.joongang.co.kr/article/17333467#home.
3 Byunghwa Kim, "[Kaesong Industrial Complex Shutdown] North Korea Responds to Government's Cease of Operations," *Hankuk Ilbo*, February 15, 2016, https://magazine.hankyung.com/business/article/201602150103b. Also see, Dongjoo Seo, "Why the Kaesong Industrial Complex Had to Shut Down," Republic of Korea Policy Briefing, February 18, 2016, https://www.korea.kr/news/reporterView.do?newsId=148809542.
4 Mark E. Manyin, "The Shutdown of the Joint North/South Korean Kaesong Industrial Complex," Congressional Research Service (CRS), February 11, 2016, https://sgp.fas.org/crs/row/IN10442.pdf.
5 Ibid.

6 See, for example, Younghee Kim, "It's Time to Give Up THAAD," *Joongang Ilbo*, June 30, 2016, https://www.joongang.co.kr/article/20247169#home.
7 Rora Oh, "[Breaking] North Korea Will 'Take Physical Countermeasures Once THAAD Deployment Location Is Confirmed'," *Chosun Ilbo*, July 11, 2016, https://www.chosun.com/site/data/html_dir/2016/07/11/2016071100523.html.
8 See, for example, Myunghyun Koh, "THAAD: An Inevitable Decision," *The Asan Institute for Policy Studies*, July 15, 2016, http://www.asaninst.org/contents/%EC%82%AC%EB%93%9Cthaad%EB%B6%88%EA%B0%80%ED%94%BC%ED%95%9C-%EC%84%A0%ED%83%9D/. Also see, Taewoo Kim, "The THAAD Issue Should Be Decided According to Security and National Interest Considerations," *IFS Post*, May 22, 2017, https://www.ifs.or.kr/bbs/board.php?bo_table=News&wr_id=506.
9 Heekyong Yang and Hyunjoo Jin, "As Missile Row Drags On, South Korea's Lotte Still Stymied in China," *Reuters*, June 16, 2017, https://www.reuters.com/article/lotte-china/as-missile-row-drags-on-south-koreas-lotte-still-stymied-in-china-idUSL3N1JC3BA. Also see, Kye-wan Cho, "In the First Half of 2017, THAAD Retaliation Caused $4.3 Billion in Losses for S. Korean Companies," *Hankyoreh*, July 6, 2017, http://english.hani.co.kr/arti/english_edition/e_business/801752.html.
10 Hyunjoong Kim, "Support, Then Oppose... Moon's Vacillation on THAAD," *New Daily*, March 7, 2017, https://www.newdaily.co.kr/site/data/html/2017/03/07/2017030700057.html. Also see, Minsang Kim, "Moon Jae In to THAAD-Opposing Lee Jae Myung, 'It's Alright to Be Direct, but...'," *Joongang Ilbo*, March 21, 2017, https://www.joongang.co.kr/article/21392617#home.
11 Jisang Le, "[Korea Gallup] THAAD Deployment 53% 'Support' vs 32% 'Oppose'... Support Increases," *Joongang Ilbo*, June 16, 2017, https://www.joongang.co.kr/article/21672605#home. Also see, Toil Kim, "Changes in Public Opinion on THAAD Deployment," *Yonhap News*, June 16, 2017, https://www.yna.co.kr/view/GYH20170616000500044; Gweewon Lee, "52% Support THAAD Deployment, 35% Oppose," *Yonhap News*, March 12, 2017, https://www.yna.co.kr/view/AKR20170312064600001.
12 "Moon Jae-In's Policy on the Korean Peninsula," *Policy Issues*, Ministry of Education, South Korean Government, https://www.unikorea.go.kr/eng_unikorea/policyIssues/koreanpeninsula/goals/.
13 Kyungjoon Park, "President Moon Claims South Korea Will Be in the Driver's Seat for Inter-Korean Relations, Prompting Speculation for a 'New Berlin Statement'," *Yonhap News*, July 3, 2017, https://www.yna.co.kr/view/AKR20170703069851001.
14 Jin Huh, "[Full Text] President Moon's 'New Berlin Statement'," *Joongang Ilbo*, July 6, 2017, https://www.joongang.co.kr/article/21735593#home.
15 Bridget Martin, "Moon Jae-In's THAAD Conundrum: South Korea's 'Candlelight President' Faces Strong Citizen Opposition on Missile Defense," *Asia-Pacific Journal*, Vol. 15, No. 1, https://apjjf.org/2017/18/Martin.html.
16 Bonnie Berkowitz and Aaron Steckelberg, "North Korea Tested Another Nuke. How Big was It?" *Washington Post*, September 14, 2017, https://www.washingtonpost.com/graphics/2017/world/north-korea-nuclear-yield/?utm_term=.1152f8514008.
17 John R. Bolton, *In the Room Where it Happened: A White House Memoir* (New York: Simon & Schuster, 2020), p. 78.
18 "Panmunjom Declaration for Peace, Prosperity and Unification of the Korean Peninsula," *ROK Ministry of Foreign Affairs*, April 27, 2018, https://www.mofa.go.kr/eng/brd/m_5478/view.do?seq=319130&srchFr=&amp%3BsrchTo=&amp%3BsrchWord=&amp%3BsrchTp=&amp%3Bmulti_itm_seq=0&amp%3Bitm_seq_1=0&amp%3Bitm_seq_2=0&amp%3Bcompany_cd=&amp%3Bcompany_nm=&page=1&titleNm=.
19 "Moon's Approval Rating Tops 80 Pct: Survey," *The Korea Times*, May 22, 2017, https://www.koreatimes.co.kr/www/nation/2017/05/356_229771.html. Also see, Thomas Maresca, "South Korea's Moon Jae-in is More Popular Than Ever," *USA Today*, May

10, 2018, https://www.usatoday.com/story/news/world/2018/05/10/south-korea-moon-jae-approval-rating-popularity-north-korea/597557002/.
20 "The Spring of Panmunjom, Opening an Era of Peace and Prosperity," *Hankyoreh*, April 27, 2018, https://www.hani.co.kr/arti/opinion/editorial/842457.
21 "Summit Sparks Pyongyang Noodle Cravings," *The Korea Times*, April 29, 2018, https://www.koreatimes.co.kr/www/nation/2018/04/113_248173.html.
22 John R. Bolton, *In the Room Where it Happened: A White House Memoir* (New York: Simon & Schuster, 2020), p. 81.
23 Whan-woo Yi, "Kim Jong-un Vows to Dismantle Nuke Test Sites in May, Allow US Inspection," *The Korea Times*, April 29, 2018, http://www.koreatimes.co.kr/www/nation/2018/04/113_248150.html.
24 "The Inter-Korean Summit That Passed Nuclear Issues to US and NK and Prioritized Aid to NK," *Chosun Ilbo*, April 28, 2018, https://www.chosun.com/site/data/html_dir/2018/04/27/2018042702874.html.
25 Ji-won Park, "65% of South Koreans Trust Kim Jong-un's Denuke Pledge," *The Korea Times*, April 30, 2018, https://www.koreatimes.co.kr/www/nation/2018/04/113_248198.html. Also see, "It's Too Early to Discuss Ending Mandatory National Service," *Segye Ilbo*, April 30, 2018, https://www.segye.com/newsView/20180430006951.
26 Ibid.
27 "Hoping for a Good Trump-Kim Summit," *Kyunghyang Shinmun*, March 9, 2018, http://news.khan.co.kr/kh_news/khan_art_view.html?artid=201702222159025&code=990101%27%20target=%27_self.
28 "[Editorial] The Trump-Kim Summit That Will Determine the Fate of the Korean Peninsula," *Joongang Ilbo*, March 9, 2018, https://www.joongang.co.kr/article/22428951#home.
29 "[Editorial] The Trump-Kim Summit That Will Determine the Fate of the Korean Peninsula," *Joongang Ilbo*, March 9, 2018, https://www.joongang.co.kr/article/22428951#home.
30 "Joint Statement of President Donald J. Trump of the United States of America and Chairman Kim Jong Un of the Democratic People's Republic of Korea at the Singapore Summit," Ministry of Foreign Affairs, Republic of Korea, June 12, 2018, https://www.mofa.go.kr/eng/brd/m_5478/view.do?seq=319135&srchFr=&%3BsrchTo=&%3BsrchWord=&%3BsrchTp=&%3Bmulti_itm_seq=0&%3Bitm_seq_1=0&%3Bitm_seq_2=0&%3Bcompany_cd=&%3Bcompany_nm=&page=1&titleNm=.
31 A *Chosun Ilbo* article on June 12 posits that Kim's latest peace gesture signals his willingness to accept—or at least work with—US demands of CVID, but wonders what Kim requested in exchange. In terms of security, the article notes two rhetorical shifts from the Trump administration; for more detail, see, "[Editorial] It's Time to Explain to North Korea What Is Being Offered in Exchange for Denuclearization," *Chosun Ilbo*, May 11, 2018, https://www.chosun.com/site/data/html_dir/2018/05/11/2018051102934.html.
32 Michael Burke, "Rubio Defends Trump on North Korea: 'No Deal is Better Than a Bad Deal,'" *The Hill*, February 28, 2019, https://thehill.com/policy/defense/431997-rubio-defends-trump-on-north-korea-no-deal-is-better-than-a-bad-deal/.

5
GAMBLING ON GREAT POWER RELATIONS

Gilbert Rozman

The four years from 2016 to 2019 saw both a high point in expectations that Seoul could reshape geopolitics in Northeast Asia and a low point in awareness that it remained at the mercy of the great powers and North Korea with little agency to pursue its dreams. The period can readily be divided into two: the troubled Park-Moon transition shaken by a downturn in China-ROK ties and the roller-coaster diplomatic ride of the following two years, when Moon gambled both on North Korea and also on great power outreach, audaciously making Seoul the center of transformation. In the background were Donald Trump, a wild card in Washington, emboldened China-Russian joint assertiveness, and Abe Shinzo, with whom Park had cut a deal but Moon never connected.

This chapter separates the two periods and covers ROK relations with China, Russia, and Japan successively for each period, keeping the context of ROK-US and ROK-DPRK relations well in mind. The highs and lows with each great power are clearly indicated: with China, a low in 2016 with no high despite some respite in the second period; with Japan, a high in 2016 descending to a new low in 2019; with Russia, momentary promise but mostly a low ebb; and with the United States, a mirage of positive summitry annually set against a drumbeat of sub-surface tensions.

Two realities of South Korean foreign policy were driven home in this period more than at any other time. First, Seoul kept anticipating a big payoff from its economic clout and geopolitical outreach, assuming it could be a driving force of change in Northeast Asia. Second, it could not escape the reality of being sandwiched between great powers whose aspirations contradicted those it harbored and could leave it feeling isolated and beleaguered with little warning, taking advantage of their own policy preferences toward an often-belligerent North

DOI: 10.4324/9781003394792-6

Korea. Combined, these realities made the period 2016–2019 feel like both the best of times and the worst of times.

The period 2016 to 2019 saw South Korea draw more attention from the outside world than at any previous time apart, perhaps, from the period of democratization leading to Seoul Olympics diplomacy in 1987–88. Its internal turmoil and "candlelight movement" symbolized democracy, its THAAD deployment leading to China's unofficial sanctions and anger set the tone for "wolf warrior" belligerence, its downward spiral with Japan thwarted US alliance-building, and its diplomatic finesse with the US and North Korea led to the negotiations of the decade. Seoul was in for a wild ride: there was no stability to relations with China, Japan, North Korea, or Russia. Ties to the US were more stable, but they could not avoid repeated foreign policy spillover.

The Troubled Transition in 2016–17

Not only was the impeachment of Park a drawn-out affair, Moon's first year was marked by US doubts, Japanese alarm, Chinese pressure, and the "fire and fury" of North Korean belligerence and US threats. Until the end of 2017 there was no clarity on how a progressive president would cope with such a barrage of problems and seemingly zero-sum challenges. The US-China divide, the Japan-ROK slippery slope, and the US-DPRK war scare all posed inescapable dilemmas.

At the start of 2016, four time bombs hung ominously over ROK foreign policy in Asia. Despite the upbeat mood over Park-Xi relations, the agreement with Japan over the "comfort women," and the popularity of US President Barack Obama, many had a sense of foreboding over what was to come. China was threatening if Seoul deployed THAAD, public opinion did not accept the "comfort women" deal with Japan, and the US was calling for a regional alliance, linked to Japan and the South China Sea. Moreover, North Korea was assumed to be ready to undertake threatening moves and even a possible peace offensive, which would expose divergent policies among the great powers.

The winter of 2015–16 had seen a series of transformative developments for ROK foreign policy. On December 28 Seoul and Tokyo finalized their "comfort women" agreement; on January 6 North Korea carried out its fourth nuclear test, and in the aftermath, China refused to answer Park's phone call, Park closed the Kaesong Industrial Complex and abruptly approved deployment of THAAD. Although a new Security Council resolution toughened sanctions on the North, it took 50 days to conclude, and China ensured flexibility in implementing sanctions by inserting the phrase "North Korean people's welfare," a humanitarian clause that leaves enforcement in doubt. Given increased US-China tensions, China-Russia coordination, and Japan-US cooperation, South Korea had lost diplomatic room for maneuver. A turning point had been reached, but it proved difficult for South Koreans to grasp apart from a spike in anxieties. If Park's goals had failed, the alternative of doubling down on the US alliance offered little satisfaction for a state which over 25 years had counted on having realized a leadership role through diplomatic diversification.

Park Geun-hye came under fire not only for previous policies that had failed but also for having no answer to increasing challenges. Chinese Foreign Minister Wang Yi in a speech on February 17 called for a peace agreement to replace the armistice on the peninsula, which was seen as a blow to those focused on denuclearization, a sign that Beijing would only implement sanctions on its own terms and had marginalized Seoul. This was one of many signs that relations with Beijing had been damaged along with hopes for talks with Pyongyang. Moscow's tilt toward Pyongyang was a further blow to Park's agenda. The sharp backlash against her deal with Abe weakened her too.

Through the spring of 2016 the sense kept building that Park's foreign policy agenda could not gain support at home or abroad. China and Russia kept up their barrage of warnings against the deployment of THAAD along with calls to negotiate with North Korea at odds with deterrence. China revealed a difference of opinion on almost every aspect of North Korea besides nuclear weapons. US hopes for trilateral security cooperation with Japan were overshadowed by the mounting anger against the December 28 agreement in South Korea, exacerbated by criticism of new Japanese textbooks, interpreted as proof that the deal made Abe more confident he could distort history. Protection of the "comfort woman" statue by the Japanese embassy in Seoul became a symbol of opposition as did indictments for libeling the victims against a Japanese reporter and an author. Tenser US-China relations added to concern about the THAAD fallout.

The early summer of 2016 saw the actual decision to deploy THAAD, the international court ruling against China on the South China Sea, Brexit, and Donald Trump's ascent as the candidate of the Republican Party. Assumptions of recent years were shattered, one by one. Some critics saw Park dragging South Korea into a US-China struggle, in which China would draw closer to North Korea. Others saw the US forging a regional security framework and pressuring Seoul to join. Inter-Korean conflict was now subsumed in a broader regional stand-off, in which Seoul has little say. The worldview cultivated not only over the Park years but ever since the end of the Cold War was in doubt; yet ideological polarization blurred this recognition. As Park's position was weakened for domestic reasons, her foreign policy decisions were more difficult to defend. Especially, her deal with Abe proved to be a convenient focus of distraction from other issues.

The fall of 2016 and early winter of 2017 saw the greatest instability in Korean foreign policy thinking since the end of the Cold War. North Korea's fifth nuclear test in September led to a wide divide in the response of conservatives and progressives, China's unofficial sanctions over THAAD led to hand-wringing but no sign of an effective response, anger toward Japan focused on Park Geun-hye's decision to join it in a GSOMIA (General Security of Military Information Agreement) with no prospect of reversing the "comfort women" agreement, and Donald Trump's election shook longstanding assumptions about the United States and the

ROK-US alliance. The foreign policy establishment offered one set of responses to this troubled time, which, however, was compounded by a leadership vacuum as Park was in free fall toward impeachment. On the rise, the progressives answered with an entirely different set of prescriptions for moving ahead.

From the center-right establishment rose a call for invigorating the alliance and cooperating more with Japan in this context. The North's nuclear threat had intensified, China was hostile to Seoul and unreliable in opposing the North's threats, and the US needed reassurance. Balancing the US for security and China for economy was no longer tenable. North Korean policy had increased Seoul's dependency on Beijing, and that should end. Given growing isolation, Seoul must double down on its alliance, joining the US on broader East Asian security issues and agreeing to trilateral security cooperation with Japan. The establishment countered the strident opposition to the deal with Japan with three arguments: (1) as in 1965 and 1998 there is serious opposition, but those deals later were accepted, and this one can be normalization 3.0, leading to a new boost in bilateral relations as the process of implementation addresses its faults; (2) the need for Japan on security has risen sharply, due both to deteriorating conditions in their vicinity and to greater uncertainty about the US, to which they could more effectively appeal together, since it is the true balancer in the region; and (3) there is no prospect of Abe sitting with the ROK at the negotiating table again, and no matter how much Koreans are dissatisfied, the purpose of the agreement was to boost national security and make trilateral cooperation easier, meaning that its repeal would strike a blow at an untimely moment to both Seoul's credibility and security.

The above arguments did not persuade progressives, who redoubled their call for dialogue over deterrence, insisted on the priority of inter-Korean relations with warnings against behavior that could seriously raise regional tensions, lumping together the "comfort women" agreement, the deployment of THAAD, and GSOMIA as weakening Seoul's position on key issues while tilting it toward the US and even Japan through Park's "imperialistic" decision-making. This resonated with other criticisms of Park for ignoring the will of the people. Emotions toward Japan could be easily aroused, and the notion that Seoul had to back away from its autonomous diplomacy was a hard sell. Naturally, as Park's fate hung in the balance, foreign affairs coverage was secondary.

All discussion of foreign policy from November 2016 was overshadowed by responses to the victory of Donald Trump. If Trump's arrival raised new uncertainty in North Korea policy, trade, and the alliance, some progressives saw hope that "strategic patience" would be cast aside or that less US pressure would open space for more autonomous foreign policy. Conservatives instead called for tightening ties to the US since no other alternative would serve Seoul's interests adequately. Yet the leadership vacuum in Seoul gave little credibility to officials trying to chart a clear course. Anxiety mounted over a hard line to North Korea raising the risk of conflict, a trade war with China putting South Korea in the crosshairs, and unprecedented pressure on Seoul from the US. Meanwhile, Abe rushed to ingratiate himself with Trump, leaving Seoul at a disadvantage, just as ROK-Japanese tensions over the demolition of a "comfort woman" statue were intensifying.

The transition from an impeached Park Geun-hye to a strongly empowered Moon Jae-in saw a gamble in some ways similar to Park's foreign policy but in other respects strikingly at odds with her approach. Outreach to North Korea stood in the forefront, albeit with far less conditionality. The US alliance was again not directly challenged, but this time utilized to facilitate interactions with the North, playing on the vanity of a new US president, Donald Trump. One big difference was in the treatment of China, which felt marginalized by Moon but won various concessions on strategic policy as he tried to remove THAAD sanctions. Another difference occurred with the repudiation of Park's "comfort women" agreement, setting back relations with Japan barely a year after they had been repaired. The sequence for Moon resembled that for Park: his second year brought a surge of rhetoric about unification—this time backed by diplomacy with Kim Jong-un—and his third year a dead end, accompanied by rising US pressure to reverse course.

The two biggest differences for South Korean diplomacy were the switch to a progressive at the top and the arrival of a US president who was narcissistic about his power to work with dictators and to proceed without concern for foreign policy professionals. Other leaders were the same: Kim Jong-un, now emboldened to flex his military might; Xi Jinping, now increasingly aggressive in his foreign moves; Abe Shinzo, even more confident of his closer relationship with the US leader; and Vladimir Putin, now more supportive of Kim and prepared to take action. It was not a propitious environment for building regional consensus. That goal of Park had been dropped. However, the narrower goal of building trust with leaders in North Korea and the US simultaneously had become the obsession and even seemed to be within reach if one did not look closely at the wide divergence between the two and at the responses of the other three leaders.

Moon Jae-in took office in May 2017 following Park's impeachment, an interim president, and his electoral victory, facing a challenging environment. He needed to proceed with caution, given the moves of the other five leaders active in Northeast Asia and the legacy he had inherited. Offending Xi Jinping, who was already imposing onerous sanctions, and Donald Trump, whose demeaning language about South Korea stung, could have been costly. Moon proceeded with care, facing also Kim Jong-un's belligerence, Abe Shinzo's distrust, and Vladimir Putin's tilt to North Korea.

As candlelight vigils whipped up impeachment demands, toppling the Park government and leading to an interim president and an early election, ominous foreign policy shadows loomed through most of 2017. The Trump shadow shook confidence in the ROK-US alliance and in vital decisions regarding US relations with Seoul's neighbors. The Xi Jinping shadow left Seoul under unofficial sanctions and "wolf warrior" criticism for its THAAD deployment. Coupled with the

Kim Jong-un shadow of unprecedented weapons tests, shaking regional security, and the self-inflicted Abe Shinzo shadow as South Koreans were consumed with overturning the agreement Park had reached with him, this was a disconcerting environment to absorb the lessons of failed foreign policies and to set a course for navigating through a treacherous regional environment.

In 2017 Moon Jae-in proceeded cautiously in preparation for the gamble he anticipated would become possible. He catered to Trump, even when squirming at Trump's "fire and fury" threats against North Korea and human rights cavalcade against it in a speech given before the National Assembly. Without damaging ties to Washington greatly, Moon also met Xi Jinping's demands for assurances on security called the "three no's," to renew summitry after the THAAD crisis in bilateral relations. That year Moon also wooed Putin with his New Northern Policy. If Japan was not soothed by Moon and saw a renewal of the discord of the early Park years, in 2017 Moon showed some restraint in his rhetoric and policies. He started by not alienating other leaders.

Trump, Xi, Abe, and Putin were, for various reasons, angry with Seoul, no matter its leadership until Moon Jae-in solidified his administration and began to find some answers. In this vacuum, progressives, emboldened by the popularity of the impeachment cause, raised hope that a path forward existed by repudiating Park's policies. In essence, they called for doubling down on outreach to Pyongyang without calling it *trustpolitik*, pulling back on THAAD to renew the wooing of China without suggesting another honeymoon, and implementing a Seoul-led regional strategy differently without calling it NAPCI (Northeast Asia Peace and Security Initiative) while rebuilding ties to Russia without labeling it a Eurasia Initiative. Somehow, renouncing the "comfort women" agreement and defying the US on THAAD and other matters would not lead to alliance tensions. The progressive case relied on the repudiation of Park's 2016 diplomacy without offering clarity on how alternative choices would be received.

Conservatives raised the alarm, but their voices could not ring loudly in the atmosphere of 2017. For many of them the key question was THAAD and not yielding to pressure from Beijing, since it was trying to force Seoul to choose between it and Washington, regarding North Korea as a buffer state and pursuing regional hegemony. Indeed, Park's weakness before China, giving it hope that it had a veto over THAAD, and the statements of progressives to cater to China, only whet its appetite to retaliate. Some went so far as to say that reviewing the THAAD decision would pour cold water on US efforts to defend South Korea. If conservatives shared the fear that going a long stretch without a newly elected president would result in US "Korea passing," Moon was met with deep skepticism.

Flummoxing strategic calculations was the perception that Trump did not value Seoul's strategic and economic contributions and was inclined to abuse US leverage over a weaker power. Trump's statements about asking Seoul to pay for THAAD, revisit the KORUS FTA, pay much more for US forces stationed in South Korea, and his other forms of "Korea bashing" left many on edge. Once

Xi had met with Trump in April and congratulated Moon on May 11 after he had taken office, there was also uncertainty about US-China and China-North Korean relations. Moon's meeting in July with Trump was treated as if it were upbeat, but an early one with Xi did not seem to reset relations at all.

Given the initiative in Kim Jong-un's hands with ICBM tests and another nuclear test, attention centered on Trump and Xi's responses as well as Moon's in the context of Security Council talks and resolutions. Blame for the inadequacy of past resolutions and new ones as well was placed on China, especially by conservatives. Trump's talk of "fire and fury" toward North Korea alarmed progressives most of all, not "respecting" South Korea's role or sovereignty. US-ROK discord was at maximum pitch, as Moon was seen as now coerced into "maximum pressure" toward Pyongyang.

The Nadir of ROK-Chinese Relations, 2016–17

If previously low points in Seoul's relationship with Beijing had been due to "soft issues" or in 2010 to China's refusal to criticize North Korea for its aggression, the plunge in relations from early 2016 was owing not only to a "hard issue" but specifically to the security triangle of the US, China, and the ROK. Seoul was accused of being Washington's henchman, of brandishing a sword pointed at China. China's tough posture reflected its newfound sense of empowerment and that South Korea was now economically vulnerable. It may have been a reaction to the excessive catering by Park, raising false expectations of the South's shift toward balance between the two great powers. Another explanation is that US-China relations were in rapid descent, and Beijing found it easier to target Seoul in a proxy attack.[1] Whatever China's motivation, the impact for South Korea was far-reaching. Having joined China's Asian Infrastructure Investment Bank but shied away from Obama's push for the Trans-Pacific Partnership and attended the September 2015 victory day parade in Beijing, Park had cast doubt on her commitment to the US with no payoff from China, to dismay at home. As Obama moved ahead with talk of "Indo-Pacific" regionalism and Kim Jong-un stepped up saber-rattling, Park had to fundamentally regroup.

Park had counted on personal ties to Xi Jinping and an atmosphere called the best period ever in China-Korean history. She had presumed a US-China complementary relationship in Northeast Asia, but China treated Seoul's ties with Beijing and Washington as zero-sum, blaming "Cold War" thinking for efforts to reenforce the alliance (even if they were to counter the threatening moves from North Korea).[2] The THAAD response brought China's message home to Koreans.

After recovering in 2013–14 from slippage, South Korean public opinion toward China entered an irreversible slide in this period. As Kim Ji-yoon wrote in April 2016 before the deepest plunge, "To many South Koreans, China is still a communist country, North Korea's friend, and a state with many problems in human rights and often unbearably arrogant." Its soft power was collapsing. "When asked if a respondent thinks that Korea and China share a similar value system, only 32.5 percent of respondents answered yes, while 64.4 percent answered 'no.' This conflicted with the conventional wisdom that Korean cultural heritage largely draws from China, in particular Confucianism, and thus these two countries are inseparable in terms of history, culture, and values. It was South Korean youth who most decidedly thought that Chinese and Korean value systems are not in conformity." Although the image of Park and Xi Jinping sharing the dais in September 2015 was still fresh and still "35.9 percent of South Koreans positively viewed Chinese leadership in Asia," public sentiment was shifting already, including over Chinese badgering about THAAD.[3]

Kim Ji-yoon highlighted a dramatic shift from 2015 to 2017. "In 2015, the proportion of the South Korean public who thought China would not take the side of North Korea was even higher than that of those who thought China would. 56.8 percent of South Korean respondents believed that China would not join the North Korean side when another war broke out, while 43.2 percent of them believed it would. It was a good year for the two countries' relations, and people's favorability score for China went up as well." She added: "The proportion of respondents who believed that China would not take sides with North Korea decreased to 33.3 percent in 2016. In the following year of 2017, it was 30.2 percent. Those who believed that China would be with the North increased to 66.7 percent in 2016 and 69.8 percent in 2017. China's image appeared much more threatening. Even for those who did not approve of THAAD deployment, China's aggressive economic retaliation was negatively perceived. It was considered an unfair and unilateral assault by a superpower… South Koreans' views of China had been damaged by the THAAD controversy, and they seem to have lost the trust in China, which had been building over time."[4] It would never revive in the ensuing period.

Having oversold its progress with China, the Park administration found itself strongly criticized when China at first opposed sanctions to address North Korea's nuclear test and long-range missile test at the start of 2016. It "suggested that heavier sanctions against North Korea would only lead to hardship for ordinary citizens. China also argued that pushing North Korea into an isolated corner might make it unpredictably dangerous. In addition, China suggested that concerned parties should rely on dialogue rather than sanctions to improve the situation. At first, China did not show sympathy with the idea that heavier penalties should be applied. As an extension, Chinese authorities repeatedly called attention to the importance of convening the Six-Party Talks as a mechanism to dissuade North Korea from developing nuclear weapons and, eventually, to denuclearize the country. In the eyes of South Koreans, all of these messages sounded as if China was taking sides with North Korea… Criticisms mounted because the Park government had claimed until that time that South Korea-China relations are at an all-time peak under the Park regime. However, the fact that Xi Jinping did not even pick up the phone when Park tried to reach him was publicized as telling proof that China was not seriously considering South Korea's legitimate concerns. A turbulent period in bilateral ties between South Korea and China was rapidly taking shape. Second, Park expressed this diplomatic backlash in January 2016, implying that South Korea would enter into substantial negotiations with the United States about introducing the Terminal High Altitude Area Defense (THAAD) system on Korean soil. As the THAAD issue is something China always raises in warnings to South Korea, bilateral ties rapidly turned sour."[5]

Despite the deterioration in China's image, some progressives held out hope that its position on South Korea could be reversed in the post-Park period. They recalled Chinese pressure on Kim Jong-un in 2013–15 and interpreted it as a fundamental change. If Park had failed to sustain better ties, Moon could do better through outreach to China and a new approach to North Korea.[6] They were aware of Beijing's clear preference for Moon, indicated in Wu Dawei's five-day visit to Seoul in April 2017. Rather than seek support for retaliation against Chinese sanctions, Moon strove for a breakthrough, announcing it on October 31 and confirming it with a December Beijing summit.[7]

South Korean thinking toward China proceeded along two tracks. On the one hand, resentment prevailed over unjustified sanctions and "wolf warrior" rhetoric as well as hysterical blogging. As Choi Kang wrote, "The majority of the South Korean public thought China was trying to interfere in South Korea's sovereignty, which could not be tolerated."[8] Yet, calculating that it must have China's cooperation to resolve the North Korean problem, the Moon administration concentrated on accommodating at least some of China's security concerns, agreeing on October 31 to the "three no's" (no participation in missile defense, no additional THAAD, and no trilateral alliance among the United States, Japan, and South Korea). Official views downplayed concern about China's policy.

Progressives tended to doubt that any great power acted in accord with South Korean national interests. If China in the first months of 2017 aroused the most frustration, that did not negate the sense that the US was to no small extent responsible, and Park was "serving a big power." Impeachment was seen as the start of a reversal. In the 25th anniversary of normalization of relations with China, an opening could be found, they assumed. Hosting Trump in November 2017, Moon could create an atmosphere conducive to momentum with Xi Jinping, too. This meant staying clear of US appeals for regional cooperation, such as talk of the Indo-Pacific, and satisfying China on security ties with Japan and missile defense restraint.[9] This combination would allow Seoul to take the initiative. For Moon, the moves in late 2017 prepared the way to put North Korea at the center over the next year.

Moon and Trump were on different tracks in their China policy. Although THAAD had dislodged the image of Seoul tilting toward Beijing, its concessions on national security left an impression of appeasement. Meanwhile, Korean progressives viewed the aggressive US posture toward China on a wide regional theater, including the South China Sea, as excessive or untimely, if not provocative. Calls for Seoul to join in a regional alignment were seen as antithetical to

Moon's policy agenda. One triangle took center stage in the final months of 2017, although North Korea loomed in the background. South Korean media closely tracked US-China relations, as Trump spoke on China and visited China, while also watching how ROK-US relations were affected. Yet the main focus was on Moon's efforts to put the THAAD issue behind China-ROK relations. US warnings against China's ties to North Korea did not keep Moon from assuring Xi Jinping that he had a different strategy to gain Kim's confidence. The fact that Trump had stirred growing economic frictions with Moon may also have encouraged Xi to agree to an arrangement to get beyond the worst part of the THAAD sanctions.[10] Conservative coverage took exception to the poor reception Moon received in China, considering it belittlement of South Korea or describing the trip as "tributary diplomacy."

Yet, it was hard to keep attention on ROK-Chinese relations, when Trump kept grabbing the spotlight—in November with a trip to Japan, South Korea, and China; in December with a new national security strategy, and repeatedly with comments on North Korea. There was increasing concern that Seoul would be pressed to take sides between Washington and Beijing and would be sidestepped on the North, although Trump in Seoul said it would not be. Also, there was mounting worry that Moon's insistence that "balanced" diplomacy was not in reference to his stance between Washington and Beijing was not true. Warning of a new "Cold War," many feared that Seoul would be marginalized in its quest for reunification. Moon's foreign policy seemed stalled in late 2017.

After the South Korean foreign minister announced the "three no's" on October 31 the path was cleared for Moon to finalize this deal in China in December. If conservatives charged that South Korea had abandoned sovereignty over its own security or had jeopardized the ROK-US alliance, progressives valued Moon's results, including agreement on principles for dealing with the North. Moon's plan was: neutralizing Xi, playing to Trump's vanity, and dismissing Abe as irrelevant.

Catering to Russia at the Eastern Economic Forum in 2016–17

In September 2016 Park made a last-ditch effort to sustain relations with Russia despite its anger over the THAAD deployment, and a year later at the same venue in Vladivostok Moon seized on his meeting with Putin to try to refocus bilateral relations on cooperation to restart diplomacy with Kim Jong-un. In Park's case, she shared a panel with Abe as well as Putin on the future of the Russian Far East. In Abe's eight years of wooing Putin, this may have been the high point of optimism that a breakthrough was within reach, as Abe stressed how Japan could contribute to the economic rise of this corner of Russia, mainly suggesting ways to improve the quality of life in cities such as Vladivostok. Park renewed talk of three-way, north-south corridors through North Korea. Neither offered much to entice Putin, given his geopolitical, not economic, obsession.

Reviewing this forum in 2017, I wrote, "Japan is primarily concerned about Russia drawing too close to China, while South Korea is worried, above all, of Russia moving closer to North Korea. Whereas Park has pulled away from years of joint statements with Putin about cooperation on the development of the Russian Far East (together with projects crossing North Korea), Abe in 2016 has told Putin that he has bold plans for cooperation that would help to turn the Russian Far East into one of the locomotives of Russia's socio-economic rise, in accord with Putin's latest priorities. There is no sign of coordination in the positions they take toward Russia…" In Vladivostok, Park encouraged Putin by calling the Russian Far East the meeting place of Asia and Europe and the new heart of Russia, but she warned that this treasure house of energy resources is not now being tapped to its potential due to North Korea. If reunited, Korea would unlock the door to its dynamism, making this a region of prosperity and peace. Park described a region at a crossroads: facing either disorder and new protectionism and isolationism or openness and integration, while Russia's 'pivot to the East' heightens the region's potential. Her appeal to Putin was to embrace integration and take advantage of Seoul's cutting-edge technology, geographical location, competitive industrial base, and eagerness to work with Russia. Yet, Park made everything conditional on resolving the most serious threat to the region coming from North Korea. She called for speaking with one voice against this threat. Changing North Korea is the best hope for the Russian Far East and creating a new Eurasia based on peace and mutual prosperity. Indeed, Park was clear about seeking development based on economic principles with support from the international community.[11] This was not a welcome message.

Angered at Park's conditional message, Putin was leaning increasingly toward Kim Jong-un. Thus, there was no prospect of improving bilateral relations. Hopes raised earlier by Park's announcement of a "Eurasian Economic Initiative" had been dashed without any sign of a reversal. Progressives paid little attention, however, still eying ways to bring Russia on board in diplomacy with the North. Compounding Moon's challenges, his meeting saw the Russian leader try to play the "North Korean card," opposing further sanctions, while Russia refused to cut oil supplies to it. In Moon's keynote address to the Eastern Economic Forum, he announced his "New Northern Policy" as well as a nine-bridge strategy for ROK-Russia cooperation. If Korean conservatives were skeptical, progressives valued wooing Putin for its North Korea impact. Days later, Russia agreed to Security Council Resolution 2375 in response to North Korea's sixth nuclear test, but not covering oil supplies.

Struggling to Capitalize on a High Point in ROK-Japan Relations

The combination of the "comfort women" agreement on December 28, 2015, and the fourth North Korean nuclear test on January 6, 2016, seemed to "have provided a new, maybe the most favorable, atmosphere for the realization of trilateral security cooperation… A high-ranking government official in South Korea said, 'I am truly relieved that South Korea and Japan concluded a deal on the comfort women issue before North Korea went on its nuclear test.'" On March 31 in Washington, Obama joined Park and Abe in committing both to implement the new Security Council resolution and to "enhance the level of three-way security cooperation." Such unity may have helped to persuade China to take a tougher line toward North Korea, while it gave new hope to the US for upgraded trilateral security ties.[12] Yet, the mood in Seoul did not focus on future opportunities.

Choi Kang wrote, "the agreement on the 'comfort women' on December 28, 2015, the fourth nuclear test of North Korea on January 6, 2016, and disappointing Chinese behavior after the test have provided a new, maybe the most favorable, atmosphere for the realization of trilateral security cooperation."[13] In 2016 neither bad ROK-Japan relations nor hope for better ROK-China relations stood in the way. He added, "Chinese reactions after this test have been particularly disappointing. Foreign Minister Wang Yi merely reiterated China's traditional three principles: denuclearization, peace and stability, and negotiations. In the eyes of most South Koreans, China appears to be primarily concerned with regime stability in North Korea, prioritizing that over denuclearization, and China is not much concerned with South Korea's own security interests. Now Park's China policy is the target of criticism from both progressives and conservatives for the failure in securing long-expected Chinese cooperation when North Korean put this to a test and for the overall misunderstanding of China's policy toward the Korean Peninsula."

Yet progressives worried that "trilateral security cooperation would bring the Cold War structure or confrontation back to the Korean Peninsula and Northeast Asia and would serve the interests of the United States and Japan, not those of South Korea. Secondly, some are likely to argue that under the trilateral security cooperation framework, South Korea will have little room to pursue its own policy initiatives toward North Korea. Korean Peninsula issues will become secondary, entrapped in a larger regional context; 'fear of entrapment' may arise."[14] Such warnings overwhelmed any strategic optimism.

I wrote in 2017 that, "The US-Japan-ROK triangle has become more acceptable, but as the weakest of the three parties and the one with the narrowest objectives, Seoul cannot avoid nervousness in regard to how the next US president may visualize the triangle. First, it may be subsumed in a broader alliance network (Australia, India, some states in Southeast Asia), countering the South Korean effort to keep the focus narrow. Second, Washington's tolerance for the moves Abe may undertake as he strives to reconstruct Japanese national identity may be at odds with Seoul's deeply felt concerns about historical memory. What US observers find tolerable as a pathway for Japan to assume responsibility as a great power may well be opposed to what South Koreans deem necessary for Japan to stay contrite about past imperialism. The way forward for this alliance triangle will likely not be smooth sailing."[15] Indeed, it was not, as Moon turned away from trilateralism.

Japanese were wary about the backlash in Seoul over the agreement, Koreans did not trust Japan's agenda if ties improved, and the US put the onus on Moon to build on the agreement. As I had written: "realignment through alliance trilateralism is a significant development in 2016. Some Koreans are hesitant to acknowledge what is now transpiring—often quietly among military and security communities—and there are still breakthroughs that have been delayed (e.g., direct intelligence sharing through GSOMIA) and public opinion that has not caught up with why and how conditions are changing... Abe's push for constitutional revision is certain to arouse disapproval in a Korean election year, and the Korean opposition is insistent that it will make rejecting and renegotiating the December 28 deal a central issue in its campaign."[16] A big problem for Koreans was the rapid improvement in US-Japan relations. "Abe's successful Washington visit at the end of April 2015 became a watershed event that turned around the mood in Korean society... Abe's success aroused a strong backlash in South Korea against the diplomatic strategy of the Park government... Abe's diplomatic engagement sent an alarming signal that South Korea might be diplomatically isolated, creating momentum for rethinking the Park administration's diplomatic stance in Northeast Asia."[17]

On Japan Moon tried to thread the needle by having his special task force reviewing the "comfort women" agreement criticize it as seriously flawed, terminating the trust fund for it, but then having his foreign minister announce at the start of 2018 that Seoul would forego renegotiations, as Moon had earlier promised. After the task force report, Japan had warned that renegotiations would leave bilateral relations in an "unmanageable" state. Moon insisted that he sought to mend ties and would take a two-track approach, separating the "comfort women" issue from all others. Abe agreed to attend the 2018 Winter Olympics opening ceremony, but that was not a sign of trust with Moon.

Casting Great Power Maneuvering Aside in 2018–19

Great power diplomacy in 2018–19 lost the vigor of 2017. As a new president, Moon had set his sights on creating a positive atmosphere for diplomacy with North Korea. In 2018 triangular ties with Kim Jong-un and Donald Trump became his obsession. Their failure in 2019, however, did not lead to reinvigoration of diplomacy with Xi Jinping, Vladimir Putin, or Abe Shinzo, each of whom shunned Moon for his own reason. With Kim Jong-un blaming Moon for the breakdown in diplomacy and Trump turning away from the peninsula, Moon became a foreign policy lame duck before his term as president had reached the halfway mark. Yet this low ebb was preceded by such a three-way diplomatic frenzy in 2018 that few noticed the great power environment.

As 2018 began Moon appeared to be sandwiched between Trump and Xi with overtures to Kim Jong-un just a desperate gambit to make an end run around the obstacles. Trump's State of the Union address, showcasing North Korean human rights abuses, his announcement of tariffs on steel and aluminum imports, and his rescinding of the nomination of Victor Cha as ambassador to South Korea did not bode well for Moon's plans. Mike Pence's visit to the Winter Olympics in Pyeongchang, where he sidestepped dinner including a North Korean official, suggested as well that a "bloody nose" strike was more likely than support for reconciliation. Having just won China and Russia's support for tougher sanctions, Trump seemed ill-inclined to endorse any diplomacy that threatened to undermine sanctions without real optimism about the results.

In March Moon's gambit suddenly paid off when Trump, without input from US officials, chose to take a gamble of his own, agreeing to meet Kim Jong-un. Suddenly, the gates were opened to diplomacy, which China rushed to enter as well. Moon sought to put Seoul in the driver's seat, but that was never an option with Trump in the picture nor was it Xi's plan. Xi quickly arranged a summit with Kim Jong-un to precede Trump's. Progressives feared that Trump would be swayed by "super-hawks" led by John Bolton, the newly named national security advisor, to refuse any compromise. Conservatives saw Kim's March 28 trip to Beijing as "Beijing-centric" intervention, which would complicate Moon's mission and weaken the recently strengthened sanctions regime. Few trusted China's motives, as it was seen as playing a broader strategic game with the US. Progressives were ambivalent. Xi could help to legitimize Moon's soft line, stressing a peace process, but, after THAAD sanctions, he could not be trusted. A second Kim Jong-un visit to China on May 7, just 40 days after his first visit, was described in Pyongyang as part of an "historical new golden era." Instead of a three-party framework, earlier suggested by the Panmunjom Declaration between Moon and Kim, there was now a balance, giving North Korea more leverage. Stories that China had relaxed sanctions and that Kim had hardened his position, postponing talks with South Korea and threatening to cancel the summit with Trump, suggested that Kim had gained confidence in light of the newly achieved Chinese support.

As Seoul and Washington calmed tensions, in part by renegotiating KORUS FTA, the "trade war" between Washington and Beijing was heating up with potentially heavy costs for Seoul. Moon banked on Trump, assuming that US-China relations were not a big factor for him or Kim Jong-un. He bypassed Xi Jinping, not joining in Trump's initiatives to counter expansionist moves by China further south but also not collaborating with Xi on North Korean diplomacy.

The June 12 Singapore Declaration heartened Moon Jae-in despite vagueness that left others doubtful that it laid a foundation for proceeding and their alarm that Trump oversold it and unilaterally pledged to end US-ROK joint military drills. Just one week later Kim was back in China to meet Xi Jinping, seeking economic assistance among other objectives. Progressives again were tempted to put a positive spin on these ties, expecting Pyongyang's confidence to lead to more serious negotiations and Beijing's support for parallel talks on denuclearization and a peace regime to be a good thing. In contrast, conservatives warned that China would endanger the pressure that had brought Kim Jong-un to the negotiating table. They suspected that Xi and Kim would find common ground on altering the regional security framework at the expense of the US. Dandong had already come alive again with North Korean merchants. How to get the US to offer more to North Korea, e.g., to allow Seoul to open a joint liaison office in Kaesong and reopen the Kaesong Industrial Complex instead of calling these steps sanctions violations, was on the progressive docket. How to keep the pressure on Pyongyang was central for conservatives, who took little hope from the Singapore Summit or from China's behavior. Moon watched the Chinese parallel track with North Korea, but he had no strategic alternative to offer Xi Jinping.

In the eight months between the Singapore and Hanoi summits, South Korean eyes were fixed on Trump, Kim Jong-un, and Moon Jae-in. Xi Jinping appeared to be trying somehow to get into the picture, but little was known about his meetings with Kim. Abe was assumed to be sulking at diplomacy that could lead in a dangerous direction, but he kept quiet. Putin also brooded on the sidelines, awaiting his first opportunity to meet with Kim. Yet Xi's role proved to be greater than many at first recognized and Abe and Putin at least received reassurances from their partners in Washington and Beijing respectively that the deal they most feared was not at all feasible.

Several themes arose that demonstrated the implausibility of any agreement. Moon Jae-in put the focus on an end-of-war declaration, which found no resonance in Washington unless real steps toward denuclearization were taken. Likewise, Moon's proposals for an "East Asian Railroad Community" and bilateral economic openings with North Korea, as if they would lead to accelerated denuclearization, were rejected by the Trump administration. Trump's charges that China was no longer helping with denuclearization and was condoning illicit border trade were a sign that US-China coordination was a thing of the past. Many feared that if UN sanctions were relaxed with or without some agreement, they could not be renewed since China and Russia were now insistent on removing at least some of them amid a downturn in their relations with the US.

The February Hanoi Summit spelled the end of Moon's illusion that he was in the driver's seat. Kim Jong-un blamed Moon for the failure, refused to include him in the summer meet-and-greet with Trump at Panmunjom, and dissed him repeatedly throughout the year. If progressive editorials after Hanoi put a positive spin on Moon's continued ability to play the middleman as Trump and Kim kept searching for a breakthrough, the reality was loss of trust with Trump and marginalization as Kim turned to Putin in an April summit and hosted Xi in a June summit. Moon's calls for a softer approach to Kim and relaxation of sanctions were more in line with Xi and Putin's positions than the US one. Meetings with Trump only exposed the wide gap between the two. At the Osaka G20 summit, meetings with Xi and Putin exposed Moon's lack of leverage, and Abe refused a bilateral meeting. There was much talk of Seoul's isolation. Xi had refused to visit Seoul despite earlier talk of doing so, even as he went to Pyongyang earlier in June. The United States, Japan, and India held a meeting to discuss the "Free and Open Indo-Pacific," but there was no US-Japan-ROK trilateral meeting.

Focused fruitlessly on the ROK-DPRK-US triangle, Moon was sidelined in the polarized atmosphere taking shape, pretending that Hanoi was a blip in the road rather than a dead end.

In 2019 Moon seemed to be on the verge of repeating Park's pivot after she found herself in a corner late in 2016. He also prioritized leaning toward the United States, however much he sought to beckon further to Kim Jong-un and not to cross a Chinese red line, as Park had done. Straddling the US-China divide and delaying steps toward Japan encouraged by the US were growing more difficult, but Moon strove to keep the door ajar for a possible progressive successor to follow.

Accommodating China, but Not Allaying the Tension in Bilateral Relations

The deepening US-China trade war put Seoul in a difficult position, damaging cooperation over North Korea and threatening South Korean exports, 39 percent of which go to the two countries. If Chinese exports to the US drop, South Korean intermediate goods to China drop as well. Pressure was felt too over Huawei technology, which the US warned allies against using. In his meeting with Moon Xi warned that external pressures should not affect China-ROK cooperation, a sign that he was trying to force Seoul into making a choice between Beijing and Washington in the trade war.

Signs of an upgrading of China-DPRK relations were widely recognized in Seoul. In September 2018 at the 70th anniversary celebration of the founding of North Korea, China sent its third highest-ranked official. On November 17, when Moon and Xi met, they promised to cooperate closely for the success of the US-DPRK summit, adding "the second US-DPRK summit and Kim's return visit to Seoul will mark a watershed in solving the problem on the Korean Peninsula." These words pressed Kim to visit as early as possible, along with Xi's plan shared with Moon that he would visit both Seoul and Pyongyang in 2019. Kim's travel to Beijing for a fourth summit with Xi Jinping on January 8–9, 2019, was seen as a prelude to Kim's Hanoi visit with Trump. The Xi-Kim summit was followed by a four-hour banquet in honor of Kim's birthday and 70 years of diplomatic ties. With Xi joining Kim for lunch the next day and agreeing to visit North Korea, newspapers in Seoul saw a strong bond emerging. Although Moon quickly praised the summit in Beijing as having a positive impact on the forthcoming Kim-Trump summit, Korean conservatives were doubtful, arguing that this threatened that North Korea could take a different path backed by China, getting sanctions relief and support for a nuclear freeze, not denuclearization. Given Trump's new pressure on Seoul to pay almost double for the US troop presence or face the threat of troop reductions, Moon was being squeezed. Grasping for straws, progressives even saw the visit as paving the way to a multilateral peace regime in line with Kim's New Year's message, economic reforms given that Kim went to a technology zone in Beijing, and US-China cooperation after the Trump-Xi summit of late

2018, leading Trump to say that Xi had agreed to work with him 100% on North Korea. South Koreans were split on China's actual intentions.

Xi's visit to Pyongyang, more than any of Kim's visits to China, raised concern about China's intentions. Coming a day before Xi's meeting with Trump in Osaka, was this a move to link the North Korean issue to the US-China trade war? Was it a signal that Washington and Seoul would be bypassed in favor of Pyongyang as Beijing took charge of future diplomacy? Or, as progressives claimed, was Xi trying to jump-start talks between Washington and Pyongyang as Seoul remained an integral part of more diplomacy? Before long, Seoul's marginalization soon became clear, as Chinese sources blamed the US and Seoul for not only the failure at Hanoi but also diplomatic efforts that had sidelined Beijing. China could no longer be viewed as a positive force in diplomacy.

China drew attention again in the second half of December. At a Security Council meeting to discuss North Korea's provocations, China proposed easing of sanctions in order to keep the momentum going for US-North Korea talks. A week later, Moon Jae-in held a summit with Xi Jinping ahead of the China-Japan-ROK trilateral summit, where Xi argued that "China and South Korea should join forces in making North Korea and the United States maintain dialogue momentum." Moon stated that he "appreciated China's important role for denuclearization of the Korean Peninsula and a peace settlement," and he hoped that the two countries "can work together even more closely." The two sides also discussed the new UNSC draft resolution that was proposed by China and Russia. Progressives agreed that sanctions relief should be at the top of the agenda, also calling on Xi to mediate between the US and North Korea as Moon had sought, while conservatives said China should join against belligerent behavior, criticizing its mixed messages.

Watching Russia Turn More toward North Korea

Far more important than Putin's Osaka meeting with Moon was his April Vladivostok summit with Kim Jong-un. It sent the message that Kim has Russia as well as China as alternatives to the US and South Korea. Kim blamed the US for the collapse of the Hanoi talks and set a course for bypassing it, while Putin favored multilateral talks to offer North Korea security guarantees at odds with the strategies of Seoul and Washington. In violation of Security Council Resolution 2397, Putin claimed that North Koreans were "working successfully" in Russia and hinted at steps to counteract the sanctions. If progressives struck a positive note, as if Putin was playing a constructive role rather than endorsing Kim's delayed approach to denuclearization, Russia's meager economic role left little reason to dwell on this summit. Two months later the Xi visit to Pyongyang mattered much more.

South Korea mattered little to Russia as attention shifted to ways to capitalize on the failure of the Hanoi Summit.[18] This was viewed as a temporary setback caused primarily by US domestic politics. The ball was in the US court. Progressives in Seoul were regarded as a positive force, but both the US and Korean conservatives were blamed. It was assumed that Seoul had no power to exercise its sovereignty. Similarly, Trump was seen as throttled by the establishment in the United States. Yet, because of the Vladivostok summit, Russia was back in the game. Not only that, Russia was now teaming with China at an unprecedented level on North Korean matters. A diplomatic meeting of Russian, Chinese, and North Korean officials in October 2018 was one of many indications.[19]

For Seoul, interest in the Eastern Economic Forum had waned. Moon did not attend again after his visit in 2017. Preparations for the 2018 forum envisioned a three-way gathering with both Moon and Kim Jong-un joining with Putin, but Kim showed no interest and Moon was still keen on his own follow-up summit with Kim. Meanwhile, Washington was accusing firms in the Russian Far East of sanctions violations, and Seoul was cooperating in enforcement to Moscow's displeasure. The divide between the two sides over North Korea had widened, spilling over to economic ties. In 2019 each side dismissed the other as peripheral to its strategic objectives in Northeast Asia.

ROK-Japan Relations Falling into an Abyss

Concerns about ROK-Japan relations heated up at the end of 2018. There was the South Korean highest court's decision on forced wartime labor by a Japanese firm and a dispute over the use of radar against a Japanese plane over international waters. These issues followed Moon's decision to disband the "comfort women" foundation established with the 2015 agreement, although Moon said that the agreement would not be scrapped. Japan's warning against a declaration to end the Korean War was interpreted as a negative influence on US-DPRK talks. Rather than coordinate with Tokyo on his New Southern Policy, Moon stressed at the November APEC summit that he sought to raise ties to ASEAN countries and India to the level of relations with neighboring countries. Worsening ROK-Japan ties, however, had potential to impact ROK-US ties if Trump had been attentive.

Park Cheol Hee observed a polarizing split in the coverage of Japan.[20] For progressives, it had become almost irrelevant in their pursuit of a peace regime. China was needed, not Japan. For conservatives and many young Koreans who weighed current culture above distant history, the Moon policy unnecessarily antagonized Japan and harmed bilateral ties with the US. They were not pro-Japan but against demonizing it. In 2018 a series of incidents drove relations to a new low: denial of the legitimacy of the 2015 accord, refusal to accept a flag on a Japanese military vessel, a laser pointed dangerously at a Japanese aircraft, and worst of all, an October court verdict for compensation by Japanese corporations to Korean forced laborers in the war years at odds with Japan's interpretation of the 1965 normalization treaty. Even security cooperation was now put in jeopardy, as in the near rejection of extending intelligence sharing. Japan's export controls in mid-2019 on critical components to South Korean industry left relations even further strained.

The second half of 2019 saw ROK-Japan relations at their nadir. After Moon and Abe did not hold a bilateral meeting at the G20, Abe just days later went further in his retaliation for the Seoul court ruling in October 2018 on forced labor, imposing restrictions on the export of three chemicals needed in the semiconductor industry. Seoul sought Washington's intervention and then declared it would withdraw from the intelligence-sharing agreement GSOMIA with Tokyo, but this angered Washington since it affected national security in Northeast Asia. This threatened withdrawal hung over the ROK-US alliance for months, as did the gap in approach to North Korea and host-nation support, until Moon finally agreed in late November to maintain the military intelligence-sharing pact. Backing down, Moon had failed to pressure Japan and had damaged his image in the US.

As 2020 began, Moon was still searching in vain for an opening with North Korea, struggling to find some space as US-China pressure to take sides was mounting, at a loss to explain his New Northern Strategy given Putin's behavior, and bloodied by his failed attempt to find an exit from the collapse in ROK-Japanese relations. No great power leader seemed amenable to a new diplomatic initiative. Moon remained fixated on Trump, hoping he would renew overtures to Kim Jong-un.

Conclusion

Park's earlier foreign policy had hit a dead end, and she started to take new steps from late 2015.

In 2016 Park abruptly changed course, but it was too little, too late. In 2017 Moon started quite cautiously, delicately maneuvering between difficult challenges, but he was undeterred. In 2018 he made a bold bet on Kim Jong-un and Donald Trump, appearing to put Seoul in the driver's seat in a spurt of diplomacy. Yet this optimism reflected a misreading of both Kim and Trump and an underestimation of Xi Jinping's response. The euphoria continued into 2019 without any proof that diplomacy would end well. After February 2019 Moon was isolated: scorned by Kim Jong-un, pressured by Trump for bilateral reasons and his threat to trilateralism with Abe, and bypassed by Xi Jinping, who chose to visit Pyongyang but not Seoul and called on Moon to defy Trump and relax sanctions on North Korea while also staying clear of the US-China trade war.

The habit persisted of promising far more than could be delivered. Park had her comeuppance in 2015, feeling obliged to do an about-face with Japan, then with China and Russia, nullifying her "honeymoon" with Xi and "Eurasian initiative" with Putin in 2016. Moon reached even higher, as if he could bridge the gap between Trump and Kim Jong-un, only to see his plans crashing down in 2019. Catchy slogans and marginal goals had failed to come to grips with the serious differences existing between other countries. Seoul lacked the leverage to achieve its dreams.

In the second half of 2019 the foreign policy environment for South Korea was bleak. Not only was there no hope of budging Kim Jong-un or Donald Trump on their principal objectives, ties with Abe and Putin had further deteriorated, and the arrangement reached with Xi Jinping late in 2017 had only put a band-aid on a gaping wound. The only imaginable way forward was to plead with Trump to agree to a new agenda that might, as a long shot, capture Kim Jong-un's attention. This approach would extend to Trump's successor. With the other four regional actors, Moon had no clue what to do in order to manage a continuously deteriorating security environment.

Notes

1. Chung Jae Ho, "South Korea's Strategic Approach to China (or lack of it)," in Gilbert Rozman, ed., *Joint U.S.-Korea Academic Studies. A Whirlwind of Change in East Asia: Assessing Shifts in Strategy, Trade, and the Role of North Korea* (Washington, DC: Korea Economic Institute, 2018), pp. 72-90.
2. See-Won Byun, "The Impact of Chinese National Identity on Sino-South Korean Relations," in Gilbert Rozman, ed., *Joint U.S.-Korea Academic Studies. The Sino-ROK-U.S. Triangle: Awaiting the Impact of Leadership Changes* (Washington, DC: Korea Economic Institute, 2017), pp. 97-111.
3. Kim Jiyoon, "Can't Buy Me Soft Power (with Hard Power): China's Appeal to South Koreans," *The Asan Forum*, April 15, 2016.
4. Kim Jiyoon, "South Korean Public Opinion," *The Asan Forum*, February 27, 2018.
5. Park Cheol Hee, "Reviving the US-Japan-Korea Triangle in South Korean Diplomacy," *The Asan Forum*, April 29, 2016.
6. Kim Heung-kyu, "A View from South Korea on Sino-ROK Relations," in Gilbert Rozman, ed., *Joint U.S.-Korea Academic Studies: The Sino-ROK-U.S. Triangle* (Washington, DC: Korea Economic Institute, 2017), pp. 26-35.
7. Choi Kang, "South Korea," *The Asan Forum*, April 24, 2018.
8. Ibid.
9. Kim Taehwan, "China's Sharp Power and South Korea's Peace Initiative," in Gilbert Rozman, ed., *Joint U.S.-Korea Academic Studies. The East Asian Whirlpool: Kim Jong-un's Diplomatic Shake-up, China's Sharp Power, and Trump's Trade Wars* (Washington, DC: Korea Economic Institute, 2019), pp. 142-59.
10. Jin Linbo, "Chinese Views of Korean History in the Cold War Era," in Gilbert Rozman, ed., *Joint U.S.-Korea Academic Studies: A Whirlwind of Change in East Asia* (Washington, DC: Korea Economic Institute, 2018), pp. 150-62.
11. Gilbert Rozman, "Trilateralism and Realignment: Reassessing Three Triangles with South Korea," in Gilbert Rozman, ed., *Joint U.S.-Korea Academic Studies: The Sino-ROK-U.S. Triangle* (Washington, DC: Korea Economic Institute, 2017), pp. 131-43.
12. Park Cheol Hee, "Reviving the US-Japan-Korea Triangle in South Korean Diplomacy," *The Asan Forum*, April 29, 2016.
13. Choi Kang, "US-ROK-Japanese Trilateral Security Cooperation," *The Asan Forum*, February 12, 2016.
14. Ibid.
15. Gilbert Rozman, "Trilateralism and Realignment."
16. Ibid.

17 Park Cheol Hee, "Reviving the US-Japan-Korea Triangle in South Korean Diplomacy."
18 Artyom Lukin, "Why Did the Hanoi Summit Fail and What Comes Next? The View from Russia," *The Asan Forum*, 2019.
19 Robert Sutter, "Sino-Russian Relations, South Korea, and North Korea," in Gilbert Rozman, ed., *Joint U.S.-Korea Academic Studies: The East Asian Whirlpool* (Washington, DC: Korea Economic Institute, 2019), pp. 18-32.
20 Park Cheol Hee, "South Korean Views of Japan: A Polarizing Split in Coverage," in Gilbert Rozman, ed., *Joint U.S.-Korea Academic Studies: East Asian Leaders' Geopolitical Frameworks, New National Identity Impact, and Rising Economic Concerns with China* (Washington, DC: Korea Economic Institute, 2020), pp. 172-85.

6
RETURN OF PROGRESSIVE NARRATIVES

Eun A Jo

In 2016, conservative president Park Geun-hye's *trustpolitik* crumbled with North Korea's nuclear tests. This triggered a barrage of policy reversals, including decisions to (1) deploy the US anti-ballistic missile system, Terminal High Altitude Area Defense (THAAD), (2) enter a military intelligence-sharing agreement—General Security of Military Information Agreement (GSOMIA)—with the United States and Japan, and (3) conclude a "comfort women" agreement with Japan (actually, days earlier). By this point, all hopes of leveraging Chinese support to deal with North Korea had elapsed and Park had returned to a deterrence-focused approach. Amid growing domestic turmoil that eventually culminated in Park's impeachment and imprisonment; however, South Korean foreign policy would suffer yet another whiplash in early 2017.

Progressive president Moon Jae-in came to power in a climate of mounting uncertainty with a "candlelight" mandate. He had the delicate task of reviewing Park's foreign policy decisions—many of which bore accusations of procedural illegitimacy—as well as delivering his own "Moonshine" agenda. The Trump presidency and the onset of "fire and fury" brinkmanship only added to Moon's urgency. A series of high-profile summitries thus followed, in large part as a result of Moon's public outreach. Yet, opinions were divided, some declaring them timely interventions and others finding them excessive diplomatic concessions.

In the two periods marking the downfall of the Park presidency and the rise of Moon's, South Korea's foreign policy was in for a wild ride: (1) from the botched *trustpolitik* to "Moonshine" on North Korea; (2) from fears of Korea passing to grievances of Korea bashing by Trump's America; (3) from a breakdown in courtship with China over THAAD to its recovery; and finally (4) from a "final and irreversible" deal on history issues with Japan to a recharged row. Partisan

DOI: 10.4324/9781003394792-7

narratives on these shifts were remarkably consistent at times and remarkably innovative at others, reflecting the uncertainty of the times.

The Park Presidency

In her 2011 *Foreign Affairs* essay, Park had promised a "new kind of Korea"—one bonded by trust, rather than merely power or ideals. Departing from a conventional party platform, her policy of *trustpolitik* would pursue in tandem capacity-building for deterrence and trust-building for diplomatic outreach. As she stressed: "To ensure stability, *trustpolitik* should be applied consistently from issue to issue based on verifiable actions, and steps should not be taken for mere political expediency."[1] *Trustpolitik* was, in essence, a policy of constructing and enforcing norms of engagement.

In practice, this required a much better working relationship with China than one that her conservative predecessor Lee Myung-bak had left behind. With bipartisan support for her efforts, Park sought closer ties with Beijing through a series of grand gestures—such as attending the 2015 Victory Parade—and strategic dialogues. Yet, there appeared to be a diplomatic ceiling: when push came to shove in January 2016, with the North's fourth nuclear test, Beijing refused to reign in Pyongyang, prompting Park to announce: "We can no longer expect much from China."[2] In this sense, various policy reversals that came in the wake of this incident—the THAAD deployment, the signing of GSOMIA, and even the passage of the "comfort women" agreement just before—indicated Seoul's reembrace of Washington and its trilateral regional security framework with Japan as the only viable mechanism of deterrence against the North.

These policy realignments, however well-intentioned, were poorly timed. With growing public indignation over Park's domestic political scandals, many of her decisions were recast as illegitimate and even diversionary. Those who found them in any way meritorious were quickly sidelined, and the progressive opposition, armed with public support, repudiated them in full force. By the time Park left office in disgrace and Trump entered his in disbelief, conjectures surrounding South Korea's foreign policy trajectory—vis-à-vis North Korea, the United States, China, and Japan—were as rife as they were divisive.

North Korea

With its nuclear tests in 2016, Pyongyang made clear its unwillingness to play by Park's *trustpolitik* paradigm. Disappointment was felt across ideological lines, though blame fell on different entities: if the conservatives focused more squarely on the hostile strategic environment and, in particular, the rigidity of key powers—that is, China and the United States—the progressives condemned Park for her diplomatic failure and urged continued engagement with China. Each decision Park made in response to the North's nuclear provocations was assessed with its broader implications for the regional security environment in which South Korea's autonomy as a "shrimp between the whales" appeared increasingly tenuous.

Conservative commentators questioned the willingness of regional powers to resolve the North's nuclear conundrum. A January 11 *Joongang Ilbo* columnist noted that China and the United States have stringently maintained their original frameworks for dealing with North Korea despite repeated failure.[3] Implicit in this analysis was, thus, that Park's attempts to innovate were botched precisely by the lack of trust from which she believed the region suffered. On that same day, a *Chosun Ilbo* columnist similarly opined that cooperation on this issue had reached a dead end, with China's continued rigidity regarding the international sanctions regime—a necessary component of *trustpolitik*—and the United States' lukewarm approach to nuclear diplomacy under the guise of "strategic patience."[4] Naturally, the advice for the Park administration was to independently prepare for any military contingency even as it sought multilateral diplomatic efforts to deter the North.

Progressive voices, on the other hand, faulted the imbalance in Park's *trustpolitik* and its disproportionate emphasis on sanctions against North Korea as the primary culprit of its failure. A *Hankyoreh* columnist, for instance, insisted that Chinese support for sanctions had been building, but the international demand for Chinese pressure has outpaced its willingness to exert it.[5] Such a dynamic could, in fact, undermine the effectiveness of the sanctions regime, because the necessary legwork of bringing all relevant parties to a policy consensus through sustained dialogue has been neglected. In this view, Park's failure to capture US attention and leverage China's influence on Pyongyang was responsible for the backlash.

The ideological divide grew wider with Park's decision to close Kaesong Industrial Complex (KIC). For the conservatives, the measure was both necessary and reasonable. On February 12, a *Joongang Ilbo* columnist argued that it served as an effective penalty against the North for its nuclear test; the economic consequences of the KIC's closure weighed far more heavily against the North.[6] The restricted cash flows, it argued, would have direct and indirect impact on the Kim regime, including through the loss of employment for 50,000 workers and of black markets, which would undermine regime viability in the long term. Though similarly heralding the decision, a February 15 *Donga Ilbo* article was more skeptical about its effectiveness. It would have some symbolic utility in signaling Seoul's resolve, but it would not change either Pyongyang's behavior or China's response. The measure was, however, seen as unavoidable by conservatives. The former foreign affairs minister Han Sung-joo said as much in an interview with *Chosun Ilbo* on February 17: "It is complicated, but it is a necessary and inevitable move. It is quite convincing that the money invested in the complex was exploited to develop nuclear arms. It is self-contradictory to keep operating the complex under the circumstances."[7]

Unsurprisingly, the progressive narrative was far less enthusiastic about the closure of the KIC. On February 11, *Hankyoreh* condemned the decision as a desperate and reckless move.⁸ The day before, Seoul had already announced new sanctions against the North. The KIC could have served as a platform for maintaining engagement even as such pressure was applied, but the door to dialogue had now closed entirely. At the same time, former unification minister Jeong Se-hyun stated, in an interview with *Kyunghyang Shinmun* on February 11, that the closure did little to advance *trustpolitik*.⁹ There was already a widespread belief in China that Washington is using sanctions against North Korea as a broader strategy to coerce Beijing into complying with a US-led regional security framework; in this instance, Beijing would see Seoul's unilateral decision to close the KIC as just another tool of US containment strategy, aimed first and foremost against China.

Partisan narratives in the wake of North Korea's nuclear advances reaffirmed the enduring rift between the two ideological camps in South Korea about the right approach to deal with North Korea. The progressives continued to push for engagement, depicting the North's provocations as an outcome—rather than a driver—of the South's mixed signals and deterrence-heavy approach. At the same time, conservatives felt vindicated in their deep-rooted cynicism about the North's intentions and, to that extent, skepticism about the viability of Park's *trustpolitik* paradigm. Thus, when she finally reversed the policy, conservatives pointed to the hostile strategic environment as the cause of its failure, not Park's lack of strategic foresight.

United States

The North's nuclear provocations forced partisans to double down on their narratives concerning the US alliance. These largely followed the traditional fault lines in partisan narratives on foreign policy, though they also revealed a growing consensus in the mainstream partisan narratives—the futility of economic sanctions, which had been the primary tool of coercion—which prescribed divergent policy responses, ranging from dialogue to deterrence. Meanwhile, Trump's election and "America First" rhetoric engendered a critical development in the fringes of conservative thinking in support of self-nuclearization, even at the risk of harming the US alliance and the international non-proliferation regime.

Following the second nuclear test in September 2016, conservative coverage called for a series of military actions, including strengthened US nuclear deterrence and trilateral security framework. In a September 13 *Donga Ilbo* article, Choi Kang argued that Seoul needed to expedite cooperation with the United States and Japan to facilitate information sharing and crisis management.¹⁰ Choi also recommended establishing a Nuclear Planning Group or redeploying tactical nuclear weapons in the South to bolster US nuclear guarantees and moderate arguments for self-nuclearization. The next day, *Donga Ilbo* further emphasized the importance of trilateral security cooperation and, in particular, the signing of the two military agreements GSOMIA and the Acquisition and Cross-Servicing Agreement (ACSA), which had long been delayed due to Seoul's tenuous support.¹¹

Finally, the author added that fears of Japan's remilitarization were misplaced, especially when China has been seeking hegemony in the region.

Meanwhile, progressive coverage called for caution and dialogue. On September 21, a *Hankyoreh* columnist argued that dialogue—and only dialogue—had so far worked in dealing with North Korea, delaying its nuclear development over the last two decades.[12] Any change in tactics must thus aim to have more and better dialogue, not less. More concretely, the author recommended building dialogue in a step-wise manner, first around a verification strategy for a nuclear freeze and later around a comprehensive agreement on denuclearization or a peace treaty. Underlying this assessment was an unsaid assumption that Obama's "strategic patience" and Park's *trustpolitik* had failed, because they were driven by an unrealistic objective: the dismantlement of the North's nuclear forces and, thus, the Kim regime. Once again, the responsibility lay with Seoul and Washington to revive dialogue.

One interesting convergence in the partisan narratives was the futility of economic sanctions, albeit for different reasons. Conservatives believed that additional sanctions would not stop Kim, because they were not accompanied by credible military threats.[13] For this reason, they stressed that Seoul (and the United States) needed to solidify its missile defense and nuclear deterrence. Progressives similarly asserted that sanctions were impractical and potentially even dangerous; they had so far done little to impede the North's nuclear development and in fact made South Korea its key target. Even at the height of sanctions, Pyongyang had managed to advance its nuclear capabilities at historic speed and scale; from this perspective, compelling the North to abandon its weapons was as foolish as it was illusory. Instead, dialogue should be aimed at normalizing relations such that hostilities would become both unnecessary and undesirable.

In this polarizing moment, news of Trump's election generated both anxiety and a sense of opportunity in South Korea. In general, conservatives were warier about the implications, ranging from possible estrangement to total abandonment. In *Joongang Ilbo* on November 10, an observer posited that Trump would pursue retrenchment, narrowing US commitment in the region to the maritime theater.[14] Similarly, Kim Taehyo in *Chosun Ilbo* on the same day argued that Trump would seek some form of "offshore balancing" and rely on regional powers like Japan to check potentially hostile challengers like China.[15] Even though Kim believed that such a concept was unlikely to materialize at the time—given the history of US values diplomacy—he acknowledged that Trump was uninterested in promoting human rights or democracy abroad. A *Chosun Ilbo* columnist thus advised on November 26 to prepare for the worst, as Trump had promised during the campaign to undo much of the military and economic foundation of the US-South Korean alliance, in favor of a "better deal."

By contrast, progressive narratives surrounding Trump's election were more cautiously optimistic. On November 24, Shin Bong-gil opined in *Hankyoreh* that Trump's disregard for existing institutional arrangements—and the uncertainties this boded for policies on North Korea, the alliance, and trade—could offer an opportunity for Seoul. All Trump cared about were short-term transactional gains, which meant there may be an opening for South Korea to undertake painful, but necessary, transitions in the alliance structure to finally regain some autonomy. Whether by retrenchment or inattention, the Trump administration would force Seoul to be more independent in its dealings with North Korea, and it was time that it took concrete steps to curtail what the author described as "excessive" dependence on the United States.

Trump's election in many ways catalyzed South Korea's search for autonomy, albeit for different reasons. As conservatives questioned the credibility of US security guarantees to the South and anxieties about abandonment grew, calls for indigenous (nuclear) weapons systems gained steam. Progressives, on the other hand, saw Trump's domestic orientation as a boon for Seoul to extricate itself from postwar entanglements with Washington. What had long served as foreign policy common sense—its ties to the United States—appeared to be unraveling by this point.

China

China's failure to reign in Pyongyang, despite its continued nuclear provocations, raised questions about Beijing's intentions. What role did it play—a facilitator or a spoiler—in North Korean denuclearization or the broader inter-Korean peace process? If, in the conservative narrative, China was and always will be a spoiler despite sincere efforts to engage it, in the progressive narrative, China remained the crucial facilitator for any regional security problem. The prescriptive implications of these partisan narratives for Seoul's foreign policy once again diverged, between a strengthened military deterrence approach and a more energetic diplomatic engagement approach.

These debates reemerged when, in response to the North's nuclear testing, the Chinese foreign minister Wang Yi called for a "nuclear-free" Korean Peninsula and a peace agreement to end the ongoing armistice. On February 17, 2016, a *Donga Ilbo* article condemned the speech as a tactic to delay sanctions mechanisms at the UN Security Council and detract attention from denuclearization.[16] The suggestion, the author argued, was also insincere, as it would require the South to simply accept the North as a nuclear state. Likewise, a *Joongang Ilbo* article the next day raised alarm about the "Chinese way" of dealing with North Korea.[17] The principles of non-interventionism and multilateralism allow Beijing to disguise its "inherent unilateralism" in pursuing a non-decision and, thus, non-coercion against North Korea.

By contrast, a February 19 *Kyunghyang Ilbo* article supported China's proposal as a solution to the more fundamental problem in inter-Korean relations: North Korea's insecurity. The proposition was, in fact, nothing new: previous joint statements between the two Koreas had already articulated a peace agreement as an aspiration. The article thus argued that to reassure (and denuclearize) the North, the vestiges of Cold War era confrontation should be resolved first. Sanctions alone could not prevent the arms race from spiraling into a conflict, even though they may serve as effective punishment in the short term. Mapping strategies to achieve regional peace in the long term—with China's help—was key.

The debates intensified as Seoul decided to deploy THAAD on July 7, 2016. Progressives immediately warned against it, claiming that it would destroy Park's credibility as well as diplomatic identity. On July 15, a *Kyunghyang Shinmun* observer noted that, though the effects of THAAD were uncertain, the scale of its backlash was both clear and massive. Indeed, as part of her *trustpolitik* paradigm, Park had pursued the "Korean Peninsula Trust Process," "Northeast Asia Peace and Cooperation Initiative," and "Eurasia Initiative"—each of which had sought to deepen multilateral engagement with China and Russia. These efforts were now irrevocably compromised, leaving no diplomatic option but to depend on the United States.

A centrist outlet, *Hankook Ilbo*, had also cautioned against it on July 11, asserting that this could drag South Korea further into the Sino-American battle over the regional order. Throughout her tenure, Park had been sending mixed signals to China, from attending its military parade in 2015 to deploying THAAD, which it claims is weakening its nuclear deterrent. Park's decision could now raise North Korea's strategic value for China, which would likely retaliate in various ways.

Conservatives similarly acknowledged the unnecessary complication that Park's earlier diplomacy introduced, yet downplayed China's possible retaliation. On July 16, a *Chosun Ilbo* commentator argued that Beijing would take a symbolic—rather than material—action to signal its displeasure;[18] and whatever the cost, Seoul should bear it for the sake of national security. What is more concerning, in fact, was Seoul's declining credibility as an ally. Despite continued negotiations with the United States, Seoul repeatedly insisted that there was "nothing requested, negotiated, and decided." From the beginning, Seoul should have clarified that any decision would reflect its interests, given the North's ongoing provocations. Instead, Park played a double game, giving China a ruse with which to be uncooperative and the United States reasons to distrust Seoul's reliability.

Seoul's drastic U-turn in its policy orientation vis-à-vis China suggested Park's growing disenchantment with *trustpolitik*. Conservatives welcomed the administration's return to the traditional alliance-centered approach to North Korea, though many worried that the damage had already been done. Combined with Trump's election and the rise of the "America First" paradigm in the United States, a sense of detachment was growing more palpable.

Japan

The primary source of friction in South Korea's relationship with Japan during this period concerned the "comfort women" agreement (December 2015) and later,

GSOMIA (November 2016). The "comfort women" agreement had proclaimed that the issue had been resolved in a "final and irreversible manner," with Japan's contribution of a billion yen toward supporting the surviving "comfort women" in the South. Various Japanese politicians also interpreted the deal as stipulating the removal of "comfort women" statues. The deal generated significant controversy in South Korea, particularly during its implementation process and with the signing of GSOMIA, earlier efforts for which had been foiled due to public opposition.

Progressive coverage condemned the deal as both illegitimate and immoral. On December 30, Shin Joobaek in a *Kyunghyang Shinmun* article portrayed the deal as little more than a means to bolster trilateral military cooperation, allowing the Abe administration to escape international criticism. Similarly, a *Hankyoreh* article a day later characterized it as hastily reached, without consulting the victims and taking their wishes into account. Given the public ire, the deal was unlikely to put "history issues" to rest. Instead, it would exacerbate the conflict as Japan now had an excuse to evade responsibility and Koreans would continue to demand justice. In the longer run, this would only make cooperation with Japan more difficult.

Meanwhile, conservative outlets emphasized the benefits of the deal and called for caution. A *Chosun Ilbo* article on December 31 acknowledged—in fact, applauded—that the deal had emerged from conversations with the United States and Japan about strengthening trilateral cooperation. Yet, the agreement was fragile given the "extreme sensitivity" in South Korea. Managing public opinion was thus crucial for its implementation; and to this end, the article warned Japanese officials to refrain from making incendiary remarks that could lead to the breakdown of the deal. Other conservative commentators, such as Nam Kijung in a *Hankook Ilbo* article on December 29, were more optimistic, casting the deal as a starting point for the two countries' "future-oriented relationship."

With the July 28 launch of the Foundation of Reconciliation and Healing—tasked with disbursing the funds—public criticisms of the deal mounted. *Kyunghyang Shinmun* noted on August 31 that the foundation's main objective was to disguise Japan's legal responsibility by distributing the funds as assistance rather than compensation. Further, Japan's demands for removing the statues have only grown louder, making it clear that the funds accompanied little remorse. The next day in *Hankyoreh*, Nam Kijung advocated for a temporary suspension in the implementation of the deal, conditional on three demands: first, Abe needs to recognize the deal as representing Japan's view on history; second, the source of the funds must be specified to clarify the nature of the compensation as legal damages to the victims; and third, Japanese politicians must stop asking for the removal of the statues. Without the abovementioned conditions, implementing the deal would further delegitimize it and the spirit of reconciliation it was intended to sustain.

Conservative commentators nonetheless supported the deal as a pragmatic alternative to the ongoing stalemate over history issues. On August 1, a *Donga Ilbo* article likened the "comfort women" agreement to the 1965 normalization treaty, which had similarly suffered tremendous opposition but set the two countries on a mutually beneficial path. With proper implementation by the foundation, the current deal could also serve as a springboard for deepening their relationship.

By the time GSOMIA was passed in November 2016, the public backlash appeared insurmountable. Park's decision was assessed within the broader context of her domestic political scandals, amplifying dissenting voices that these foreign policy maneuvers were procedurally undemocratic and, thus, illegitimate. Many recalled the previous attempts in 2012 by the Lee Myung-bak administration to close the deal in secret, for which he was similarly denounced. As calls for Park's impeachment grew, the fate of these last-minute agreements with Japan seemed, too, in peril.

The Moon Presidency

On March 10, 2017, Park was removed from office following the endorsement of the Constitutional Court of the parliament's impeachment vote. In the midst of such mayhem, concerns mounted about the political vacuum in Seoul and its growing diplomatic isolation. It was in this climate of uncertainty and instability that Moon Jae-in took office. From the intensity of North Korean military provocations, the frictions in the US-South Korean alliance under the Trump presidency, the onslaught of Chinese retaliation for THAAD, to the backlash over the "comfort women" agreement with Japan, the Moon administration was besieged by foreign policy crises. A sense of urgency was unmistakable.

Given his "candlelight mandate," Moon sought first and foremost to review the controversial decisions that his predecessor had made vis-à-vis China and Japan and then accelerated his own "Moonshine" agenda with North Korea and the United States. On the former, the Moon administration emphasized the importance of transparency to regain public trust in executive decision-making processes. On the latter, he sought to project South Korea's role as an indispensable mediator. Within the first two years of his tenure, Moon's diplomacy had facilitated a series of high-profile summits that seemed to place South Korea back on the "driver's seat." A sense of diplomatic victory was widespread.

China

Following the advanced deployment of THAAD under the interim president Hwang Gyo-ahn, relations with China took a turn for the worse. Both sides of the ideological spectrum in South Korea broadly agreed that the decision was poorly executed, without the necessary diplomatic legwork to reassure Beijing. Some conservative commentators, however, came to Hwang's defense, claiming that Seoul should not have to justify its security decisions to China. Despite a long and painful economic coercive campaign by Beijing to reverse the THAAD decision, Moon maintained the deployment and later, managed to forge a degree of rapprochement. But calls to diversify South Korea's economic ties to reduce vulnerability to Chinese retaliation were rampant by this point.

Progressive coverage blasted the underlying military rationale behind the THAAD deployment and emphasized the unintended costs of its abrupt implementation. A February 20 *Hankyoreh* article, for instance, argued that North Korean short-range missiles could fly undetected, rendering South Korea's missile defense system—consisting of the Kill Chain, KAMD, and THAAD—effectively useless. THAAD was, in this view, more intended to protect the United States forces in Okinawa and Guam rather than the South Korean people. On March 13, Choi Jong-geon in *Hankyoreh* also asserted that THAAD stripped Seoul of its only leverage to bring the Trump and Xi administrations to resolve the North Korean nuclear issue. By forcing its implementation, Hwang jeopardized Seoul's diplomatic standing as well as economic health, which was already under significant strain.

Conservative outlets generally conceded that the implementation was unnecessarily hurried, though without questioning the military utility of the THAAD system. On March 7, a *Joongang Ilbo* columnist acknowledged that reaching a settlement with Beijing was critical for Seoul as it sets new alliance boundaries with Washington under Trump, who had already floated ideas of unilateral and preemptive strikes against North Korea. That same day, the former foreign minister Yoon Yung-kwan also commented in *Chosun Ilbo* that Beijing's attempts to gain hegemony further complicated Seoul's position in the region. For this reason, policies concerning THAAD had to be carefully pursued to maximize Seoul's influence over not just North Korean denuclearization but the broader developments in regional security. Conspicuous in this coverage was a sense of anxiety regarding the shifting terms of alliance under the Trump administration and the diminishing scope of policy autonomy for Seoul in the face of an assertive China.

With South Korea's pledge to the "three no's" principles—no additional THAAD units; no joining the US missile defense system; and no trilateral military alliance with the US and Japan—China finally rolled back its economic coercive campaign and committed to improving bilateral relations. But by this point, both ideological camps in South Korea had grown wary about the implications of the THAAD incident for future contingencies in which South Korean defense efforts become tied to broader regional competition between its ally, the United States, and strategic partner, China.

Indeed, though progressive voices generally welcomed the limited rapprochement, they also recognized the need for a mechanism to resolve differences in the longer run. A *Hankyoreh* editorial on October 31 celebrated the "practical" decisions of the two parties to repair relations, allowing South Korea to keep the existing THAAD launchers by providing assurances that it will not participate in US encirclement of China.[19] But *Kyunghyang Shinmun* on the same day noted that, if Seoul's THAAD decision had posed a shock to China, the "three-no's" principles would surely disappoint the United States. South Korea needed concrete measures to navigate what will remain conflicts of interests.

Conservative voices, meanwhile, saw the "three no's" principles as overly accommodating and even harmful to South Korean sovereignty. A *Kookmin* article on October 31 described "three no's" as "short-sighted": Without knowing what kind of North Korean provocation is underway, making such promises was simply imprudent. The article also condemned China for failing to apologize for its retaliation over THAAD; there was no mention of compensation for the losses accrued by South Korea, or of promises not to reoffend.[20] Similarly, other conservative editorials in *Donga Ilbo* on November 1 and *Chosun Ilbo* on November 11 portrayed Seoul as the decisive loser in the diplomatic bargain with China. They mourned Seoul's loss of sovereignty over security matters as this incident had only proved the efficacy of coercive tactics for China.

During the Moon-Xi summit on December 14, 2017, the two leaders agreed to four basic principles on North Korea. These principles included: (1) unacceptability of war on the Korean Peninsula, (2) commitment to its denuclearization, (3) commitment to the peaceful resolution of the North Korean problem, and (4) recognition that improved inter-Korean relations are key to achieving peace. Besides agreeing to these principles, Moon and Xi considered a range of measures to repair the strained ties, including establishing a hotline between the two leaders.

Contrary to expectations that Xi would push Moon aggressively—particularly prevalent among conservative outlets prior to the summit—Xi refrained from touching on sensitive topics, including the "three no's" and "freeze-for-freeze." Arguably in return, Moon refrained from demanding that Xi place an oil embargo on North Korea.

Following the summit, the Blue House released an internal assessment of Moon's China trip, painting it as successful. Conservative outlets, including *Chosun* on December 18, argued that the Moon administration's self-evaluation was overly optimistic.[21] *Chosun* pointed out that of the four principles to which Xi agreed during the summit, three have been Beijing's preferences since 1993—no war, denuclearization, and resolution by peaceful means. In other words, Beijing's current stance is not a product of Seoul's diplomatic efforts, but rather, long-held strategic judgment. A more centrist outlet *Kookmin*, on December 17 further noted that while emotional approaches to assessing Moon's trip can be found from both sides, it is undeniable that few concrete measures have been agreed to toward fulfilling the aforesaid principles.[22]

Progressive coverage criticized the main opposition party for their emotional analyses of Moon's China trip. A *Kyunghyang* article on December 15 cited the leader of the opposition Hong Joon-pyo, who described Moon's recent trip as "tributary diplomacy"; the article views such remarks as inflammatory yet empty in substance.[23] Given that the conservatives were in many ways responsible for the current state of South Korea-China relations—by blindly supporting alliance ties with the United States and allowing the deployment of THAAD in particular—*Kyunghyang* found Hong's attitude inappropriate. *Hankyoreh* shared this view.[24] Even while conceding that Beijing's treatment of Moon was subpar, the article argued that expectations of a grand welcome were unrealistic to begin with. More important, the article saw the opposition party's derisive remarks as a political attempt to simply derail Moon's commitment to repair ties with Beijing.

In this way, much of the partisan debate surrounding China concerned the THAAD fallout and the implications of South Korean "three no's" compromise for its foreign policy autonomy going forward. Though assessments over who won or who lost followed closely existing ideological expectations, there appeared to be an emerging consensus that South Korea was facing an impossible security-economic dilemma, in which efforts to regain security in the face of continued North Korean provocations resulted in economic losses imposed by an increasingly assertive China. Seoul's ability to avoid these trade-offs seemed dubious at best, and commentators from both sides called for economic diversification to dampen the blow going forward.

Japan

If relations with China had regained some semblance of normalcy under Moon, relations with Japan progressively deteriorated. Relying on a so-called "two-track approach"—disaggregating diplomatic and historical issues in conducting bilateral relations—Moon sought to circumvent any discussions of sensitive issues with Tokyo. This only lasted so long, as a South Korean independent commission found that the 2015 "comfort women" agreement was unsound, and later, the Supreme Court ruled that individual victims of forced labor could seek reparations from Japan. These so enraged Tokyo that, in the summer of 2019, it unleashed a barrage of informal sanctions against South Korea, rendering bilateral relations at an impasse.

On December 27, 2017, Moon's Special Task Force, assigned to review the 2015 South Korea-Japan agreement on "comfort women," announced that the deal was concluded in a "seriously flawed" manner and could not resolve the two countries' dispute over the historical issue. The agreement entailed a one-time payment of approximately $8.3 million by Tokyo to meet the needs of the "comfort women" survivors in South Korea, and branded the deal a "final and irreversible" resolution to the decades-old issue. In response to the findings of the Special Task Force, Japanese Foreign Minister Kono Taro responded that any revision or renegotiation of the 2015 agreement would render bilateral relations in an "unmanageable" state, leading to speculations about Moon's next steps.

Progressive coverage expressed extreme disappointment regarding the undisclosed aspects of the 2015 agreement, in which the then-president Park agreed to: (1) persuade organizations working on behalf of the "comfort women" to accept the payment; (2) strive to remove the "comfort woman" statue in front of the Japanese embassy in Seoul; (3) stop funding additional "comfort woman" statues in third countries; and (4) stop using the term "sexual slaves" to refer to the "comfort women." Lamenting how Park discarded the demands of the surviving "comfort women" in conceding to Japanese terms, a *Hankyoreh* article on December 27, 2017, painted the 2015 deal as a "historic crime."[25] Further, the article condemned Abe for failing to apologize for Japan's wartime atrocities and urged him to take legal responsibility. Given that one of Moon's campaign promises was to renegotiate the 2015 agreement, *Hankyoreh* found Moon in an intractable, and perhaps contradictory, position to reopen the dispute while simultaneously seeking to mend ties with Japan.

Conservative coverage found fault with both the 2015 agreement and its review, concerned about its implications for South Korea-Japan relations. A *Joongang* article on December 28, 2017, acknowledged that the deal was concluded in a rushed manner and that its characterization of the resolution as "final and irreversible" was inappropriate.[26] Yet, the article also recognized that the Task Force released sensitive documents—merely two years after the conclusion of the deal—potentially harming the legitimacy and reputation of the South Korean government. *Joongang* asks rhetorically, "which country would be willing to conclude a politically sensitive, secret deal with Seoul?" A more centrist *Kookmin*, on December 27, 2017, shared the sentiment: Even though the flaws of the agreement are manifest—and Japan's attitude of entitlement should be corrected—repudiating the deal would be costly and could possibly damage South Korea-Japan relations beyond repair.[27] A better path forward, in these commentaries, was for Moon to work to compensate the victims internally and cooperate with Tokyo to restore the broken trust rather than unilaterally rescinding the agreement.

Amid intense debate in Seoul about the prospects of the 2015 deal, South Korean foreign minister Kang Kyunghwa announced during a press conference on January 9, 2018, that the Moon administration will not seek renegotiations. Nonetheless, Seoul requested of Tokyo a "voluntary and sincere apology" to the victims. In response, Abe stated that he cannot accept Seoul's unilateral demands that Tokyo take measures beyond the initial terms of the 2015 agreement and claimed that Tokyo will not move "even a millimeter on the deal." Further, Kono stressed that future bilateral agreements will be difficult if the Moon administration simply rejects the commitments of its predecessors. In revealing his decision to attend the opening ceremony of the Pyeongchang Olympics, Abe also declared that he intended to convey his firm stance on the 2015 deal and demand that Moon abide by its terms, pushing in particular for the removal of the "comfort woman" statue.

Partisan narratives remained hotly divided, as conservatives criticized the Moon government for "stirring the pot" for political gain and progressives expressed frustration over unmet expectations of reopening negotiations with Japan. Editorials from *Chosun Ilbo* and *Joongang Ilbo* on January 10, 2018, portrayed Moon's earlier protests against the "comfort women" deal as a ploy to further delegitimize his conservative predecessor, even at the risk of undermining South Korea's diplomatic credibility and security priorities.[28] By contrast, progressive outlets like *Kyunghyang* and *Hankyoreh* blamed the intractable nature of the conflict—fueled by Park's blunder—for Moon's predicament.[29] Neither, however, saw Kang's announcement as a final resolution to the history issues.

Indeed, following the 2018 Supreme Court ruling in South Korea, which stipulated that individual victims could seek redress from Japanese entities regardless of any government-to-government settlement, history issues once again resurfaced. The ruling effectively nullified the Japanese argument that all outstanding issues of reparations had been resolved through the 1965 normalization treaty. If the 2015 "comfort women" agreement had only nominally survived—its enforcement mechanism now dismantled—the issue of forced labor had found new legal momentum and thus, prompted new diplomatic controversy.

A backlash was anticipated by many across ideological lines. At the same time, progressive editorials emphasized the indispensability of the ruling; besides paving the way for victims to pursue justice, the ruling helped rectify the troubled history of South Korean-Japanese normalization.[30] Conservative commentators, while acknowledging the weight of the ruling, were warier about the diplomatic implications of future legal battles. Both *Chosun Ilbo* and *Joongang Ilbo* noted the possibility of involving third parties for mediation or even taking the case to the International Court of Justice.[31] In such cases, history issues would continue to agitate relations, to the detriment of regional security.

North Korea

From the moment of his inauguration, overtures to the North were consistent. From his "Berlin Declaration" to subsequent remarks on Independence Day, Moon made clear his intentions to revive inter-Korean dialogue. But it was only in the aftermath of the North's sixth nuclear test and the specter of US preemptive strikes that diplomacy took center stage. With Kim Jong-un's momentous New Year's Address and a string of summits that followed in the aftermath of the 2018 Pyeongchang Olympics, hopes of a diplomatic breakthrough on denuclearization and broader peace process abounded.

The contours of "Moonshine" policy took shape as Moon pushed for peace talks between the two Koreas. Speech after speech, he spoke of "permanent peace," which entails the denuclearization of the Korean Peninsula, security guarantees for the North, and deepening economic and cultural exchanges. These overtures were largely welcomed by progressives, who believed that incremental gestures such as resumption of family reunions and cessation of hostilities around the Military Demarcation Line would help build momentum for longer-term commitments toward peace. Conservatives, by contrast, found these as little more than bargaining chips for the North to draw concessions from the South. This pattern of behavior has only enabled Pyongyang to advance its nuclear program. Seoul, they warned, should remain wary of any efforts by Pyongyang to lift sanctions.

On September 2, 2017, North Korea conducted its sixth nuclear test at the Punggye-ri site, claiming to have detonated an "H-bomb" miniaturized to fit onto an ICBM, much to the skepticism of experts. In response to the test, Trump tweeted that "North Korea is a rogue nation which has become a great threat and embarrassment to China," while also admonishing South Korea that "appeasement with North Korea will not work." On the other hand, despite calling the test "severely disappointing," Moon insisted: "we will not give up and will continue to push for the denuclearization of the Korean Peninsula through peaceful means working together with our allies." Concerns about Korea scaring, bashing, and passing were at their zenith in the aftermath of the sixth nuclear test.

One crucial development in partisan debates over the sixth nuclear test regarded the utility of self-nuclearization in South Korea. Many in the conservative camp argued that the test "crossed the red line," justifying all options—including military ones—in response. In their view, the traditional sanctions approach had failed; Moon must thus aim to stop—not control—Pyongyang's nuclear pursuits, even if by imposing regime change or developing Seoul's own nuclear weapons. Progressives found these suggestions dangerous, debasing efforts toward denuclearization on the Korean Peninsula and triggering a possible nuclear arms race in Asia. For all his talk of dialogue, Moon had deployed THAAD, expanded South Korea's missile capabilities, and acquired high-tech military assets—moves that only validated Pyongyang's insecurities, some of his supporters complained.

Amid Trump's threats of "fire and fury," Kim delivered his New Year's Address, which suggested conditional talks with Seoul during the 2018 Pyeongchang Olympics. This followed the reopening of inter-Korean lines of communication in Panmunjom, which had been shut for nearly two years since the closure of KIC in 2016. Welcoming the North's overture, Seoul proposed holding high-level talks on January 9, 2018, which Pyongyang accepted. Trump told Moon in a phone call that he supports the talks and agreed to postpone their military exercises, but also reaffirmed his commitment to the campaign of maximum pressure against Pyongyang.

Conservatives treated the developments with caution, frustrated in particular by Trump's about-face on North Korea. A *Joongang* article on January 8, 2018, claimed that Trump's support for the talks could be a double-edged sword, particularly because he suffered domestic opposition in agreeing to delay the military exercises for the successful completion of the two Koreas' upcoming exchanges.[32] If the talks do not amount to meaningful outcomes and merely result in the North's participation at the Olympics, Seoul could be blamed for buying Pyongyang the time it needs to advance its nuclear weapons program. Even more disquieting, it may give Trump a reason to resort to military options. Such concerns were scant in progressive coverages, which instead criticized conservative outlets for refuting Trump's backing of the talks.[33]

As high-level talks unfolded before the Pyeongchang Olympics, partisans debated the meaning of the North's olive branch for denuclearization. Pyongyang had argued that its nuclear weapons were not directed at its "brethren" South Korea, but the United States, and thus should not be a topic of discussion in inter-Korean talks. Progressives focused on the symbolic significance of the North's Olympics participation and the opportunity this could bring for eventual dialogue on the more sensitive issues, including denuclearization. Conservatives, meanwhile, saw it as Pyongyang's ploy to drive a wedge between Seoul and Washington. As a *Chosun* editorial had foretold at the time, a "time of reckoning" was coming.[34]

Even as the third ever inter-Korean summit was held at the peace village of Panmunjom on April 27, 2018, the same partisan thinking persisted. The summit had transpired on the heels of a flurry of diplomatic and cultural exchanges that followed the North's participation at the Pyeongchang Winter Olympics. During the summit, the two leaders signed the "Panmunjom Declaration," which stated their objectives in three categories: (1) improving inter-Korean relations through joint cultural, economic, and social projects; (2) reducing military tension and eliminating the threat of conflict; and (3) establishing a "peace system" to bring a formal end to the war and denuclearize the Korean Peninsula. Media responses to the summit were largely positive, though differences were noticeable in their emphases: progressive outlets characterized the summit as a successful "first step" toward peace, while conservative outlets focused on denuclearization as the core (or at times the sole) objective of the summit.

It is worth noting that the Panmunjom summit had generated substantial shifts in public mood regarding the North's intentions for peace. According to one public opinion survey, 64.7% of the respondents stated they trusted the North's commitment to denuclearize, while only 28.3% stated they were skeptical.[35] These results demonstrated an astonishing reversal of opinion: a similar survey before the summit had painted the very opposite picture, with an overwhelming majority of 78.3% responding they distrusted the North's peace gesture. Other trends were notable, too: real estate prices near the border spiked upward, and talk of abolishing military requirements was spreading rapidly among the younger generation.

In this triumphant mood, inter-Korean diplomacy charged ahead, culminating in the Pyongyang Declaration. The jointly signed peace agreement included a cessation of military hostilities, economic cooperation, family reunions, exchanges in arts and sports, a reference to a nuclear-free Korea, and Kim's potential visit to Seoul by the end of the year. The most noticeable part of the agreement was North Korea's promise to "permanently" dismantle its nuclear facilities and allow international experts to "observe" the dismantlement; as for additional measures regarding denuclearization, including the permanent dismantlement of the Yongbyon nuclear facility, North Korea expressed its willingness to carry them out as long as the United States takes corresponding measures following the spirit of the US-DPRK joint statement signed during the Singapore Summit.

It was only after the Pyongyang Declaration was made that conservative coverage of Moon's diplomacy began to split. Some like *Chosun* continued to see Pyongyang's promises as empty and Seoul's concessions as imprudent.[36] Inter-Korean projects, such as reopening KIC and Mount Geumgang tourism, require lifting of existing sanctions, which would provide material benefits to Pyongyang despite limited progress on denuclearization. Meanwhile, *Joongang* and *Donga* acknowledged that the Pyongyang Declaration was a step forward from past agreements. They welcomed, for instance, the more specific wording on denuclearization and a commitment to achieve it in "Kim Jong-un's voice." They especially appreciated the third inter-Korean summit bearing the fruit of practically allowing international inspections, including by the United States, although the term used in the declaration was "observation." The divisions in conservative voices marked how pervasive the sense of diplomatic victory was at the time, convincing even some partisans to celebrate Moon's success.

United States

Trump's election and his "America First" foreign policy had massive ramifications for South Korean foreign policy during the early years of Moon's presidency. Concerns ranged from "Korea bashing" (blaming Seoul for the North's intransigence) to those about "Korea passing" (making peninsular decisions without Seoul's input). Trump's impulsive personality, combined with his general disregard for the establishment, made predicting US responses to North Korean provocations—and later overtures—almost futile. In late 2017, amid North Korean provocations, Trump had pledged "fire and fury"; in 2018, he took credit for the nascent inter-Korean dialogue in a tweet, "Does anybody really believe that talks and dialogue would be going on between North and South Korea right now if I wasn't firm, strong and willing to commit our total 'might' against the North?" The kind of high-profile diplomacy between the United States and North Korea, many believed, would have been challenging if it were not for Trump.

The North Korean threat of a missile strike against Guam and the specter of preventive strikes stimulated discussions about South Korea's nuclearization and alliance posture. Suggestions for bolstering nuclear deterrence varied within the conservative camp, with the mainstream voices pushing for redeploying tactical nuclear weapons and others calling for joint capitalization of US strategic assets akin to NATO's nuclear sharing.[37] The key difference in these two approaches was that the latter will guarantee information sharing, joint decision-making, and joint command-and-control in case of use. As debates about nuclearization gained steam, progressives emphasized the growing strains in the US-South Korean alliance: unilateral actions by the Trump administration were spawning suspicion and harming its legitimacy—and therefore sustainability.[38] If most discussions about nuclearization were limited to alliance-based arrangements, already on the fringes of the conservative wing, calls for self-nuclearization were brewing.

During this period, the Trump administration continued to refer to North Korea as a "rogue regime"—in public speeches at the UN General Assembly as well as in official documents such as the 2017 National Security Strategy. In it, Washington detailed four pillars of "America First" policy: (1) protection of the American people, homeland, and the American way of life; (2) promotion of

American prosperity; (3) preservation of peace through strength; and (4) advancement of American influence. These pillars linked American domestic strength to its performance overseas, subtly redefining "America First" by rejecting implications of isolationism and embracing, instead, a version of internationalism. Within this broader picture, the document also reaffirms Trump's position on North Korea, namely that the United States is ready to use "overwhelming" force against Pyongyang.

The incendiary rhetoric prompted accusations of war mongering among South Korean progressives, who drew parallels between Trump's labeling of "rogue states" to former President Bush's "axis of evil" discourse in 2002.[39] Alarmed, a *Kyunghyang Shinmun* editorial on September 20 went so far as to liken Trump to a "thug," threatening war at the very institution aimed at preserving peace, the United Nations.[40] Progressive narratives in this period also worried about Trump's escalatory approach to broader regional security issues—most evidently against another "rogue state," China—and its implications for peace on the peninsula. *Hankyoreh* warned in this light that Korea may be the greatest victim of this "new Cold War."[41]

Conservatives welcomed Trump's aggressiveness and "maximum pressure" strategy. A *Donga* editorial, for instance, portrayed his UN remarks as "principled realism," aimed at diplomatic maneuver.[42] Immediately following his speech, Secretary of Defense James Mattis subtly contradicted it to send a mixed—but according to *Donga*—calculated signal. At the same time, conservative outlets noted the growing gulf between the Trump and Moon administrations' positions on North Korea. The 2017 National Security Strategy (NSS) advocates strengthening US missile defense systems in Asia, which directly contradicts Moon's "three no's" principles. Trump's readiness to use force equally challenges Moon's "no war" stance. Ultimately, Seoul will have to confront these contradictions and choose a side—on North Korea as well as the broader developments concerning China.

Following the Pyeongchang Olympics—during which frictions persisted as the US delegation protested the North's participation in subtle ways—Trump accepted Kim's invitation for a summit. He tweeted in affirmation, "Great progress being made but sanctions will remain until an agreement is reached. Meeting being planned!" The surprise was palpable across ideological lines, albeit varying levels of enthusiasm. Progressives imagined a "big deal" on North Korea, praising Kim's practicality and Trump's bold decision-making. Meanwhile, conservatives worried about the prospects of abandonment. A *Chosun* editorial, for example, noted the possibility of a deal in which the North agrees to denuclearize in exchange for the US ending its alliance with the South.[43] Many variations of such a deal were conceivable, including Trump agreeing to lift sanctions for Pyongyang to dismantle its intercontinental ballistic missile program. By and large, however, celebrations of Moon's diplomatic competence overwhelmed calls for caution.

On June 12, Donald Trump and Kim Jong-un met in Singapore. Marking the first-ever US-North Korean summit, the two leaders shook hands and jointly announced the Singapore Declaration. The declaration reaffirmed Kim's agreement to "work toward complete denuclearization of the Korean Peninsula" in exchange for Trump's commitment to provide "security guarantees," the details of which remained unspecified. The declaration also welcomed the "establishment of new US-DPRK relations and the building of a lasting and robust peace regime on the Korean Peninsula." Toward that end, Trump announced his willingness to halt US-South Korean military exercises, which he described as "provocative."

Partisan debates centered around one key aspect of the Singapore Declaration: Trump's unilateral decision to halt joint military exercises with South Korea. If progressives saw it as a part of any "comprehensive" trajectory toward peace, conservatives deemed it a natural path for the North to become recognized as a nuclear-armed state. According to *Kyunghyang*, the summit provided the critical first step, allowing the two leaders to build rapport as well as cease any provocative activities—a moratorium on testing for the North, military exercises for the United States.[44] *Chosun*, on the other hand, remarked that the declaration was the "worst outcome for South Korea," as Trump signaled his willingness to undermine the alliance in return for small, but immediate gains.

As working-level talks floundered, partisans engaged in a broader debate about the right course of action forward. For the progressives, the most viable approach was tit-for-tat disarmament, in which Pyongyang's dismantlement of nuclear facilities and ICBMs are rewarded with partial sanctions relief, such as the reopening of KIC operations. The North's "denuclearization measures" and the US "corresponding measures" must be executed in lock step with each other to generate synergy toward peace. For the conservatives, the only sustainable approach was based on principles of complete and verifiable denuclearization that leave no room for Pyongyang's reneging, which it has done in the past. This requires, among others, a united front of Washington and Seoul to push for more-than-symbolic concessions from Pyongyang.

In hindsight, the second Hanoi Summit between Kim and Trump was set up for failure: the ambiguities of the Singapore Declaration and the tensions from the working-level talks rendered expectations implausibly high and approaches too divisive. When Trump walked away from the negotiations—asserting "no deal is better than a bad deal"—partisans in South Korea rushed to assess Moon's performance as a facilitator and draw lessons for Seoul. In conservative coverage, Moon's key flaw was failing to clarify denuclearization as the only answer to sanctions relief, giving Pyongyang the impression that it could get away with its gambit.[45] Progressives, meanwhile, elevated Moon's role as the middleman once again, holding onto their beliefs that the two parties will eventually return to the negotiating table.[46] As days went by, however, any positive spin the progressives had churned was shadowed by the dread of the returning status quo in US-North Korean relations.

Conclusion

The years 2016–2019 marked a sea change in South Korean foreign policy. Park's untimely exit and Moon's "candlelight" mandate meant that on various dimensions of foreign policy—where the executive has significant prerogatives—Seoul made notable reversals, departures, and advances. Their implications are many and still to be clarified, on questions of South Korea's relations with its friends and foes as well as place in the region.

The botched *trustpolitik* and the succeeding "Moonshine" generated some notable headlines as images of Pyongyang shifted from an untamed provocateur to a long-lost brother. Though Moon's activism helped escape the specter of war, its impact on the status of disarmament, denuclearization, and diplomacy remains hotly debated. Crucially, South Korea's alliance with the United States was more tested during this period than ever, as Trump's "America First" foreign policy in many ways dissolved existing ideological commitments. The most prominent evidence in this regard was the growing calls on the fringes of the conservative party for self-nuclearization, which saw US nuclear guarantees as no longer reliable. Partisan narratives reflected the volatility of the times.

More predictable, perhaps, were the developments surrounding China and Japan. By faulting Park's authoritarian politics, Moon could seek foreign policy reversals in the name of "candlelight" rehabilitation: recovering relations with China over the THAAD dispute with his "three no's" compromise and asserting procedural illegitimacy of South Korea's agreements with Japan on history issues. Though Moon attempted to nuance his decisions—maintaining existing THAAD deployments and choosing not to overturn Park's diplomatic and military commitments with Japan—the outcomes were as expected.

Notes

1 Park Geun-hye, "A New Kind of Korea," *Foreign Affairs*, September/October 2011.
2 *Chosun Ilbo*, February 13, 2016.
3 *Joongang Ilbo*, January 11, 2016.
4 Chosun Ilbo, January 11, 2016.
5 *Hankyoreh*, January 10, 2016.
6 *Joongang Ilbo*, February 12, 2016.
7 *Chosun Ilbo*, February 17, 2016.
8 *Hankyoreh*, February 11, 2016.
9 *Kyunghyang Shinmun*, February 11, 2016.
10 *Donga Ilbo*, September 13, 2016.
11 *Donga Ilbo*, September 14, 2016.
12 *Hankyoreh*, September 13, 2016.
13 *Chosun Ilbo*, September 10, 2016; *Donga Ilbo*, September 28, 2016.
14 *Joongang Ilbo*, November 10, 2016.
15 *Chosun Ilbo*, November 10, 2016.
16 *Donga Ilbo*, February 17, 2016.
17 *Joongang Ilbo*, February 18, 2016.
18 *Chosun Ilbo*, July 14, 2016.

19 *Hankyoreh,* October 31, 2017.
20 *Kookmin Ilbo,* October 31, 2017.
21 *Chosun Ilbo,* December 18, 2017.
22 *Kookimin Ilbo,* December 17, 2017.
23 *Kyunghyang Shinmun,* December 15, 2017.
24 *Hankyoreh,* December 15, 2017.
25 *Hankyoreh,* December 27, 2017.
26 *Joongang Ilbo,* December 28, 2017.
27 *Kookmin Ilbo,* December 27, 2017.
28 *Chosun Ilbo,* January 1, 2018; *Joongang Ilbo,* January 1, 2018.
29 *Kyunghyang Shinmun,* January 9, 2018; *Hankyoreh,* January 9, 2018.
30 *Hankyoreh,* October 30, 2018.
31 *Chosun Ilbo,* October 31, 2018; *Joongang Ilbo,* October 31, 2018.
32 *Joongang Ilbo,* January 8, 2018.
33 *Hankyoreh,* January 7, 2018.
34 *Chosun Ilbo,* January 10, 2018.
35 *Segye Ilbo,* April 30, 2018.
36 *Chosun Ilbo,* September 20, 21018.
37 *Segye Ilbo,* August 14, 2017; *Maeil Kyeongjae,* August 15, 2017.
38 *Kyunghyang Shinmun,* August 14, 2017.
39 *Hankyoreh,* September 20, 2017.
40 *Kyunghyang Shinmun,* September 20, 2017.
41 *Hankyoreh,* December 19, 2017.
42 *Donga Ilbo,* September 21, 2017.
43 *Chosun Ilbo,* March 10, 2018.
44 *Kyunghyang Shinmun,* June 12, 2018.
45 *Joongang Ilbo,* March 2, 2019.
46 *Hankyoreh,* March 1, 2019.

7
SHIFT TO THE NEW MISSILE AGE: 2020–2022

Sue Mi Terry

For South Korean policy toward North Korea, the 2020–2022 period proved to be a watershed. Ever since the Sunshine Policy began in 1998, leaders in Seoul had envisioned some sort of breakthrough with the leadership in Pyongyang to greatly decrease the threat from the North and to foster better relations with the South. Achieving those goals was perceived as vital to not only safeguarding South Korean security but also to allowing it to exercise greater influence on the world stage. In 2020 these hopes were left on life support following the breakdown in diplomacy between Donald Trump and Kim Jong-un. In 2022, they were relegated to history by North Korean misbehavior and the deteriorating global environment, including the Russian invasion of Ukraine and growing US-China tensions, which further split the international community and made it impossible for the great powers to come together to deal with North Korea.

Even after the collapse of diplomacy and summitry with Kim Jong-un following the failure of the Hanoi Summit in 2019, President Moon Jae-in still clung to the hope that he could make an improbable breakthrough with the North in the remaining three years of his term. The Moon administration doubled down on diplomatic efforts with the North with a sense of urgency, although its term would come to an end without a happy ending. By the time President Yoon Seok-yeol came into office in May 2022, the North had returned to an unprecedented level of provocations, including sustained and frequent ballistic missile tests. By the end of 2022, the North had launched a record number of missile tests for the year (nearly 100) and declared a new nuclear doctrine threatening a preemptive strike. South Korea was left facing a North Korea with a weapons of mass destruction program that was rapidly morphing and expanding. In the end, Moon's North Korea policy, while initially credited with facilitating nuclear diplomacy between

DOI: 10.4324/9781003394792-8

Washington and Pyongyang and easing fears of conflict, had come to be seen as having aided the Kim regime to buy time and advance its nuclear and missile technologies. 2022 ended with inter-Korea relations entering a new and more dangerous phase.

2020: From Diplomacy to Confrontation

As the two-year anniversary of the historic Kim-Trump summit in Singapore approached in June 2020, Kim Jong-un began shifting to a harder line in his public posture, including threats to resume long-range missile and nuclear tests. Kim had greeted the new year, 2020, with a warning to the world that it would soon see the North's "new strategic weapon," while vowing that the North would implement new "policies" in the coming year to boost its nuclear deterrent.[1] At a rare meeting of the ruling Korean Workers' Party, which replaced the typical, televised New Year's address, Kim railed against Washington's "hostile" policy and "gangster-like acts," which, he said, left the North no choice but to pursue a "new path."[2] In the preceding months, Kim had given the US until the end of the year to drop its hostile policy while threatening to deliver an unwelcome "Christmas gift."[3] While the end of 2019 came and went without a Christmas gift from the North and without renewed missile tests, when Kim greeted 2020, he signaled that he was about to shift to a more aggressive phase in inter-Korea relations.

Moon Jae-in was still eager to improve ties with the North. He used his New Year's address to say that "the need to find realistic ways to further advance inter-Korean cooperation has become all the more urgent" and reiterated his proposal for the two Koreas to cooperate in various areas such as jointly bidding to host the 2032 Summer Olympics, beginning sports exchanges, and reconnecting inter-Korean railways and roads.[4] Moon also said that he would continue his efforts to resume operation of the inter-Korean Kaesong Industrial Complex (KIC), which the previous Park Geun-hye administration had closed in February 2016 in retaliation for the North's nuclear and missile provocations. He also expressed a desire to resume South Korean tourism to Mount Geumgang in the North. Moon and Kim Jong-un had agreed during a summit in Pyongyang in September 2018 to reopen the KIC and Mount Geumgang tours as soon as conditions were right.

A few weeks later, in his annual New Year's press conference, Moon went even further, saying, "If exceptions from U.N. sanctions are necessary for South-North cooperation, I think we can make efforts for that."[5] Talking about sanctions exceptions for the North was clearly a carefully deliberated move by the Moon administration. On the same day, halfway around the world, Moon's foreign minister, Kang Kyung-wha, speaking to reporters in Silicon Valley following meetings with the foreign ministers of Japan and the United States, said it was essential to revive "North Korea's engagement momentum" through inter-Korean talks. She said that there were projects which, if there is a problem with international sanctions, could proceed by receiving sanctions exemptions.[6]

When Kim Jong-un did not respond to these peace gestures, and as the COVID-19 outbreak began, Moon used his annual speech commemorating Korea's March 1 Independence Movement to say that he was looking forward to cooperating with North Korea on healthcare, so that the two Koreas could battle the virus together. North Korea's response to these overtures by Moon was to have the most active month of missile testing to date. It conducted nine tests in March 2020, even though Washington and Seoul cancelled joint military exercises. A day after Moon's March 1 address on possible inter-Korean cooperation on COVID-19, Pyongyang launched two short-range ballistic missiles (KN-25s),[7] which were followed by three more KN-25 tests on March 9,[8] two KN-24 tests on March 21,[9] and then two final KN-25s on March 30.[10] This series of short-range missiles in March signaled the North's intent to follow through with Kim's promise to deploy a "new strategic weapon."

Shortly afterward, on the eve of a key state anniversary in the North and parliamentary elections in the South, the North launched cruise missiles—the first such test in nearly three years.[11] Even with a barrage of tests by the North, the Moon administration could not be swayed off the path it was on, of trying to find some sort of a breakthrough with the North. When the ruling Democratic Party won a landslide victory in the South's parliamentary elections in April, gaining 180 out of 200 seats, the Moon administration was more determined than ever to forge ahead with inter-Korean cooperative projects. In a news conference on May 10 marking his third year in office, Moon declared his desire to become a "negotiator" again: "Let's not just look at the U.S-North Korea dialogue, but now find what can be done between South and North."[12] Then, on May 21, Moon's first chief of staff, Im Jong-seok, gave a revealing interview to a Korean magazine about Moon's mindset: "President Moon will try to push ahead to get things done, while sufficiently communicating with the U.S., even if there are negative views."[13] Im added that South Korea has to think about what it would do if the dialogue between the United States and North Korea did not work out. Im was a key figure in the Moon government's inter-Korean relationship and was deeply involved in the three inter-Korean summits between Moon and Kim. Clearly, he was indicating that the Moon administration was willing to be at odds with Washington if it meant making even incremental progress on inter-Korea relations, the Trump administration having maintained that the improvement of inter-Korean relations should take place in tandem with the pace of denuclearization.

Going even further, the Ministry of Unification declared that the May 24 sanctions measures that were enacted in the wake of the North's attack on the South Korean corvette, the *Cheonan*, in 2010 would no longer be an obstacle to promoting inter-Korean cooperation. This was the first time in a decade that the South Korean government had officially stated that it could ease the May 24 measures that banned all inter-Korean exchanges and cooperation. To achieve this goal, the Moon administration prepared a draft amendment to the inter-Korean Exchange and Cooperation Act that would simplify the process of contacting Pyongyang, while conducting a survey to register the DMZ, an emblem of inter-Korean conflict, as a UNESCO World Heritage site.[14]

The North was unmoved by all these gestures. The Kim regime underscored that it was not interested in Moon's attempt to preserve the Korean détente and began to dramatically escalate tensions the following month. Early in June, Kim's sister, Kim Yo-jong, threatened to pull out of an inter-Korean military accord, withdraw from the KIC, and abolish the joint liaison office if South Korea failed to stop its citizens and North Korean defectors from sending anti-Pyongyang leaflets across the border.[15] Calling the North Korean defectors involved in the anti-North leaflet campaign "human scum" and "rubbish-like mongrel dogs," she demanded that the Moon administration ban civilian leafleting.[16]

Just hours after Kim Yo-jong's tirades against the leaflet balloons, the Moon administration obliged the regime by saying it would take immediate action to prohibit the sending of leaflets; a spokesperson of the Ministry of Unification even said implausibly that "most leaflets have been found in our territory, causing environmental pollution and increasing burden on local people to get rid of them."[17]

Yet even after the Moon administration responded to Kim Yo-jong's derisive dressing down by saying Seoul would indeed ban the activist groups from sending leaflets, the North still followed through with its threats on June 8 by cutting off all channels of communication with the South, including the inter-Korean military communication hotline, the inter-Korean general hotline, and the hotline between Moon and Kim.[18] Soon after, on June 16, the North made good on Kim Yo-jong's threat and literally blew up the "useless" inter-Korean liaison office located at Kaesong—a four-story office building that had cost the Moon administration $70 million to build and that served as a de facto embassy and communications channel for the two Koreas.[19] A statement released by North Korea described the move as "the latest punishment measure conducted in the wake of cutting off all communication lines between the North and the South."[20] Simultaneously, the North declared the South to be an "enemy" and threatened to move troops into the demilitarized zone, refused to participate in future inter-Korean talks, and vowed to develop its nuclear weapons.[21] With this dramatic ramping up of tensions on the Korean Peninsula, the cooperative spirit of the 2018 summits became a dead letter by the end of June.

The destruction of a rare symbol of cross-border cooperation marked a sharp escalation from Pyongyang and a setback for Moon, who had made his effort to coax the Kim regime to give up nuclear weapons the hallmark of his presidency. As Professor Lim Jae-cheon said at the time, "Moon's peace and reconciliation policy appears to have failed," and it appeared "Moon probably will have great difficulty in reviving relations for the rest of his term."[22] Most Korea watchers in the US and South Korea concluded at the time that the demolition of the liaison office was simply the most explosive moment of an escalating pressure campaign by the North intended to push Moon to split from Washington and ease sanctions against the Kim regime.[23]

Yet the Moon administration still could not be discouraged from its pursuit of diplomacy. Even North Korea's brutal killing of a South Korean Ministry of Fisheries and Maritime Affairs official, Lee Dae-joon, on September 21 would not affect the Moon administration's desire to make progress with Pyongyang. Trying to make the North look better, the Moon administration asserted that Lee was on sea duty near Yeonpyeong Island in the Yellow Sea and claimed that he tried to defect when he was killed by North Korean soldiers and his body was burnt at sea. (The Yoon administration's Board of Audit and Inspection would find in October 2022 that there was insufficient evidence to claim that Lee was a would-be defector.)[24]

A few weeks later, on October 10, the North held a long-awaited military parade to mark the 75th anniversary of the Workers' Party of Korea, where it revealed more North Korean military technology—both conventional and WMD—than ever before, including new anti-tank guided missiles, a new air defense radar system, a new submarine-launched ballistic missile, the Pukguksong-4, and scores of short-range and medium-range ballistic missiles. The centerpiece was its new "strategic weapon," dubbed by experts a "monster" weapon, the Hwasong-15, the largest liquid-propellant, road-mobile intercontinental ballistic missile in the world.

Clearly the message that the North was sending with such a display was that it was in a position of strength, that it was making incredible progress on its nuclear and missile programs, and that time was on its side despite the raging pandemic, its strict border closure with China, typhoons, and other challenges. In fact, in a speech, Kim emphasized that "time is by our side."[25]

By the end of 2020, the South Korean National Assembly, dominated by Moon's party, adopted legislation criminalizing the sending of anti-regime leaflets, USB sticks, Bible verses, and even US dollars into North Korea via balloons.[26] The new South Korean law imposed stiff fines (up to almost $30,000) and even jail terms (up to three years), despite fierce criticism by conservatives and human rights activists abroad that South Korea was sacrificing civil liberties and freedom of expression. This was perceived as a highly partisan, divisive decision in South Korea. Ruling party lawmakers said the legislation was simply intended to avoid unnecessarily provoking the North and to ensure the safety of people who live near the border. Opposition lawmakers, however, saw this as evidence that Moon was appeasing Pyongyang. Opposition National Assembly members protested and refused to participate in the vote. The ruling party was nevertheless able to use its three-fifths parliamentary supermajority to bring the issue to a final vote.

2021: Seoul's Last-Ditch Efforts for a Breakthrough

Moon faced an unenviable environment heading into the final year-plus of his presidency. North Korea remained utterly impassive in the face of his outreach, and he was running out of time, but he remained undeterred in his desire to achieve a breakthrough with the North. He carved out a significant chunk of his 2021 New Year's speech to promoting "principles of mutual security guarantees, common prosperity and zero tolerance for war," and assuring Kim Jong-un that he was determined to meet with Kim "at any time and any place."[27]

The North's response was to make it clear to the Moon administration that it was still unhappy with Seoul even after the adoption of the "gag" law in December. At the rare Workers' Party Congress (the first since 2016), Kim criticized Moon for making "nonessential" offers to cooperate on the pandemic, humanitarian issues, and joint tours. Kim Yo-jong continued to ridicule Moon, describing him as "clueless" and an "idiot" and calling the Moon administration a "truly weird group."[28]

The Party Congress report contained a laundry list of the North's newest armaments: a nuclear-powered submarine, intercontinental ballistic missiles, reconnaissance satellites, "multi-warhead," "hypersonic gliding-fight missiles," and "ultramodern tactical nuclear weapons." At the same time, the Party Congress also passed a resolution to "further strengthen our nuclear deterrence."[29] The Kim regime then greeted the incoming Biden administration by launching two cruise missiles and two short-range ballistic missiles in March 2021, the first since it tested a barrage of short-range missiles a year prior.[30] Nevertheless, a month later, Moon, in an interview with *The New York Times*, urged the new Biden administration to not "kill the 2018 Singapore agreement."[31]

Following a months-long policy review, the Biden administration finally announced on April 30 that it would take a "calibrated, practical approach" toward North Korea with a goal of denuclearization.[17] It said it will pursue "diplomacy, as well as stern deterrence" and said it had at the same time reached out to the North, saying that it is open to talks without preconditions. The Biden administration emphasized that it still supported inter-Korean engagement and said that it was exploring diplomatic options for North Korea with South Korea and Japan.[18] The Biden administration said it was also open to using humanitarian aid to incentivize North Korea's return to talks.[19]

The Biden administration, however, did not make the bigger concessions that North Korea has demanded—such as sanctions relief—or take greater political and diplomatic risks to jump-start a diplomatic process. It also remained unclear what the Biden administration meant exactly when it said that it was exploring "something in the middle" between the Trump administration's "all or nothing" policy and the Obama administration's "strategic patience policy."[32]

On May 10, in a speech to mark four years in office, Moon again indicated his willingness to breathe new life into the Korean peace process. On May 21, Moon had his first in-person summit with newly elected Biden in Washington. As the US-ROK Leaders' Joint Statement was announced, the public and media attention largely shifted from a "vaccine swap" arrangement, which was said to be the major achievement of the summit, to a reaffirmation of the 2018 Panmunjom Declaration and Singapore Joint Statement.[33]

There finally appeared to be some sort of brief breakthrough with the North when, at the end of July 2021, the Moon administration declared that the two Koreas were restoring four communication lines that Pyongyang had cut off a year ago when the North severed all inter-Korean governmental communication.[34] Soon after, however, the North stopped answering routine South Korean calls in apparent protest of the joint US-South Korea military exercises scheduled for August. Still, the initial resumption of inter-Korean calls marked a slight improvement in inter-Korea relations since a sharp deterioration in mid-2020.[2] At the time, various Korea watchers speculated that the Kim regime was again using rapprochement to extract economic concessions and aid from Seoul as it was facing significant domestic challenges brought on by natural disasters and halting of trade with China, which reportedly had dropped by more than 80 percent due to North Korea closing its borders as a COVID-19 prevention measure.[35] In fact, perhaps the most significant development in 2021 was that the North's self-imposed COVID quarantine reduced external trade more than international sanctions ever could.

The North for the remainder of the year remained non-responsive to all overtures from the South—as well as to US overtures. By September, the North returned to testing, including a new type of long-range cruise missile, short-range missiles, and, on September 28, a new "hypersonic" missile, the Hwasong-8, followed two days later by a new type of anti-aircraft missile.[36] In October 2021, North Korea fired a submarine-launched ballistic missile and then began answering military and liaison office communication lines again.[37]

2022: The Year of Testing

2022 began with the North firing off a barrage of missiles—hypersonic missiles (some launched from train cars), short-range ballistic and cruise missiles, and intermediate-range ballistic missiles (IRMB) in January—as the North was getting ready to celebrate important triple anniversaries: Kim Jong-il's 80th birthday in February, Kim Il-sung's 100th birthday and the 10th anniversary of Kim Jong-un's reign in April (Kim becoming first secretary of the ruling Workers' Party of Korea). After the IRBM launch on January 30, the North renewed testing again, testing a Hwasong-17, the latest generation ICBM on February 27.[38] For the Moon administration, which allocated the bulk of its political capital to achieving a breakthrough with the North, these missiles in close succession ahead of the presidential election in March dashed any remaining hope of returning to dialogue with Pyongyang and leaving a positive legacy for its North Korea policy.

With the election of Yoon Suk-yeol, the candidate of the opposition conservative People Power Party, in the presidential election on March 9, South Korea's policy toward North Korea was now poised to significantly shift away from Moon's approach of the past five years. Moon approached North Korea issues as a peacemaker pursuing dialogue above all else; Yoon signaled, even before he was elected, that he would prioritize strengthening the military alliance with the US, build up South Korea's own advanced missile programs, and enhance extended deterrence of North Korea's nuclear program.

Specifically, Yoon pledged during his campaign that his administration would strengthen the US-ROK military alliance by invigorating joint military drills and deploying additional THAAD anti-missile launchers. During his New Year's press conference on January 11, hours after the North conducted its second missile test of the new year, Yoon even said that he backed achieving "preemptive strike capabilities" in the event of a conflict with the North.[39] Yoon was referring to reviving the so-called "three Ks," the three-axis system of the South Korean military response system designed to defend its territory by: first, developing a "kill chain" that preemptively strikes North Korean nuclear weapons and missiles; second, intercepting incoming missile strikes using the Korean Air and Missile Defense (KAMD) system; and third, employing a "mass retaliation" campaign to eliminate the North's command-and-control centers. The three-axis system was announced in 2013, shortly before North Korea's third nuclear test, but the Moon administration in 2019 replaced this term with a "system for responding to nuclear weapons and weapons of mass destruction," which Moon hoped would sound less offensive to the North Koreans.[40]

At the same time, Yoon also vowed to build up surveillance and reconnaissance capacities to monitor North Korean territory and promised to equip the South Korean military with "ultra-precision and hypersonic missiles."[41] The North's response was to keep the missiles coming. A few days before the presidential election, it tested its reconnaissance satellite systems, then a projectile following the election on March 16, and multiple rocket launchers and an intercontinental ballistic missile on March 24.[42] In April, the North fired two short-range ballistic missiles; it later indicated that the "new type tactical guided weapon" was developed as a means of delivering "tactical nukes."[43] A month later, after launching a submarine-launched ballistic missile on May 7, the North launched three more ballistic missiles on May 25 while Biden was flying back to Washington, D.C. after a visit to Japan and Korea. The launches continued throughout the summer. Notably, in June, the North fired eight short-range ballistic missiles from different locations in North Korea.[44]

Once Yoon was in office, while he made clear that South Korea's role going forward would not be that of a mediator between Washington and Pyongyang, his approach toward the North was *not* "all hardline, all the time." Yoon did try to continue some aspects of Moon's North Korea policy, including his desire to interact economically with the North as a means of incentivizing denuclearization. Yoon announced his initiative to install a trilateral South Korea-US-North Korea liaison office in the Panmunjom area and pledged to provide humanitarian support to North Koreans. In his first Liberation Day Speech as president on August 15, Yoon presented his vision of an "audacious initiative" that would improve North Korea's economy and North Koreans' livelihoods if Pyongyang ceased "the development of its nuclear program and embarks on a genuine and substantive process for denuclearization."[45] If this occurs, Yoon pledged that South Korea would implement a large-scale food program, aid with power generation, carry out projects to modernize ports and airports for international trade, enhance North Korea's agricultural productivity, and offer assistance to modernize hospitals and medical infrastructure, while also implementing international investment and financial support initiatives.[46]

Predictably, the North ridiculed these proposals, and Yoon's "bold plan" went nowhere. Two days after Yoon made his "audacious" proposal, North Korea called him "simple" and "childish," and fired two cruise missiles off its west coast.[47] Then in August and September 2022, South Korea and the United States held their largest joint military drills amid escalating tensions on the Korean Peninsula, the Ulchi Freedom Shield (UFS), along with a joint maritime counter-special operations exercise, which had been on hiatus since 2018. Yoon said that "only exercises that mimic real life can firmly protect South Korea's national security and the people's lives."[48] The UFS, held from August 22 to September 1, unveiled some significant changes, including the integration of the government's civil defense drills and the resumption of field training. The US-South Korea-Japan joint trilateral maritime exercise involving the nuclear-powered aircraft carrier USS *Ronald Reagan* was subsequently held in the waters off the eastern coast of the Korean Peninsula from September 26 to 29, demonstrating America's "clear commitment to the alliance."[49]

Although the alliance highlighted these joint military drills as "defensive" in nature, the North predictably denounced them as "practice to invade North Korea."[50] The North's state news agency, the Korean Central News Agency (KCNA), threatened a military escalation and said: "the United States and South Korea seem to be hoping that Pyongyang will conduct a nuclear test as soon as possible."[51] Tensions surrounding the Korean Peninsula rose further as North Korea launched another barrage of short-range ballistic missiles (SRBMs) toward the East Sea on September 25, a day before the ROK-US-Japan combined maritime exercise. The missiles were believed to be KN-23's, similar to the Russian Iskander.[52]

Even more concerning than the record number of missile tests was the North's announcement on September 8 of legislation at the Supreme People's Assembly that effectively threatened preemptive nuclear strikes. Stressing the importance of the new law, Kim Jong-un expressed his determination not to give up nuclear weapons and accused the United States of aiming to topple the regime.[53] The Nuclear Forces Policy Act stated five conditions for preemptive use of nuclear weapons. The conditions included when nuclear or other weapons of mass destruction attacks have been carried out or are imminent; when a nuclear or non-nuclear attack by hostile forces against the leadership or the national nuclear force command body has been carried out or is imminent; when a military attack has been carried out or is imminent on the country's critical strategic targets; when there is an unavoidable necessity to prevent the expansion and prolongation of war and seize the initiative in war; and when a catastrophic crisis occurs that threatens the existence of the country and the safety of the people, leaving no choice but to respond with nuclear weapons.[54]

The Yoon administration and South Korean media outlets understandably expressed concern over the new doctrine. In the face of the North's "outright and offensive nuclear threat," a call for bipartisan efforts to respond decisively to the unstable security environment increased.[55] The government stressed the importance of prioritizing military readiness and strengthening America's extended deterrence.[56]

On October 4, North Korea test-fired an intermediate-range missile that overflew Japan for the first time in five years, possibly to showcase its military accomplishments ahead of the 77th anniversary of the founding of the Workers' Party of Korea. The missile flew around 4,500 kilometers to a maximum altitude of around 970 kilometers, the longest range yet by a North Korean missile that can potentially target the US forces in Japan and Guam. This was just one of seven rounds of ballistic missile launches, from September 25 to October 9. Kim Jong-un personally guided these drills of his tactical nuclear weapon units, simulating strikes on South Korean airports, ports, and military command facilities with ballistic missiles using various platforms including an underwater silo.[57]

The North Korean media stated that the seven rounds of military drills demonstrated the North's ability "to hit and wipe out the set objects at the intended places in the set time." Regarding dialogue and negotiations, the state media quoted Kim as saying that "we do not have anything to talk about nor do we feel the need to do so."[58] These seven rounds of ballistic missile launches made clear North Korea's intention to coerce South Korea and the United States. On October 12, the North followed with testing of "long-range strategic cruise missiles" that it said were deployed with units operating "tactical nukes."[59]

North Korea marked November with the most blasts ever, with at least 46 ballistic and other missiles launched, half of them on November 2 alone.[60] On November 18, the North fired off the Hwasong-17, the newest, most powerful, and largest road-mobile ICBM in the world. A month later, on December 16, the North successfully tested a powerful, "first of its kind" solid-fuel rocket engine.[61] This was an important capability for the North as it allows the North a much shorter window for the US and South Korea to potentially preempt a missile launch. Liquid fuel missiles are more vulnerable to monitoring and even preemptive strike because they take longer to launch. Kim Jong-un guided the test personally. In its five-year plan set forth by the Eighth Party Congress in January 2021, the North announced that developing a solid-fuel intercontinental ballistic missile (ICBM) that can be launched from both land and sea was one of its five priority tasks. It now seems to be on its way to achieving that capability.[62] Two days later, the North launched two medium-range ballistic missiles from the same site where the new rocket engine was tested.

In response to North Korea's unprecedented, year-long bluster and missile barrage, the Yoon administration began raising the possibility of redeploying US tactical nuclear weapons to South Korea and of abolishing the confidence-building measure and denuclearization agreements with North Korea. In response to a press question on October 12 about the possibility of redeploying US tactical nuclear weapons, Yoon said that his government was "listening diligently" to ideas from academia and the government in South Korea and the US and looking carefully at various possibilities.[63]

On the same day, Chung Jin-suk, a head of the ruling People Power Party's emergency standing committee, argued in a Facebook post that South Korea should abolish the 1992 Joint Declaration of the Denuclearization of the Korean Peninsula and the 2018 military agreement with North Korea if the North conducts a seventh nuclear test, while Kim Ki Hyun, a representative from Yoon's conservative party eyeing selection as the next party leader, argued on October 19 during a radio interview that South Korea should look into all measures including redeploying US tactical nuclear weapons, nuclear-sharing, or developing an independent nuclear force.[64]

Washington's reaction to South Korea's growing calls to redeploy tactical nuclear weapons was muted. US Ambassador to South Korea Philip Goldberg said during a public forum held in Seoul that "all this talk about tactical nuclear weapons, whether it comes from Putin or Kim Jong-un, is irresponsible and dangerous," while National Security Council spokesperson John Kirby, during a press briefing, declined to comment on whether the US would consider redeploying tactical nuclear weapons to South Korean soil. Meanwhile, State Department spokesperson Ned Price said only that Biden "affirmed the US extended deterrence commitment to the ROK… including nuclear, conventional and missile defense capabilities."[65]

In late December, South Korea's National Assembly approved a 4.4 percent hike in defense spending for 2023, bringing Seoul's total defense budget the following year to about $45 billion. The increase included funding for new preemptive strike capabilities. Meanwhile, Japan made even more dramatic changes in its own national security strategy in response to the increased threats from both North Korea and China. Under the plan unveiled by Japanese Prime Minister Kishida Fumio in mid-December 2022, Japan will increase its defense spending by more than 50 percent over the next five years, shattering its decades-old doctrine of limiting defense spending to one percent of GDP. Japan also plans to acquire long-range counterstrike capabilities it has long shunned, including several hundred US-made Tomahawk cruise missiles that could reach targets in both China and North Korea.

2022 wrapped up with more North Korean missile tests, including two more short-range ballistic missiles on December 23 and three more short-range missiles on December 31, bringing to nearly 100 the number of missiles tested that year—a record-breaking number. On December 26, the North also violated South Korean airspace by flying surveillance drones across the border for the first time in five years. Some of the drones entered the northern end of the 2.3-mile no-fly zone surrounding the presidential office in Seoul. That incursion prompted the South to scramble jets, fire warning shots, and fly its own drones into North Korean airspace. As 2023 began, there were indications that South Korea was preparing for a nuclear test.[66] Clearly, Moon's policies had failed. Could Yoon do any better?

Conclusion

The years 2020–2022 were a period when the North Korean nuclear and missile threat grew at an unprecedented rate while the United States and South Korea struggled to find an effective response. While Trump largely abandoned attempts at a diplomatic breakthrough after the failure of the 2019 Hanoi Summit and the onset of the COVID pandemic, Moon held on until the very end of his tenure to the illusion that denuclearization and genuine peace on the Korean Peninsula were in sight. His hopes were dashed, and indeed his eagerness for outreach may have encouraged Kim to think that he could expand his WMD arsenal and carry out provocations without repercussions.

The international environment became even more favorable for North Korea, and China and Russia became less likely than ever to cooperate with the United States and its allies in strengthening sanctions on North Korea, in the aftermath of the Russian invasion of Ukraine. Previously, Beijing and Moscow were at least at times willing to join forces with the United States to penalize North Korea following provocations (e.g., in the fall of 2017), even as they helped North Korea evade sanctions. Since the start of the Ukraine war, however, both Xi Jinping and Vladimir Putin refused to not only enforce existing sanctions but also vetoed any further action against North Korea at the UN Security Council. Even additional nuclear tests or nuclear and missile developments by North Korea would be unlikely to prompt a serious reaction from China and Russia. This represented a critical juncture in regional dynamics—with Beijing and Moscow now viewing Pyongyang's provocations more as a means to gain advantages over Washington than as a concerning threat to regional stability.

Meanwhile, the Ukraine war raised the specter of North Korean aggression to a new level; it may have prompted the Kim regime to consider a new "first-use" nuclear doctrine, in addition to the development and operational deployment of tactical nuclear weapons, by taking a page straight out of Vladmir Putin's playbook. Kim likely took note of Putin's nuclear saber rattling to deter NATO and the United States from direct involvement in the war and imagined that the United States could be forced to back off with nuclear threats.

Yoon, upon taking office, took a tougher stance, but it did not pay dividends, either. Biden, for his part, was preoccupied with the Russian invasion of Ukraine and China's growing intransigence and was aware that it was nearly impossible to make any progress with North Korea. So his administration failed to come up with an effective North Korea policy. That left Biden and Yoon discussing, with Kishida, how to bolster "extended deterrence" of North Korea to prevent Kim from using his expanding WMD arsenal. But, while important, such moves could not stop Kim from continuing to expand his nuclear and missile stockpiles at an alarming rate.

By the end of 2022, North Korea had become one of only three countries—along with China and Russia—capable of hitting the US mainland with nuclear-tipped ICBMs. It was also rapidly working to develop the ability to launch multiple reentry vehicles (MIRV) that could frustrate US missile defenses. The Hwasong-17 is designed to carry multiple warheads and could thus theoretically strike Manhattan and Washington at the same time. The risk that a miscalculation by Pyongyang could lead to a conflict was growing, particularly given its lack of communication with Washington and Seoul.

Notes

1 "Report on 5th Plenary Meeting of the 7th C.C., Workers Party of Korea," *KCNA*, January 1, 2020, https://kcnawatch.org/newstream/1577829999-473709661/report-on-5th-plenary-meeting-of-7th-c-c-wpk/.
2 Simon Denyer, "Two Years after Trump Summit, Kim Vows to Boost North Korea's Nuclear Deterrent," *The Washington Post*, May 24, 2020, https://www.washingtonpost.com/world/asia_pacific/two-years-after-singapore-kim-vows-to-boost-north-koreas-nuclear-deterrent/2020/05/24/729778fc-9da1-11ea-be06-af5514ee0385_story.html.
3 Simon Denyer, "North Korean Warns United States of an Unwelcome 'Christmas Gift,'" *The Washington Post*, December 3, 2019, https://www.washingtonpost.com/world/north-korea-warns-united-states-of-an-unwelcome-christmas-gift/2019/12/03/ad406634-1599-11ea-80d6-d0ca7007273f_story.html.
4 2020 New Year's Address by President Moon Jae-in, January 7, 2020, https://overseas.mofa.go.kr/hk-en/brd/m_1494/view.do?seq=756682&srchFr=&srchTo=&srchWord=&srchTp=&multi_itm_seq=0&itm_seq_1=0&itm_seq_2=0&company_cd=&company_nm=.
5 Hyung-jin Kim, "SKorea's Moon Could Seek Exemption of UN sanctions on NKorea," Associated Press, January 14, 2020, https://apnews.com/article/asia-pacific-united-nations-north-korea-international-news-moon-jae-in-a38da362d176402226844fec7c13d5cb.
6 Sang-mi Cha, "South Korea Says Pushing Ahead with North Korea Engagement Despite Stalled Talks," *Reuters*, January 15, 2020, https://www.reuters.com/article/us-northkorea-usa-southkorea-idUSKBN1ZE0QF. Also see "Kang Kyung-wha Stresses Need to Restore Inter-Korean Dialogue," *Hankyoreh*, January 16, 2020, https://english.hani.co.kr/arti/english_edition/e_northkorea/924728.html.
7 Michael Elleman, "North Korea's Recent KN-25 Launches," *38 North*, March 6, 2020, https://www.38north.org/2020/03/melleman030620/.
8 Joseph Dempsey, "Assessment of the March 9 KN-25 Test Launch," *38 North*, March 20, 2020, https://www.38north.org/2020/03/jdempsey031020/.
9 Ankit Panda, "The Return of the KN-24: Unpacking North Korea's March 21 Missile Test," *NK Pro*, March 22, 2020, https://www.nknews.org/pro/the-return-of-the-kn-24-unpacking-north-koreas-march-21-missile-test/.
10 Ankit Panda, "North Korea Conducts 4th Missile Test in March 2020," *The Diplomat*, March 30, 2020, https://thediplomat.com/2020/03/north-korea-conducts-4th-missile-test-in-march-2020/.

11 Hyung-Jin Kim, "North Korea Fires Barrage of Missiles in Weapons Test," Associated Press, April 14, 2020, https://www.defensenews.com/global/asia-pacific/2020/04/14/north-korea-fires-barrage-of-missiles-in-weapons-test/.
12 Cited in Sean Lee, "Moon Jae-in Holds on to His Dream of North Korea Diplomacy: South Korea's President is Poised for One More Push to Improve Inter-Korean Relations," *The Diplomat*, June 2, 2020, https://thediplomat.com/2020/06/moon-jae-in-holds-on-to-his-dream-of-north-korea-diplomacy/.
13 Ibid.
14 Ibid.
15 Timothy W. Martin, "Kim Jong Un's Sister Threatens South Korea Over Leaflets," *The Wall Street Journal*, June 4, 2020, https://www.wsj.com/articles/kim-jong-uns-sister-threatens-south-korea-over-leaflets-11591267505.
16 "Kim Yo Jong Rebukes South Korean Authorities for Conniving at Anti-DPRK Hostile Act of 'Defectors from North'," *Rodong Sinmun*, April 6, 2020, https://kcnawatch.org/newstream/1591257669-272137200/kim-yo-jong-rebukes-s-korean-authorities-for-conniving-at-anti-dprk-hostile-act-of-defectors-from-north/.
17 "South Korean Balloons: Plans to Stop People Sending Cross-Border Messages," *BBC News*, June 4, 2020, https://www.bbc.com/news/world-asia-52917029.
18 "KCNA Reports on Cutting off All North-South Communication Lines," *KCNA*, June 8, 2020, https://kcnawatch.org/newstream/1591650988-850028113/kcna-report-on-cutting-off-all-north-south-communication-lines/.
19 "N. Korea Blows Up Joint Liaison Office in Kaesong," *Yonhap News Agency*, June 16, 2020, https://en.yna.co.kr/view/AEN20200616008253325?section=nk/nk.
20 "Ominous Prelude to Total Catastrophe of North-South Relations," *KCNA*, June 17, 2020, https://kcnawatch.org/newstream/1592344056-859499527/ominous-prelude-to-total-catastrophe-of-north-south-relations/.
21 "Our Army Will Provide Sure Military Guarantee for All External and Internal Measures of Party and Government: Spokesman for KPA General Staff," *KCNA*, June 17, 2020, https://kcnawatch.org/newstream/1592344056-981767238/our-army-will-provide-sure-military-guarantee-for-all-external-and-internal-measures-of-party-and-government-spokesman-for-kpa-general-staff/. Also see Minjoo Kim, "North Korea Blows Up Joint Liaison Office, Dramatically Raising Tensions with the South," *The Washington Post*, June 16, 2020, https://www.washingtonpost.com/world/asia_pacific/north-korea-liaison-office-kaesong-explosion-demolish-dmz/2020/06/16/7c7a2dc0-af9d-11ea-98b5-279a6479a1e4_story.html.
22 John Power, "Moon Jae-in's Vision of Peace with North Korea Goes Up in Smoke," *South China Morning Post*, June 20, 2020, https://www.scmp.com/week-asia/politics/article/3089859/moon-jae-ins-vision-peace-north-korea-goes-smoke?module=perpetual_scroll_0&pgtype=article&campaign=3089859.
23 Hyonhee Shin and Josh Smith, "North Korea Destroys Inter-Korean Liaison Office in 'Terrific Explosion'," Reuters, June 16, 2020, https://www.reuters.com/article/north-korea-southkorea-idINKBN23N0EL.
24 Seo Ji-eun, "Koreas State Audit Agency Requests Investigation of 20 Officials in Fisheries Official Case," *JoongAng Daily*, October 16, 2022, https://koreajoongangdaily.joins.com/2022/10/16/national/politics/Korea-fisheries-murder/20221016185742341.html.
25 "Supreme Leader Kim Jong Un Delivers Speech at Military Parade," *KCNA*, October 10, 2020, https://kcnawatch.app/newstream/1602334499-856510497/supreme-leader-kim-jong-un-delivers-speech-at-military-parade/.
26 "South Korea Bans Flying of Leaflets Toward N. Korea by Balloon," *Courthouse News Service, Associated Press*, December 14, 2020.
27 2021 New Year's Address by President Moon Jae-in, January 13, 2021, https://usa.mofa.go.kr/us-en/brd/m_4497/view.do?seq=761783.

28 Kelly Katsulis, "Party Congress over: Kim Yo Jong Insults Seoul and Talks Military Parade Rumors," *NK News*, January 12, 2021, https://www.nknews.org/2021/01/party-congress-over-kim-yo-jong-insults-seoul-and-talks-military-parade-rumors/?t=1610501004490. Also see Jeong-ho Lee, "Kim Jong Un Sister Slams 'Weird Group' in South Korea for Spying," *Bloomberg*, January 13, 2021, https://www.bloomberg.com/news/articles/2021-01-12/kim-jong-un-s-sister-slams-south-korea-for-spying-on-pyongyang#xj4y7vzkg.
29 Choe Sang-hun, "Kim Jong-un Uses Party Congress to Double Down on Nuclear Program," *The New York Times*, January 13, 2021, https://www.nytimes.com/2021/01/13/world/asia/north-korea-kim-jong-un-nuclear.html.
30 "N. Korea Fires 2 Short-Range Ballistic Missiles into East Sea: JCS," Yonhap News Agency, March 25, 2021, https://en.yna.co.kr/view/AEN20210325000656325?section=nk/nk.
31 "After Trump 'Failed,' South Korean Leader Hopes Biden Can Salvage Nuclear Deal," *The New York Times*, April 21, 2021, https://www.nytimes.com/2021/04/21/world/asia/biden-north-korea-nuclear-deal-president-moon.html.
32 "Biden Dismisses Trump, Obama Approaches in Charting New North Korea Policy," *ABC News*, April 30, 2021, https://abcnews.go.com/Politics/biden-dismisses-trump-obama-approaches-charting-north-korea/story?id=77425459.
33 "U.S.-ROK Leaders' Joint Statement," *The White House*, May 21, 2021, https://www.whitehouse.gov/briefing-room/statements-releases/2021/05/21/u-s-rok-leaders-joint-statement/.
34 Timothy W. Martin and Dasl Yoon, "North Korea Reopens Communications Hotline with South Korea, Breaking a Year of Silence," *The Wall Street Journal*, July 27, 2021, https://www.wsj.com/articles/north-korea-reopens-communications-hotline-with-south-korea-breaking-a-year-of-silence-11627359601.
35 "Kim Jong-un Says North Korea's Economic Plan Failed," *BBC*, January 6, 2021, https://www.bbc.com/news/world-asia-55563598.
36 "N. Korea's 'Hypersonic Missile' Appears to be at Early Stage of Development: JCS," Yonhap News Agency, September 29, 2021, https://en.yna.co.kr/view/AEN20210929005552325?section=nk/nk. Also see "N. Korea Test-Fires New Anti-Aircraft Missile: State Media," Yonhap News Agency, October 1, 2021, https://en.yna.co.kr/view/AEN20211001000553325?section=nk/nk.
37 "Kim Jong-un Says North Korea's Economic Plan Failed," *BBC*, January 6, 2021, https://www.bbc.com/news/world-asia-55563598.
38 Choe Sang-Hun, "Tracking North Korea's Missile Launches," *The New York Times*, January 2, 2023, https://www.nytimes.com/article/north-korea-missile-launches.html.
39 "Yoon Says Preemptive Strike is Only Answer to N. Korea's Hypersonic Missiles," *Hankyoreh*, January 12, 2022, https://english.hani.co.kr/arti/english_edition/e_national/1027059.html.
40 "Defense Ministry Changes Terminology for 'Three-Axis System' of Military Response," *Hankyoreh*, January 13, 2019, https://english.hani.co.kr/arti/english_edition/e_national/878208.html.
41 Yoon Suk-yeol, *Facebook Post*, January 16, 2022, https://www.facebook.com/sukyeol.yoon/posts/223370563330218.
42 Choe Sang-Hun, "With U.S. Focus on Ukraine, North Korea Launches a Powerful New ICBM," *The New York Times*, March 24, 2022, https://www.nytimes.com/2022/03/24/world/asia/north-korea-missile-icbm.html.
43 Choe Sang-Hun, "North Korea Launches 2 Short Range Missiles," *The New York Times*, April 16, 2022, https://www.nytimes.com/2022/04/16/world/asia/north-korea-missile-launch.html.

44 Choe Sang-Hun, "North Korea Launches a Volley of Short-Range Missiles," *The New York Times*, June 5, 2022, https://www.nytimes.com/2022/06/05/world/asia/north-korea-missile.html.
45 Yoon Suk-Yeol, "Address by President Yoon Suk Yeol on Korea's 77th Liberation Day," Speeches, Office of the President, Republic of Korea, August 15, 2022, https://eng.president.go.kr/speeches/k4bSEz3J
46 Ibid.
47 Choe Sang-Hun, "North Korea Launches Two Missiles in First Test Since June," *The New York Times*, August 17, 2022, https://www.nytimes.com/2022/08/17/world/asia/north-korea-missile-launch.html.
48 "US, ROK Begin Largest Joint Drills in Years After North Korea Brandishes Nukes," *NK News*, August 22, 2022. https://www.nknews.org/2022/08/us-rok-begin-largest-joint-drills-in-years-after-north-korea-brandishes-nukes/?t=1672104646414.
49 "USS Ronald Reagan in S. Korea for Joint Drills Against N. Korean Threats," Yonhap News Agency, September 23, 2022, https://en.yna.co.kr/view/AEN20220923000453325.
50 "한미연합연습 '을지자유의 방패' 1일 마무리," *Hankyoreh*, September 1, 2022, https://www.hani.co.kr/arti/politics/defense/1057092.html.
51 "'반격' 한·미 군사훈련 2부 시작에…북 선전·공식매체 '방어 아닌 침략' 맹비난," *Kyunghyang Shinmun*, August 29, 2022, https://www.khan.co.kr/politics/north-korea/article/202208291453001.
52 "北, 美항모 반발 이스칸데르 미사일 쏴…내일부터 연합훈련," Yonhap News Agency, September 25, 2022, https://www.yna.co.kr/view/AKR20220925015551504.
53 "김정은 '미국이 노리는 건 정권 붕괴…절대 핵 포기 못해'," Yonhap News Agency, September 9, 2022, https://www.yna.co.kr/view/AKR20220909015452504.
54 "김정은이 법으로 밝힌 '핵 사용 5대 조건'은," *Hankyoreh*, September 9, 2022. https://www.hani.co.kr/arti/politics/defense/1058180.html.
55 "'선제적 핵공격' 법에 못박은 북한의 위험한 도박," *Joongang Ilbo*, September 13, 2022, https://www.joongang.co.kr/article/25101137#home.
56 "北 핵무력 법제화, 국제사회 고립만 심화시킬 것," *Segye Ilbo*, September 12, 2022, https://www.segye.com/newsView/20220912517615.
57 Choe Sang-Hun, "North Korea Says It is Building Underwater Nuclear Weapons Silos," *The New York Times*, October 10, 2022, https://www.nytimes.com/2022/10/10/world/asia/north-korea-underwater-nuclear-missiles.html.
58 "KCNA – Respected Comrade Kim Jong Un Guides Military Drills of KPA Units for Operation of Tactical Nukes," *NK News KCNA Watch*, October 10, 2022, https://kcnawatch.app/newstream/1665358635-402491168/respected-comrade-kim-jong-un-guides-military-drills-of-kpa-units-for-operation-of-tactical-nukes/.
59 Choe Sang-Hun, "Tracking North Korea's Missile Launches," *The New York Times*, January 2, 2023, https://www.nytimes.com/article/north-korea-missile-launches.html.
60 Choe Sang-Hun, "North Korea Launches 23 Missiles, Triggering Air-Raid Alarm in South," *The New York Times*, November 1, 2022, https://www.nytimes.com/2022/11/01/world/asia/north-korea-missile-launch.html.
61 "경애하는 김정은 동지의 지도밑에 국방과학원 전략적의의를 가지는 중대시험 진행," *Rodong Sinmun*, December 16, 2022, https://kcnawatch.app/newstream/1671141020-238965489/%EA%B2%BD%EC%95%A0%ED%95%98%EB%8A%94-%EA%B9%80%EC%A0%95%EC%9D%80-%EB%8F%99%EC%A7%80%EC%9D%98-%EC%A7%80%EB%8F%84%EB%B0%91%EC%97%90-%EA%B5%AD%EB%B0%A9%EA%B3%BC%ED%95%99%EC%9B%90-%EC%A0%84%EB%9E%B5/.
62 Choe Sang-Hun, "North Korea Party Congress Opens With Kim Jong-un Admitting Failures," *The New York Times*, January 5, 2021, https://www.nytimes.com/2021/01/05/world/asia/north-korea-kim-jong-un-party-congress.html?searchResultPosition=4.

63 "Yoon Suk-yeol Admits to Looking at New Deterrence Options," *Korea Joongang Daily*, October 13, 2022, https://koreajoongangdaily.joins.com/2022/10/13/national/politics/Korea-tactical-nuclear-weapons-extended-deterrence/20221013181545418.html.
64 "김기현 '국회의원도 전쟁터 나가야…육십 넘었지만 총 들고 나올 것'," *KBS News*, October 19, 2022, https://news.kbs.co.kr/news/view.do?ncd=5581824.
65 "Talk of Tactical Nuke Redeployment 'Irresponsible': US Ambassador," *Korea Herald*, October 18, 2022, https://www.koreaherald.com/view.php?ud=20221018000650; "(LEAD) U.S. Remains Open to Dialogue with N. Korea Despite Kim Remarks: NSC Spokesperson," Yonhap News Agency, October 12, 2022, https://en.yna.co.kr/view/AEN20221012000251325.
66 Sue Mi Terry, "The New North Korean Threat," *Foreign Affairs*, January 13, 2023. https://www.foreignaffairs.com/north-korea/new-north-korean-threat.

8

EDGING TOWARD BIPOLARITY

South Korea's Regional
Reorientation, 2020–2022

Gilbert Rozman

The Moon to Yoon transition drew South Korea closer to the United States and even to Japan, while seeing a marked falloff in relations with Russia and looming difficulties with China. If the switch from progressive to conservative, as in 2008, accounted for some of the change, no less important were global and regional developments. The Ukraine war had a polarizing effect, but so too did the "extreme competition" between China and the United States. Donald Trump's "trade war" gave way to Joe Biden's "high tech decoupling," at the same time as Kim Jong-un's missile provocations ended the prospects for diplomacy critical to Seoul's outreach to Beijing. If Moon Jae-in was adamant about keeping the door open to Pyongyang and to regional diplomacy, Yoon Suk-yeol increasingly agreed to embrace bipolarity to the anger of China. Yoon went well beyond previous ROK presidents on US, Japanese, Indo-Pacific, and NATO relations.

Repeatedly, Seoul showed itself capable of bending toward its ally, the United States, without closing its options for regional diplomacy with room for flexibility. At no time had this proven to be more difficult than in 2020 to 2022. Given the obsession with North Korean diplomacy of the Moon Jae-in administration, accompanied by its perceived need to keep China and Russia in a cooperative mood, limiting the tilt to the US sought by Donald Trump in 2020 and again by Joe Biden in 2021 was not far out of line with precedent. Waiting out events proved harder in 2022, however, when Biden was rallying allies to make Russia a pariah and to decouple from China in dual-use tech, notably involving advanced semiconductors. Under a conservative leader the tilt toward Washington was greater from May 2022, crossing lines that China had repeatedly drawn. If Seoul's response feel short of Tokyo's tight embrace of Biden's agenda, and some Koreans sought to

DOI: 10.4324/9781003394792-9

draw the line in order to keep the economic cost of defying China more manageable, there was no sign that Yoon stood in the way of the ongoing polarization.

Moon's May 2021 summit with Biden was huge, paving the way for the big shift in 2022 under Yoon. It was transitional in reorienting Seoul toward US-led regionalism. Yoon went further and added a critical values component, refocusing from a "peace regime" prioritizing the Korean Peninsula toward a shared vision with the United States in facing regional and global dangers. The starting point was support for a rules-based order, facing North Korea as an unmitigated threat with values not obscured. With semiconductors at the forefront in the new high-tech competition, South Korea suddenly drew attention as a major player, not a "shrimp among whales." It was becoming easier for Seoul to push back against China's zero-sum arguments.

Under Park Geun-hye and Moon, Seoul was reluctant to join the emerging US regional agenda. In 2022 Yoon leaped ahead on regional cooperation but left some room for wavering. Alliance relations became more wide-ranging in Asia and beyond and more multi-dimensional including economic security. In May, Yoon agreed with Biden to a values-based and regionally oriented alliance more comprehensive than Moon's understanding with Biden a year earlier. At a three-way summit in November with the US and Japan, Yoon's support for trilateralism exceeded anything seen from Seoul earlier. The overall trend in 2022 defied China's repeated warnings. Beijing had warned Seoul against joining US initiatives, whether the THAAD missile defense system, the "Free and Open Indo-Pacific" strategy, freedom of navigation exercises, support for Taiwan, technological decoupling, criticism of China's human rights behavior, or trilateral defense moves with Japan. Yoon was more daring in defying Beijing, but he still exhibited some caution as bilateral relations could suffer serious setbacks. The fact that China sided with Russia on the essentials of the Ukraine war and was viewed as threatening Taiwan in a more urgent manner cast a chill on Sino-ROK relations. So too did China's "zero-COVID" lockdowns and new market-suppressing controls. Despite Chinese appeals to join in a neighborhood push against US protectionism, Yoon generally accepted the economic security agenda of the US, as civil-military dual-use items drew closer scrutiny. Washington sought a collective approach to industries of the future—research designs, export controls, restricted investments that could lead to technology leakage, and supply chains to reduce economic vulnerability. This holistic US approach—called invest, align, compete—put US as well as Chinese pressure on South Korea.

China's deteriorating image in 2022 made Seoul's transition easier. China's lockdowns, loss of economic dynamism, drift toward greater authoritarianism and centralization, and isolation on the side of Russia all suggested that it had already peaked. Reducing dependency on it seemed to be a good idea. Yet fear of both economic costs and retaliation led to caution. Few in Seoul seemed prepared for the full extent of de-risking Washington had in mind in its Indo-Pacific Economic Framework and security reassessments, dealing with Beijing as well as Pyongyang.

The ROK habit of focusing on the US as the driving force, giving China and Russia the benefit of the doubt as their help was sought with North Korea and for ROK-driven regional plans, had skewed discussions of the downward spiral in regional stability. Rather than point to how China caused the polarization underway, many in Seoul had blamed Washington for complicating their economic prospects. China sought to seize on this thinking by proposing more regional trade integration to counteract protectionism and vociferously arguing that the US is treating its ally as a vassal. Yet, in 2022 such appeals mixed with implicit threats proved less effective than in earlier years. Driving the shift were three forces: leadership change, geopolitical factors, and a refocus on economic security—Yoon's ascent, Sino-US and Russo-US tensions, and a US technology agenda.

The period 2020–2022 saw an extraordinary number of twists and turns centered on ROK-US relations but extending across the region. 2020 spelled the end of the Trump-Moon consensus on North Korea as Sino-US relations plummeted, putting Moon's regional agenda in jeopardy. 2021 saw a disconnect between Biden's quest for a regional framework and Moon's desperate appeals to join in a new offer to North Korea. Relations were in a rut over regional differences. Then, in 2022, the combination of Biden and Yoon found greater accord, but the challenges of transformation they faced dwarfed earlier ones. Joint affirmation of the alliance kept getting stronger. In 2020, the pandemic heightened Sino-US tensions and drew new attention to supply chain vulnerability, as Trump, Moon, and Xi eyed each other from a distance. In 2021, Biden reconfigured ties to both Moon and Xi, affecting the triangle through multilateralism and new stress on regional economics and values. Finally, in 2022, the Yoon election, Ukraine war, and focus on economic sanctions and technological decoupling proved even more disruptive. In the course of three contrasting years, foreign policy had shifted more than at any time in decades.

The Year 2020

From 2017 through 2019 Moon Jae-in was preoccupied with relations with North Korea, and he tried to keep a low profile as regional tensions deepened over other bilateral challenges. When tensions over the South China Sea, East China Sea, and Taiwan accelerated, Moon stayed on the sidelines. Xi Jinping kept up pressure on Moon, demanding that he avoid entanglement in Sino-US controversies after Moon had conceded in late 2017 on three key points of Xi's concern. In the cases of Russia and Japan, Moon felt relatively little pressure from Trump to follow the US line, tangling more directly with Abe and keeping the door open to Putin. Intent on keeping his opening with Kim Jong-un alive, Moon benefitted from Trump cutting him some slack. Unlike the Park Geun-hye period when regional diplomacy was a high priority, Moon had decidedly narrowed his sights.

In the year 2020, the widening gap between Washington and Beijing put greater pressure on Seoul. Not only had the trade war intensified, the pandemic exacerbated signs of an ideological struggle. For at least four reasons, Moon Jae-in found it harder to stay aloof. First, the Korean public's negative attitudes and business dissatisfaction toward China strongly favored leaning closer to the US. Second, Trump's cavalier threats toward South Korea, e.g., if it did not raise host-nation support drastically, left a weakened leader struggling to do more to satisfy an ally. Third, the tightening Japanese embrace of the United States left Moon wary of allowing this triangle to become even further unbalanced. Finally, Moon was at an impasse with North Korea and considered his last hope to be Trump's support for an "end of war" declaration. Although the pandemic brought in-person diplomacy to a halt, Seoul was tilting rather more to the US.

Trump, Abe, and Xi each had soured on Moon in their own way—leaving him little prospect of overcoming a lame duck image in foreign affairs in 2020. Yet, he ploughed ahead, holding three optimistic assumptions: Kim Jong-un was waiting for an initiative from Washington and Seoul to resume diplomacy; Trump could be persuaded to okay an "end-of-war" declaration that would jumpstart diplomacy; and Xi Jinping was agreeable to visit Seoul in 2020 to breathe new life into bilateral relations and to support diplomacy with Kim Jong-un. The fact that expectations were much lower in foreign capitals and within the South Korean public left Moon's quixotic pursuits with no prospect of success, even before the numbing effect of the pandemic froze diplomacy.

Toward the end of 2020, critical forces of transformation were advancing against desperate attempts to salvage Moon's legacy. Three forces defied Moon's efforts: the unbridgeable gap between the US and North Korea; the accelerating divide between China and the US; and the intensifying regional coordination between the US and Japan, isolating Moon. As these forces gained momentum, aspirations alive in 2019, when he was thwarted, grew further out of reach.

Against the backdrop of conservatives and progressives offering diametrically different advice on what to do about rising North Korean-US tensions, relations with other countries took a back seat. Having only at the end of 2019 retracted his threat to withdraw from GSOMIA sharing of intelligence with Japan, Moon hesitated to take new steps. As for China and Russia, they had at the end of 2019 called on the Security Council to ease restrictions on North Korean workers abroad, on exports of seafood and textiles, and on inter-Korean projects. If progressives were inclined to go along, Moon did not dare to break from US-led maximum pressure so blatantly.

A now-delayed Xi visit to Seoul had been desperately sought to boost cooperation on North Korean policy.

Foreign policy was on hold. The pandemic effect and the wait for US elections left policy in limbo. Ties to Japan remained troubled, although Abe's announcement at the end of August that he would step down was seen as hopeful. Divergence in regional strategy as well as policy toward North Korea cast a dark shadow over ROK-US relations, compounding the unresolved negotiations over host-nation support. This was not a time for complacency given expectations that challenges would, before long, worsen due to deeper Sino-US, North Korean-US, and ROK-Japanese tensions.

Regional Framework

Deepening Sino-US rivalry posed the central foreign policy dilemma for Moon Jae-in. Pressure was mounting to join in exclusive economic arrangements, to make clear Seoul's position on the PRC national security law for Hong Kong, to meet with the G7 to address concerns over China, and to coordinate as a US ally to counter the military build-up of China. As conservatives debated how to double down on the alliance despite Trump's one-sided demands, the Moon supporters insisted on balancing US and Chinese ties, resisting US plans for an economic bloc, or joining in condemning repression in Hong Kong. After Moon accepted Trump's invitation to an expanded G7 with China as the focus, China's foreign ministry spokesperson issued a sharp warning. Moon strove to remain ambiguous on supply chain decoupling, a US economic bloc, and even regional security issues. On the national security law Seoul did not join 27 countries that raised concerns that it would erode the human rights of Hong Kong citizens. On Xinjiang's Uyghur human rights abuses, the National Assembly only urged the international community to establish a cooperative regional order and seriously consider Korea's future role. Avoiding choosing sides prevailed over standing on clear principles. Yet Moon's December 2019 visit to China ended with a skirmish after the PRC foreign minister quoted him as saying to Xi that "Hong Kong affairs and issues concerning Xinjiang are China's internal affairs."[1] Seoul quickly denied that Moon had made such a pro-China comment.

On September 25, 2020, Foreign Minister Kang Kyung-wha said it is "not a good idea" to join the US-led Quad aimed at keeping China in check. "We don't think anything that automatically shuts out, and is exclusive of the interests of others, is a good idea," Kang said in response to a question asking if South Korea is open to join the Quad-Plus. This was the first time a high-ranking official publicly expressed a negative view on the Quad. In contrast, *Chosun Ilbo* bemoaned that the Quad foreign ministers' meeting held in Tokyo without South Korea on October 7 epitomizes "Korea passing."[2]

On foreign policy, conservatives pressed their criticism of Moon and welcomed Biden's election as an opportunity to overcome bilateral tensions and also repair the trilateral South Korea-US-Japan security framework. Capitalizing on public favor for the US over China (nearly 5:1), they urged the Moon administration to scrap its "pro-China" foreign policy and come up with a value-based foreign policy supportive of Biden's emerging regional agenda, but Moon was loathe to commit himself.

China

The pandemic brought no relief to tensions with China. Travel restrictions on foreigners aroused early charges and countercharges with Beijing. Supply chain disruptions focused attention on economic dependence on China. When on February 20 Moon and Xi spoke by phone, they agreed on a joint response to COVID-19, and Seoul soon did not impose a total ban on Chinese entrants, as a visit from Xi still appeared on the horizon. Dong Xiangrong applauds the inter-government cooperation over the pandemic, such as opening a "fast track" for businessmen, but she finds an "obvious cognitive mismatch in public opinion." Unlike Chinese praise for South Korea's handling of it, the South Korean "assessment of China's response to the pandemic is seen in China as unreasonably negative." She links this to "media ideologues accusing China of human rights violations, conspiracy, and discrimination against South Koreans inside China. In addition to blaming China for responsibility linked to the pandemic, they convey a broader critique, which is influencing the Korean public." Citing an October 6, 2020, Pew poll, she stresses that "79 percent of respondents in South Korea gave a negative assessment of China's response to the pandemic… From the spring of 2019 to the summer of 2020, South Koreans who have an unfavorable view of China rose by 12 percent to 75 percent." Separately, Dong wrote that netizens were aroused to turn on each other, e.g., over rival claims that their country was the real origin of pickled vegetables (paocai or kimchi) and the BTS singing group's speech on accepting a prize, recognizing the suffering of Koreans and Americans on the 70th anniversary of the Korean War but not of Chinese who lost their lives in the war. Dong links these clashes in 2020 to years of cultural tensions between Chinese and South Koreans coupled with the aftereffects of the THAAD clash in 2016–17, leading to a drop in the sale of Korean cars in China, and to new strains in the geo-economic environment facing the two sides. After South Korean opinion had shifted to view China as anti-reunification and a military threat, she called these nations just "superficial friends."[3]

Woo Jong Yeop puts the emphasis on geopolitics linked to global supply chains. The impact came from the growing pressure from the United States and China, as they responded to the pandemic. He writes, "Never before has Seoul faced a dilemma similar to the push and pull awaiting between Washington and Beijing, while the Pyongyang factor adds more difficulty."[4]

Yang Jiechi visited Busan on August 21 to meet with Moon's new national security adviser Suh Hoon and explained China's position regarding current US-China relations. Reportedly, he asked Seoul to remain at least neutral in the intensifying rivalry while championing multilateralism and free trade.[5] Yet, China's pressure was backfiring, as it continued earlier restrictions, e.g., over the "Korean Wave" and THAAD, while calling for closer economic integration, seen warily in Seoul.

Seoul is targeted by China differently than Tokyo for at least four reasons: (1) it is considered a more integral part of the Sinocentric order, given historical ties and geography; (2) vulnerability to North Korea gives China more leverage; (3) its economic dependency is greater; and (4) it is not viewed as a power of the same order as Japan or with the same high degree of internal political cohesion as Japan.[6] In the opinion of Eun A Jo, Moon had responded with "double allegiance," but "as

Seoul continues to pursue North Korea, satisfying both sides of the increasingly belligerent conflict will become a tough—possibly untenable—balancing act." She emphasizes that "China's cooperation on North Korea will be tied to South Korea's deference, even at the expense of the United States," and that "neither Biden's win in the upcoming presidential election nor Xi's attempts to capitalize on the narrowing scope of the US-South Korea alliance is propitious for Moon's strategy of double allegiance."[7] Indeed, Moon's approach was reaching a dead end.

Japan

The pandemic was a missed opportunity for ROK-Japan cooperation, argues Scott Snyder. Moon proposed a regional response in the fall of 2020, but did not mention Japan. Thus, "the pandemic response appears to have become a new venue for Japan-South Korea political competition."[8]

Why did Moon take little interest in Japan? According to Park Cheol-hee, for progressives, Japan's "role is negligible or minimal at least in the process of establishing a peace regime on the Korean Peninsula ... progressives remain quite generous regarding Chinese moves while they remain extremely critical toward Japan's motives ... They blamed the United States for entangling South Korea in a regional security front."[9] Park finds that progressives view Japan but not China through the prism of history, but he discerns a growing backlash among conservatives and the younger generation against demonizing Japan and for resisting further China's pressure.

Claiming that the Korean government is helpless to intervene in court proceedings, Seoul warned Tokyo that if it did not accept the court ruling that Japanese companies must compensate forced labor victims, their assets would be liquidated. In return, Japan's government refused to conduct business as usual until Seoul found a different solution. This issue halted all normal diplomacy.

On September 24, Moon and Suga held an official phone call—the first conversation between the leaders of the two countries since the trilateral summit in late December 2019. Moon proposed that the two countries work together to find an "optimum" solution to the wartime forced labor issue, called for Japan to withdraw its "unjust" export restrictions, and stressed the need for Tokyo to "respond actively" to Seoul's efforts to host the Korea-Japan-China trilateral summit this year. In response, Japan called on Seoul to find a solution for the forced labor issue that does not liquidate the seized assets of Japanese firms, adding that Suga would not attend a trilateral summit in Seoul unless South Korea put a stop to the liquidation of Japanese corporate assets in that country.

The Year 2021

With North Korea and China on lockdown and Japanese leadership in flux, South Korean eyes were focused on the new US president Joe Biden. Unlike Trump's transactional, bilateral approach and attraction to diplomacy with Kim Jong-un,

Biden took a regional, Indo-Pacific strategic prism. The two leaders struggled to find common ground: Moon persisting in his North Korean obsession, and Biden raising multilateral initiatives in managing China. Isolated, Moon gave ground gradually.

As the Biden administration was taking shape, Moon spoke by phone on January 26 with Xi and expressed hope that Xi would visit South Korea as soon as the COVID-19 situation stabilizes and looked forward to the constructive role of China in resolving the North Korean problem through dialogue. In response, Xi said that he supports inter-Korean and US-North Korean dialogue and emphasized the important role of South Korea in a political resolution of the North Korea issue.[10]

In the wake of Biden's inauguration, diplomatic activities in March and April, brought into sharp focus the dilemma of a middle power wedged between the US and China, unambiguously heading toward multifaceted confrontation, as illustrated by their March, face-to-face high-level talks in Alaska. South Korea's balancing act will be constrained to an unprecedented extent, many warned.

Amid the March 18 2+2 meeting between Seoul and Washington, conservatives appealed to the government to strengthen ties with the US while guarding against both North Korean and Chinese aggression, but progressives were wary that the US aimed to send China a warning. The meeting failed to adopt a statement that listed North Korea human rights issues and "denuclearization of North Korea," due to South Korea's demand to replace it with "denuclearization of the Korean Peninsula." A day later, in response to the acrimonious Sino-US talks in Anchorage, commentators in South Korea expressed concern about a "new Cold War," and its negative impact on solving the North Korean issue, while making it hard to maintain strategic ambiguity between the two powers. As calls to support the US grew, progressives demurred, blaming it for trying to check China.

After on February 24 signing an executive order on supply chains, Biden on April 12, at a virtual CEO summit on semiconductor and supply chain resilience, said, "the Chinese Communist Party aggressively plans to reorient and dominate the semiconductor supply chain." Clearly, a world-leading chipmaker could not continue to keep business out of politics. Samsung Electronics was a summit participant and urged the ROK government to develop a survival strategy by mobilizing all diplomatic resources, rather than leaving the sole responsibility to companies to answer Biden.[11]

The May 21 summit between Moon and Biden was the most critical event for ROK foreign policy in 2021, testing the notion of "strategic ambiguity" amid deepening US-China competition. Criticisms from the right against this policy had grown louder as Biden was appearing to undermine Moon's "Korean peace process." Rumors that Moon was turning down US demands for participation in the Quad fueled conservative views that Moon was choosing North Korea and China over the alliance. Biden's meeting with Japanese Prime Minister Suga just a month earlier had set a rather high bar.

Providing flexibility for Moon to pursue his own inter-Korea policy, Biden agreed to abolish the bilateral missile guidelines, which capped South Korea's ability to develop longer range missiles. In return, Moon gave ground. The news media sounded the alarm that this new-found sovereign right could cause a backlash from China and Russia as if Biden's intention was to contain China through South Korea. The main takeaway was that Moon had abandoned "strategic ambiguity" by supporting the US on three regional issues (ASEAN's role in the region, stability in the Taiwan Strait, and democratization in Myanmar) and supporting the Quad. Some forecast gloomy days for Sino-ROK relations, worrying about Moon holding hands with Biden on regional issues.[12]

Yet, on the whole, optimism prevailed that Moon had threaded a needle, overcoming a spell of passive diplomacy by satisfying Biden, who gave him room to maneuver with Pyongyang in return for a "global alliance," and not crossing China's red line. The US gained a boost from Korean firms' investments linked to semiconductor supply chains. The security alliance was being transformed to address technology issues, although some warned of a new round ahead in the Sino-US trade war, drawing Seoul further to the US side, and others found Moon's diplomacy still ambiguous on China compared to that of the G7 countries, including Japan. China's response was anxiously awaited.

Attention focused on two issues: China's official opinion on the ROK-US Joint Statement mention of the Taiwan Strait and the South China Sea, and the prior plan for Xi Jinping's visit to South Korea. In addition to China's foreign ministry criticism of broaching the Taiwan issue, Amb. Xing Haiming stressed the importance of "genuine multilateralism," open and inclusive, condemning the Quad as fake multilateralism that excludes and targets a specific country. Xi's visit went unmentioned.

Moon's foreign policy, apart from the US, was near a standstill. China showed its intention to revive its alliance with North Korea. Japan's LDP, ahead of the general election, found the feud with South Korea useful to appeal to its ultra-conservative voters. A Japanese official insulted Moon, as talks collapsed for a summit at the Tokyo Olympics, while the Chinese ambassador brusquely interfered in politics, attacking a presidential candidate's defense of the sovereign decision to deploy THAAD, while intimating that if Seoul does not take a zero-sum approach to ties to the US and China, it will pay. Relations with both Tokyo and Beijing were more troubled at summer's end than before. Meanwhile, North Korea and Russia were growing more belligerent.

Regional Framework

After three decades of active regional diplomacy, Seoul was isolated again. Yet, Moon remained cautious about joining in Biden's plans for Indo-Pacific regionalism, the Quad, or trilateralism with Japan. Each would have acknowledged a degree of polarization that risked his plans, especially for winning China's cooperation on North Korea. At stake for progressives was a longstanding view on how to weave between the great powers while prioritizing values such as peace, coexistence, and reconciliation, which contrasted with the Cold War, where the "us" versus "them" mentality was built on ideological blocs. As a "middle power," South Korea needed to maintain its neutrality.[13] On March 12, in response to the first virtual summit of the Quad, conservative newspapers urged the government to join as a "Quad-Plus" partner. The Quad summit joint statement referred to "denuclearization of North Korea," raising concern about South Korea being left out of discussions on the issue. Feelings of isolation were mounting with only conservatives offering a clear answer.

When AUKUS was announced, South Korea's muted response was not close to Japan welcoming the creation of AUKUS nor China calling it "extremely irresponsible." Foreign Minister Chung Eui-yong stressed the importance of US-China cooperation, rather than developing two blocs in Asia, a Chinese one and a non-Chinese one. Moon Chung-in in a column titled "Four Shadows of AUKUS" expressed concern over its long-term impact in the region and said its "four shadows"—emerging hierarchy among the US allies, exclusive support for Australia's development of nuclear-powered submarines, increasing possibilities of an arms race and nuclear proliferation in the region, and increasing uncertainty in regional security—served as an ominous signal of a new Cold War.[14]

On September 24, Biden hosted the leaders of the three other members of the Quad, broadening cooperation in space, 5G, cyber threats, and infrastructure. On October 13, asked whether the US had asked Seoul to join, ambassador to the US Lee Soo-hyuck said that the US did not intend to expand this grouping. *Conservatives* disagreed, saying that South Korea naturally falls within it.[15] Moon attended the "Summit for Democracy" but was more cautious in his language than Biden. As the summit was seen as a US effort to counter two uninvited countries, China and Russia, media outlets raised concerns over the growing tension between the US and China or were even dubious about Moon Jae-in's attendance there. Progressives also reacted warily to the first Xi-Biden summit, virtual as it was, and to the planned US diplomatic boycott of Beijing's Winter Olympics.

Russia

Even as US relations with Russia worsened in 2021, Moon Jae-in continued to value that country for its potential contribution to diplomacy over North Korea vital for the Korean Peninsula peace process. He was loathe to pull back from the New Northern Policy, centered on Russia. As the US rallied allies to deliver a message to Moscow of the dire consequences of an assault on Ukraine, Seoul stayed aloof, as if Moscow were only bluffing. Preparations for sanctions were not a focus.

China

The year 2021 saw Chinese warnings to Seoul but no major change in relations. On February 5, Amb. Xing Haiming expressed opposition to anti-China coalitions, including the Quad. "China deems forming a small group internationally or instigating a new Cold War in an attempt to exclude, intimidate, and isolate a third country as well cutting off its ties with others will inevitably force the world into division and confrontation," he said, explaining that Seoul's relations with Washington and Beijing are "both important."[16] Thus, he warned against joining Biden's agenda.

The conservative camp faulted Moon's China policy, e.g., for remaining silent about Beijing's claim that it entered the Korean War to defend peace, its attempts to claim sovereignty over the "West Sea," and its crackdown in Hong Kong, while repeatedly protesting Japanese distortions of history. Many argued that Seoul should positively consider participating in the US-led Indo-Pacific Strategy and in the Quad since the alliance is the basis of ROK foreign and security policy.

In an exchange between foreign ministers, Wang Yi cast South Korea and China as "eternal neighbors" and said that the two should focus on strengthening cooperation in various fields such as 5G, big data, green economy, artificial intelligence, integrated circuits, new energy, and the health industry. Wang said, "China, along with South Korea, will seek a process for a political resolution of the Korean Peninsula issue through dialogue." Progressives welcomed this sign of Moon's "balanced diplomacy," rather than picking sides, and keeping alive hopes for diplomacy with North Korea. *Chosun* strongly criticized the administration's obsession with "magic bullets," such as Xi Jinping's visit to Seoul and resumption of US-North Korea dialogue. Chung Eui-yong had urged Xi to visit Seoul, but the Chinese side made no mention about such a visit in its briefing after the meeting.[17] Influential progressive Moon Chung-in argued that the more intense the US-China conflicts become, the more limited South Korea's options will be, so it should move ahead toward alleviating their conflicts, through what he audaciously termed "transcendental diplomacy."[18]

When on July 1, China celebrated the 100th anniversary of the founding of the Chinese Communist Party, *conservatives* warned that China's illiberalism, including removal of term limits for its leader, repression of the Uyghurs and Hong Kong, and "wolf warrior" diplomacy, had invited international anger. Noting glorification of participation in the "War to Resist US Aggression and Aid Korea" at the anniversary, conservative *Seoul Kyungjae* editorialized that walking on eggshells toward China shrank South Korea's standing, urging a stronger alliance with the US based on shared values and openly expressed views to China.[19] Conservatives and progressives criticized China, but the latter were more wary of arousing China's ire, fearing spillover to the Sino-North Korean relationship.

On July 16, a controversy arose over an op-ed by Xing Haiming in response to Yoon Suk-yeol, the front-running presidential candidate, who had claimed that the ROK decision to deploy THAAD clearly fell within its area of sovereignty and that China should first withdraw its long-range radar near the Korean Peninsula if it wants to insist on THAAD withdrawal.[20] Stating that the deployment harmed Beijing's security interests and trust, Xing implicitly warned Seoul to defer to China's rising economic power. Park Jin, a member of the Foreign Affairs and Unification Committee at the National Assembly, wrote that by challenging a presidential candidate's stance on foreign policy, the ambassador had violated ROK sovereignty and interfered in its election.

On September 15, Wang Yi met with Moon Jae-in and Chung Eui-yong. Asked about that day's North Korean cruise missile launch, Wang said, "not only North Korea but also other countries engage in military acts." He urged restraint by all sides to prevent unilateral military action from resulting in a vicious circle on the peninsula. A week earlier, the International Olympic Committee announced that North Korea would be banned from the Beijing Winter Olympics. Despite this, Moon told Wang he hoped the Olympics would be another turning point in improving inter-Korean relations and contributing to peace in Northeast Asia. *Joongang Ilbo* underlined the gap between the announcements from Seoul and Beijing on the outcome of Wang's visit to Seoul. The Blue House's briefing omitted that "China firmly supports both Koreas in overcoming difficulties and steering clear of disruptions to improve relations." "Steering clear of disruptions" reflects both tension between the US and China and China's intention to separate ROK-US relations from diplomacy over inter-Korean relations.[21]

On November 15, Biden and Xi Jinping discussed a wide range of issues facing their countries, foreshadowing long-running competition and conflict. Progressives, who sought the support of both for security as well as the economy, appealed for additional strategic room for Seoul. After Biden, on November 18, warned of a diplomatic boycott of the Beijing Winter Olympics, Seoul was in a bind. Resisting the call for coalescing against China's repressive policies against the Uyghurs, progressives feared a boycott would impair efforts to improve relations with the North. Attendance was viewed as an extension of efforts to elicit support on an end-of-war declaration.

Progressives often echoed Chinese wording that those who did not prioritize diplomacy over deterrence were engaged in "Cold War" thinking. Rather than acknowledge threats posed by China, including its economic and cultural behavior toward South Korea, they were prone to view the US responses as the cause of setbacks to the active diplomacy they continued to desire, above all.

From early to mid-November, South Korea suffered an acute shortage of urea, used to make diesel exhaust fluid for reducing emissions, induced by China's decision to restrict exports on which South Korea was 97 percent dependent. This threatened to halt four million passenger cars and freight vehicles. The crisis exposed the danger of overdependence on Chinese raw materials and intermediary goods, leading to calls for a new mechanism to address supply chain vulnerabilities.[22]

Japan

There were modest signs from Seoul of trying to improve ties to Tokyo. Its new ambassador on January 22 called the Japanese Emperor his "Majesty the Emperor," after previously claiming that the emperor should be called a king.[23] On March 1, Moon marked the March First Independence Movement by emphasizing future-oriented development of bilateral relations at odds with his previous remarks that stressed Japan's "sincere self-reflection," but he reaffirmed the principle of resolving historical issues by stressing a "victim-centered approach." In response, Japan's chief cabinet secretary urged him to first suggest concrete proposals to settle pending bilateral issues.

In a phone call on October 15 with the new prime minister Kishida Fumio, Moon Jae-in differed on the scope of the 1965 normalization treaty but called for accelerating the search for a diplomatic solution to the forced labor and "comfort women" issues. On November 17, after a trilateral meeting of deputy foreign ministers, Japan boycotted the joint press conference on the grounds that on the same day, the South Korean National Police Agency's commissioner-general made a public visit to Dokdo. Koreans were dismayed that Japan's claim over Dokdo (Takeshima) had been growing stronger as shown by listing it as its territory in the Defense White Paper, school textbooks, and the map on the website of the 2020 Tokyo Olympics Organizing Committee.[24] At year's end, there was no sign of a turnabout in ROK-Japan relations and ample reason to think that public opinion remained wary and the Moon administration was still opposed to trilateralism.

The Year 2022

The South Korean government tilted toward the United States in 2022. There were long-term factors and precipitating ones. Two long-term factors were: the bursting of the illusion, held by progressives against all evidence to the contrary, that North Korea would entertain thoughts of peaceful coexistence and denuclearization; and the realization that China leans more closely to North Korea than South Korea, as it prioritizes driving a wedge between Seoul and Washington, not regional cooperation. Opinion toward China had shifted sharply from 2016 and toward the North from 2019. Moon delayed the inevitable by clinging to "peace diplomacy" and "strategic ambiguity" as late as early 2022, but in the face of the Ukraine war and Biden's new economic security appeals, Moon slowly yielded ground, Yoon Suk-yeol responded with greater clarity.

Yoon declared the intention of making South Korea a "global pivotal state," often interpreted as joining with the United States in an activist foreign policy while exercising autonomy in making things happen. Attention shifted from reshaping diplomacy over the Korean Peninsula to Asia more broadly. With the situation in Northeast Asia unpromising, talk of a more active role in Southeast Asia and India (expanding on the New Southern Strategy) was intensifying.

Trade is being used to advance national power and deter adversaries, altering the dichotomy between free trade and protectionism. This shift has raised questions about what constitutes national security and what types of dominance in high tech pose a security threat. Given the US inclusion of traditional security, new economic security, and human rights in calculations about trade, Seoul found alignment complicated, cooperating but seeking its own policy guidelines.

Why was Seoul inclined to buy time rather than to commit fully to the bifurcation underway? We can point to leadership, structural, and identity factors. The Yoon administration did not have the experience or top-down cohesion to proceed in an expedited manner. Yoon had scant foreign policy experience, while the presidential administration, bureaucracy, and chaebol leadership proved unwieldy to corral into a far-reaching, coordinated change of course. Of the structural factors, economic and security vulnerability to China weighed far more heavily than in Japan. The Ministry of Economy, Trade, and Industry (METI) had a long track record of working closely with companies, and the priority on economic security could more easily be swallowed. If chaebol differed on how far to embrace this, central leadership could not galvanize consensus, especially in a short turnaround time. On the identity dimension, as much as Japan had struggled for more autonomy in Asia, consensus on alliance identity as overshadowing all else remained strong and was growing. In contrast, despite strong support for the US alliance in South Korea, an alternate identity as a wielder of autonomous regional clout—whether over North Korean matters or over great power politics related to the peninsula—had become deeply embedded. If conservatives insisted that their worldview clashed with the progressive one, the degree of overlap should not be overlooked. Yet, circumstances dictated further changes in Seoul's position. By early 2023, Yoon was moving steadily toward the Biden agenda.

For progressives, leaning sharply toward the US, e.g., joining its Indo-Pacific strategy, risked China's cooperation on the North Korean nuclear issue. For conservatives, indecision stemmed from a host of factors despite a predisposition to work more closely with Washington.

The 30th anniversary of Sino-ROK normalization in 2022 passed with little recognition, while the anticipated 70th anniversary of the US-ROK alliance in 2023 was expected to lead to celebratory fanfare. Watching nervously as North Korea tested ever-more advanced missiles and relations among China, Russia, and the North strengthened, Seoul sought more reassurance from the US, not to be abandoned in the face of Chinese retaliation (as was perceived in 2016 over THAAD). Not only was extended deterrence more in doubt, as the North gained the means to attack the United States, but so too was US willingness to share the economic burdens ahead rather than to impose new rules damaging to South Korean companies. Feeling new vulnerability from old enemies in Moscow, Pyongyang, and Beijing, Seoul moved closer to Washington. The Biden administration welcomed this, but it remained concerned about a lack of clarity on key points. At the end of 2022, James Kim wrote, "Over his first 200 days as president,

Yoon Suk-yeol has toed a narrow path of tilting toward the United States without arousing retribution from China."[25]

Regional Framework

In campaigning Yoon made denuclearization of North Korea the priority. His opponent insisted that in order to pursue the national interest, Seoul must get along with Beijing. Yoon gave voice to an Indo-Pacific Strategy, participation in the Quad, as well as ROK-US-Japan trilateral cooperation. "Comprehensive strategic alliance with Washington" means moving beyond traditional security to cooperation on diverse issues, including supply chains. A shift was easier since "The South Korean public appears genuinely skeptical about China's intentions given their experience with THAAD, kimchi wars, Hong Kong, Taiwan, the COVID outbreak in Wuhan, and the Winter Olympics."[26]

Yoon veered from "strategic ambiguity," to "peace through force." The first Yoon-Biden summit in May, held less than two weeks after Yoon's inauguration, left no room for doubt that Seoul was poised to increase its cooperation, expanding the scope of joint military exercises, exchanging emerging technologies, and securing resilient global supply chains. Seoul's announcement that it would join the Indo-Pacific Economic Framework (IPEF) reenforced its decision to coordinate more closely on economic security with the United States and various other like-minded countries.

On the one hand, Biden's visit to Seoul drew praise for Yoon now actively shaping the rules of an emerging order. On the other, the progressive reaction was skeptical with a touch of alarmism, and there was a middle group nervous about aspects of Biden's trip to the region but reserving its judgment. Worries about future moves by China and North Korea cast a lingering shadow for all.

Yoon affirmed that South Korea would join IPEF, the US-led initiative to establish a resilient supply chain with partners in the region. Yoon virtually attended the summit launching in Tokyo and said that South Korea would share its experience and work together with a dozen partners in all fields covered by IPEF, a process of setting a wide range of rules related to economics and trade in the Indo-Pacific region, particularly in strengthening supply chains. He added, "It is only natural to join the process," and "If we excluded ourselves from the process to set the rules, it would cause enormous harm to our national interests." Yet, Yoon noted that there is no need to view the government's decision to join IPEF and ROK-China relations as zero-sum.[27]

For conservatives. IPEF was greeted as US reengagement on trade after its withdrawal from TPP, but it remained too vague to answer key questions. A shift away from Moon's wariness of regional goals was much welcomed; however, whereas US leaders see a historic urgency to transform an alliance that no longer fully reflected the challenges both countries face, even conservatives were wary of tilting sharply to the US, given the need for cooperation from China on both economic and security issues, warning that Seoul must not be swept into the US-led new order, but must find its own approach. The ongoing trend was to follow the US in linking economy and security and to maximize the benefits of a new technology alliance, but to retain wariness.

The progressive camp found many things of concern in Biden's visit. Some treated the US as the disruptor of the status quo, refusing to accept China's rise and containing China without sufficient reason. The ostensible reason for expanding the scope and scale of joint military exercises is North Korea, but some warned that another reason was to contain China with a three-way military framework including Japan. Suspicious of Japan's real intentions and echoing Chinese charges against the Quad—now proceeding from pandemic and climate change measures to policing the movement of Chinese ships—writers warned of aggressive intentions. IPEF aroused warnings of "economic containment" of China. Hesitant to follow the US lead fully on Ukraine and alarmed by Biden's statement on Taiwan in Tokyo, progressives charged that Biden is seeking to fundamentally alter the nature of the alliance after seven decades. They criticized a renunciation of "balanced diplomacy" by Yoon and appeared to worry about some sort of a Chinese backlash.[28]

In light of strong public support for the alliance, the visit was mostly well received. Helpful was the fact that North Korea had spurned talks, China's role in support of North Korea and Russia had further soured its image, and difficult choices had yet to be spelled out. The focus on close cooperation on technology played to South Korea's strength, as the visits by Biden to Samsung and Hyundai offices showed the US need for its ally, not pressure on Seoul. Semiconductors became a symbol of deepening technology cooperation. The summit at the Samsung Pyeongtaek campus symbolized a "semiconductor alliance."[29] If earlier asymmetry stood out with the US providing security, now the South Korean role in providing technology pointed to two-way ties.

Following Moon's ambivalence about a regional agenda and expectations of agency as a force for change in Northeast Asia, the message from Biden was not easy to accept. Rather than shaping the peninsula's future through its diplomacy, Seoul is reduced to signing onto a US-led strategy in which Tokyo is already heavily invested. Cautious responses often belied Yoon's upbeat rhetoric.

Yoon seemed to straddle between a framework opposed by China and reassurance to China and Korean economic interests that the pro-trade policies of recent decades would persist. Two keywords were linked to this pursuit: "values" to reassure the US and "prosperity" to appeal to China. Ambivalence is a sign of "strategic ambiguity" rather than "strategic clarity." Some said that strong support for the alliance signaled the latter—as it did for military deterrence of North Korea. Others argued that on regional policy or even thinking on North Korea "ambiguity" was more applicable. As much as Yoon's rhetoric added clarity on broader alliance support, reaching consensus among bureaucracies, now free of Moon's top-down approach, was proving difficult.

US regional goals drew more support from Yoon but not full endorsement. On security, Taiwan and the South China Sea received new notice, but the language was left vague. On economic or "comprehensive" security, the language was upbeat, but details needed to be clarified. And on values, a new tone arose, if limits remained on how vocal to be. A lot was left for clarification on digital trade, supply chain resilience, and high-tech decoupling. Washington prioritized security over the economy more than Seoul did in dealings with China. Suspicions abounded that IPEF was launched for "America First" unfair to US allies, including South Korea. Was the chief threat China or the deterioration of Sino-US relations, some were asking.

At the end of December, the Yoon administration released its Indo-Pacific Strategy, largely echoing the US strategy but avoiding direct mention of China's transgressions and claiming "inclusiveness" opens the door to engagement with China. Openness to closer cooperation with Japan and with Australia and India as well as stress on values aligns with US interests. The call for a more mature relationship with China based on mutual respect and reciprocity leaves the door ajar, but this puts the burden on Beijing to find common ground with a strategy it is not inclined to accept. Mention of expanded cooperation with NATO and the Quad also is consistent with US objectives. Making parallel mention of trilateral ties to the US and Japan and to China and Japan obscures the sharp distinction between the former—proceeding quickly—and the latter still largely at an impasse and requiring Beijing to cater to two US allies together by making major policy changes. While keeping an element of "strategic ambiguity" through inclusiveness, there is some sign of strategic clarity. Heartening to the US are references to "cooperation to promote rule of law and human rights," expanding comprehensive security cooperation," and "building economic security networks." Also mention of "stability on the Taiwan Strait" and "freedom of navigation and overflight in the South China Sea" affirmed principles long advocated by the US and anathema to China.

Russia

Seoul's cautious approach toward the Ukraine war threat did not end with invasion. On February 24, on the brink of war, the Ministry of Foreign Affairs noted the possibility of joining multilateral sanctions, including export controls, but set all-out war against Ukraine as a precondition. When Russia unleashed a full-scale invasion, Seoul drew the line at imposing unilateral sanctions such as financial sanctions.[30] Putin warned Yoon that if South Korea aided Ukraine militarily, it would destroy Russia-South Korea relations, presumably also leading to a shift in Russia-North Korea relations. Given that the North was soon sending ammunition to Russia and relations were drawing closer, the implications could be serious. When the US asked Yoon for ammunition for Kyiv, the response was that it could not be sent directly and thus would not signify lethal aid to Ukraine, as it replenished the stocks of others.

The Moon administration faced a supreme test after Russia launched a massive assault on Ukraine on February 24. Other US allies were already on board, but Seoul took a week of handwringing, as bureaucratic divisions bubbled to the surface. The security community recognized quickly that this was a critical test for the alliance. The METI reportedly dawdled from concern about the economic costs. The foreign ministry included those who feared that the sanctions would spell an end to three decades of diplomatic diversification and cooperation from Russia on North Korea. Some in the progressive camp seemingly saw Ukraine and its leadership, not Russia and Putin, as the cause of the mounting tension in Ukraine. The excruciating wait to join the US-led coalition aroused a sense of crisis just months prior to Yoon's inauguration as Moon's tenure ended.

Some found it hypocritical of Moon to claim that South Koreans inherited the spirit of the March 1st Movement—resistance against violence and hegemonic world order—while keeping silent about Russia's aggression against Ukraine. It seemed to be the only US ally excluded from the exemption from US export control measures before Moon finally decided on such measures.

North Korea's May 25 ICBM test and the veto cast by China and Russia at the UN Security Council, which hindered further sanctions against North Korea, raised more serious concerns over the consolidating ties between North Korea, China, and Russia. Many were alarmed that China and North Korea defended Russia, voting against suspending the country from the Human Rights Council. Concerned about the strengthening ties among the three nations, *conservatives* argued that the incoming government should put emphasis on democratic allies and the ROK-US alliance.

In his April 11 virtual speech to the National Assembly, Zelensky drew an analogy between the Korean War and the ongoing crisis in Ukraine, citing the urgency of "indispensable" weapons for its air defense that South Korea already has.[31] However, the Ministry of National Defense drew the line at sending lethal weapons. Defense Minister Suh Wook noted "limits" to military support due to the security situation on the peninsula and potential impact on South Korea's military readiness.

Given the US focus on Ukraine, Biden's visit offered reassurance that Asia was not overlooked, although it was not the Korean Peninsula but the Indo-Pacific that was showcased. The degree of South Korean support for the full range of sanctions on Russia loomed as an issue not fully resolved. Whether because of business interests or lingering fear of a further Russian tilt to North Korea, this challenge hovered in the background. If Seoul hesitated in pressuring Moscow, it was assumed that it would be more reluctant to take measures for economic security opposed by Beijing. The "wait and see" approach to Russia meant keeping channels open. Hyundai auto did not close its operations despite problems with payments. Progressives needed Russia for the next stage of diplomacy with North Korea, business interests hesitated to cut ties, and bureaucratic infighting found vested interests in resisting the security community's calls to back US sanctions.

The Ukraine war indirectly involved both Koreas, one asked by the US to apply sanctions and help to replace depleted arms stocks as well as to echo broad-based alliance rhetoric, the other willing to supply arms to Russia and eager to parrot its narrative. The war deepened the global divide and gave Moscow and Beijing a reason to further demonize the US to Pyongyang's satisfaction. Russia's nuclear blackmail set a precedent. The spate of missile tests by the North in 2022 led some to fear new provocations. The Ukraine war threatened to embolden Pyongyang at Seoul's expense.

Naturally, the New Northern Strategy did not survive the Moon-Yoon transition. In contrast, the much more successful New Southern Strategy of Moon could be rebranded under the Indo-Pacific Economic Framework being prepared by the US for rollout at the US APEC 2023.

China

The cultural clash with China was overshadowing that with Japan. If Japan's new history textbooks in March and its bid for a UNESCO world heritage site for the Sado mine aroused criticism, more attention focused on a woman wearing hanbok at the Beijing Olympics opening ceremony, which was denounced as an attempt to appropriate Korean culture, and for marring the Olympics spirit in a refereeing decision at the men's 1,000-meter short track speed skating semi-finals, when two South Korean world-record skaters were disqualified for violations, as Chinese won the medals.

On May 16, Park Jin held a virtual meeting with Wang Yi, celebrating the 30th anniversary of the establishment of diplomatic ties. On the same day at the National Assembly, Yoon Suk-yeol pledged to discuss South Korea's participation in IPEF with Biden. As a result, Wang Yi's remarks on the future of ROK-China relations came into the spotlight as a response to Seoul turning away from Beijing. Addressing fields for future cooperation, Wang argued that both sides "oppose the negative tendency of decoupling and cutting off chains" and "maintain the stability and smoothness of the global industrial and supply chains." His remarks were taken as opposition to Seoul's changing trajectory. Vice President Wang Qishan had stressed that both sides should work together to "safeguard multilateralism" during his visit to Seoul for Yoon's inauguration.[32]

Contrasts were drawn between the two May summits with Biden of Moon and Yoon. At the second, however, Seoul was faulted by progressives for tilting sharply to the US side and even turning hostile to China. The new theme of "economic security" drew criticism as a way to contain China. In 2021, the joint statement said, "our respective approaches to the Indo-Pacific region," but in 2022 Yoon praised the US strategy as if Seoul had no other and led China to think Seoul had joined in containment. On Taiwan, all that was said in 2021 was "the importance of preserving peace and stability in the Taiwan Strait." In 2022 the Taiwan Strait was called an "essential element in security and prosperity in the Indo-Pacific region." Human rights were another challenge to China, seemingly pointing to Hong Kong and Xinjiang by "sharing our mutual concerns regarding human rights in the Indo-Pacific region." Finally, on North Korea, mention of the Panmunjom Declaration and Singapore Joint Statement was omitted, shifting the framework for diplomacy, and human rights were raised more clearly. Progressives were wary of supply chains to be secured against "countries that don't share our values," i.e., Russia and China.

While abandonment was on people's minds, fearing a distracted US due to events in Europe and lack of urgency over North Korea, the summit shifted the focus for some to entrapment. Biden's remark on Taiwan in Tokyo only heightened that concern. Knowing China's tough stance on South Korean involvement in the Quad and other regional initiatives it saw as containment, fear of a repeat of the sanctions of 2016 was palpable. The shift toward a regional and global alliance aroused some criticism, coming at the expense of the focus on North Korea and reunification.

With the rising criticism from China of US-led IPEF "clique" politics, economic retaliation from China was on people's minds. Some claimed that it was no longer feasible to pursue strategic ambiguity since a country's national security was intertwined with its economy. Recalling the memory of China's economic coercion during the THAAD dispute, others insisted that the government continue to communicate closely with China and send a clear message about its position.

Following North Korea's flurry of missile launches, including the ICBM launched on May 25, the Security Council voted on a draft resolution strengthening sanctions. China and Russia used their veto. On May 27, South Korea's Ministry of Foreign Affairs expressed its deep regret, and media outlets condemned China for exonerating North Korea from responsibility. *Joongang Ilbo* expressed regret over China's representative to the UN Zhang Jun's remarks in which he addressed the US Indo-Pacific Strategy as a cause of the "latest developments on the peninsula."[33]

The dilemma of navigating between the US and China was put into sharp relief by heightened military and diplomatic tensions over Taiwan when US House Speaker Nancy Pelosi visited that island to the welcome of China's military drills. Having long tried to stay on the sidelines on Taiwan, Seoul was under new pressure to support US forces in one manner or another. Yoon already had agreed to language on "the importance of preserving peace and stability in the Taiwan Strait" in a joint statement with the US. If the US was abandoning "strategic ambiguity" on Taiwan, Seoul would find it harder to stay aloof. In Seoul after her visit to Taiwan, Pelosi was not met by Yoon—just a phone call—raising concern that Yoon was distancing South Korea from the Taiwan issue, giving China reassurance. After agreeing to language on Taiwan in May, Yoon had faced strong warnings from China on this issue, leading to his response to Pelosi.[34] Conservatives found this inconsistent with the promise to prioritize the alliance; progressives endorsed sticking to a balanced approach.

When Park Jin went to Qingdao in August to meet Wang Yi, marking the 30th anniversary of the establishment of relations, a wide range of issues was discussed, but security took center stage so soon after Nancy Pelosi's tense visit to Taiwan. Wang Yi demanded that Seoul abide by the "three no's and one restriction," the latter being on the use of the deployed THAAD system. China called for consideration of each other's core interests, unimpeded supply chains, and non-interference in each other's internal affairs—all of which Seoul was accused of ignoring in Chinese media. The reaction was to insist that the "three no's" were the approach of the Moon administration, not binding on Yoon and internal matters for the ROK. Instead of deterring the North, China was pressuring South Korea, and many responded. Yoon's efforts to avoid antagonizing Beijing might have been to no avail as Wang warned Park that Seoul should abide by the "five requirements" for relations, abstaining from the US-led semiconductor partnership "Chip 4," and additional deployment of the THAAD system on South Korean territory. Asserting its sovereignty over THAAD deployment, Seoul revealed its intention to attend a preliminary meeting for Chip 4.

Considering the fallout from US-China competition and the Ukraine crisis, media diverged in their response. Conservatives argued that it was inevitable for the US and South Korea to strengthen their bilateral cooperation for economic security and technology, turning "an-mi-gyung-jung" ("United States for security, China for economy") into "strengthening the alliance with the United States and pursuing common interests with China."[35] *Progressives* argued that strengthening the ROK-US economic security alliance should not lead to deterioration in the ROK-China relationship, urging Yoon to balance diplomacy that protects national interests with both the US and China.[36]

Seoul has inched toward recognition with Washington of a Taiwan contingency, first noting "peace and stability in Taiwan," then adding the context of "Indo-Pacific stability," and later recognizing the interests of the "international community." Beijing frowns on such statements as "interference in its internal affairs." Yoon is living dangerously by, month-by-month, testing the limits of China's patience, even as he proclaims "mutual respect" to be the centerpiece of his approach. The increasing prominence of his "alliance first" diplomacy keeps testing China. Yoon hoped to disentangle US-ROK and Sino-Korea relations,[37] but this became increasingly difficult as Sino-US tensions continued to mount. Putting aside episodic events like the Pelosi visit, Seoul's actions epitomize "alliance first," wholesale support for the US Indo-Pacific strategy and commitment to participate in the IPEF. Although Yoon's pledge to "formulate ROK's own Indo-Pacific strategy framework" signals possible differences, alignment was close.

Wang Yi and Park Jin met in August. According to the Chinese readout, Wang reiterated "the five-point commitment" to independence free of external interference; to upholding good neighborliness and friendship while accommodating each other's major concerns; to openness and win-win cooperation, and stable and unimpeded industrial and supply chains; to equality, mutual respect, and non-interference in each other's internal affairs; and to multilateralism and the principles of the UN Charter. The South Korean side reiterated the importance of cooperation on North Korean denuclearization as well as revitalization of the Korea-China-Japan trilateral dialogue. The Chinese readout did not mention these other issues

Yoon Suk-yeol and Xi Jinping held talks in Indonesia during the November 2022 G20 summit.

Yoon sought a Chinese response to North Korea's continued threats, while Chinese state media did not mention any North Korean issues but focused on economic cooperation and opposed its politicization, i.e., US policy calling on South Korea to prioritize economic security. In Seoul's report, Xi had said that South Korea and China have a common interest in the Korean Peninsula and should protect the peace, calling on South Korea to actively improve inter-Korean relations, i.e., talk with North Korea instead of conducting joint exercises with the US and Japan or implementing sanctions. Xi told Yoon the two countries should keep global industrial and supply chains unclogged and oppose politicizing economic cooperation or overstretching the concept of security. Earlier at the Korea-ASEAN summit, Yoon announced he would implement the Indo-Pacific Strategy using engagement, trust, and inclusiveness as the three principles of cooperation. The "inclusive" principle to regional order, however, seemed to exclude China.

The meeting in Bali resulted in clashing readouts. The Koreans said that Yoon started off emphasizing the "pursuit of freedom, peace and prosperity of the international community based on common values and norms."[38] He also noted the threat posed by North Korea and urged Xi to "play a more active and constructive role." The Chinese readout did not mention these talking points.[39] Instead, it emphasized the "need to enhance alignment of development strategies and work for common development and prosperity." Xi also highlighted the value of cooperation on trade, high-tech manufacturing, big data, green economy, and supply chains. Absent was any mention of values or North Korea.

In May, Yoon agreed to a joint statement more provocative, in Chinese eyes, than Moon's joint statement with Biden a year earlier. In June, Yoon bolstered ties with European states as they not only rallied against Russian aggression but warned against China's behavior, including in the Taiwan Strait. In September, at the UN General Assembly, Yoon firmly advocated for universal norms to undoubted Chinese displeasure. Then, in October, Seoul was put on the spot over a host of US-announced export controls over semiconductors, promising to impede ROK-Chinese high-tech transactions. And in November in the shadow of the East Asian Summit Yoon joined with Biden and Kishida to give momentum to trilateralism against Chinese warnings. As Beijing raised concerns, Yoon's appeals for "mutual respect" never faded. "'Mutual respect' as expressed by Yoon refers to 'South Korea not opposing China's Belt and Road Initiative and working with

Beijing in trade and commerce, [while] China... accepting, rather than opposing, South Korea's cooperative system with its allies.'" Many were left wondering if Yoon could avoid a strong Chinese backlash in the year 2023, James Kim concluded.[40]

Japan

From the moment of Yoon's election an upbeat mood prevailed in ROK-Japan relations. While a target of resolving the forced labor issue by the end of the year always seemed ambitious, security and economic ties kept advancing. Biden's input was unmistakable, culminating in the trilateral summit in the shadow of the November East Asian Summit as well as a bilateral summit of Kishida and Yoon. The "Phnom Penh Statement on Trilateral Partnership for the Indo-Pacific" brought regional strategies closer, as Yoon also joined the group led by the US and Japan known as "Partners in the Blue Pacific" to cooperate with island nations. Trilateralism tightened on behalf of the Korean Peninsula, including intelligence sharing and universal values. The three vowed to share North Korean missile warning data in real time and to launch a dialogue among the three on economic security. The joint statement covered maintaining peace and stability in the Taiwan Strait, emphasizing the three nations' commitment to stand with Ukraine, and working together to strengthen supply chains for emerging technologies. Strongly opposing any unilateral attempts to change the status quo in waters of the Indo-Pacific targeted China without mentioning it by name, as did stressing the "importance of maintaining peace and stability across the Taiwan Strait." This was the first time that the leaders of the three countries chose to adopt a comprehensive joint statement. Unprecedented trilateral coordination aligned in pursuit of a "Free and Open Indo-Pacific."

Earlier in the year candidate Yoon called for negotiating a comprehensive solution for "comfort women," forced labor, export controls, and GSOMIA, restoring the lost trust between the two countries. Improved Korea-Japan relations would lead to improved regional cooperation among Korea, the US, and Japan, he recognized.[41] In the face of relentless North Korean missile launches, Tokyo and Seoul accepted US appeals for closer trilateral security cooperation coupled with three-way naval exercises. If some progressives foresaw a chain of events leading to a new Japanese invasion, the public was shifting to support Yoon's outreach to Japan, as was Japanese public opinion.[42] One survey found the largest improvement since it began a decade ago, with the most marked change in South Korea, where fear of China has been growing rapidly.

On June 13, at a joint ROK-US press conference, Park Jin was asked whether he envisaged a US role in reviving GSOMIA between South Korea and Japan, which allowed the two countries to share information on North Korean military threats. The agreement took effect in 2016 but had been suspended in 2019 after Japan imposed export restrictions and South Korea, in turn, terminated the extension of GSOMIA. The South Korean foreign minister said he wanted "GSOMIA to be normalized as soon as possible" on the basis that South Korea, the US, and Japan need policy coordination and information sharing.[43] Conservatives saw it as a way to improve Japan ties.

The assassination of Abe Shinzo on July 8 induced Koreans to reflect on Japanese policy. Some saw a danger of the far right strengthening, which could set back diplomacy, following Yoon's meeting with Kishida at the NATO summit. One concern was further distortion of history in line with Abe's extremist image. Another was momentum for amending the Constitution and increasing military spending. On June 7, the Japanese cabinet approved guidelines for boosting military spending to 2 percent of gross domestic product, within the next five years. Some warned that this could trigger an arms race in the region, adding that Japan should not try to justify a larger defense budget by citing the Ukraine war, the North Korean threats, and the Taiwan Strait but sound out neighboring countries with which it has continued rows over historical issues.[44] Abe's death provided one more opportunity to warn of danger emanating from Japan, but most desired improved relations.

Casting a shadow on the progress made in ROK-Japan relations was the forced labor issue despite Japan's insistence that compensation was settled by the 1965 normalization agreement. The launch in early July of a consultative, public-private body on Korean victims of forced labor showed Yoon's determination to resolve the diplomatic row, perhaps even using Korean government funds for initial payments.

The meeting between Park Jin and his counterpart Hayashi Yoshimasa on July 18 was the first in person at this level since December 2017. They agreed to find a new approach to the handling of Japanese companies' assets and on the urgency of improving ties. Yoon had pledged to seek a comprehensive solution for improving the strained ties, and Kishida, who led a moderate faction within the LDP, gave some reason for hope. Media on both sides, however, were not optimistic.

By the beginning of 2023 a proposal was circulating for a South Korean foundation instead of the two Japanese corporate defendants to compensate plaintiffs over forced labor during colonial rule. As Park Cheol-hee observed, "a change in thinking underlies this change in strategy, from a hierarchical and subordinate one that framed South Korea as a victim and Japan as an aggressor to one that sees the two countries as equal actors." He saw an effort to "expand the horizon of South Korea-Japan cooperation from a narrow focus on bilateral cooperation or the Korean Peninsula, to one that includes East Asia, the Asia-Pacific region, and even the Indo-Pacific region and the whole world...This forward-looking approach is based on the idea that the pursuit of the interests of all Koreans and the national interest is the basis of diplomacy, rather than limiting the main audience of South Korea-Japan relations to victims of historical abuses."[45]

Conclusion

The years 2020–2022 were marked by a decisive, but incomplete, tilt toward the United States and away from China. Relations with Japan advanced with much promise of a solution to forced labor compensation and increased confidence that history issues were being resolved. Relations with Russia tanked following its decision to launch a full-scale war in Ukraine and acquiescence to US-led economic sanctions. After Moon's hesitation to embrace the emerging, US-defined Indo-Pacific framework, Yoon proved to be more supportive, although his call for "mutual respect" with China left some details vague. Into 2023 the momentum kept building for closer ROK-US relations.

Three key uncertainties loomed for Yoon's regional approach: defining economic security and how semiconductor restrictions on China would proceed; preparing for Chinese retaliation, keeping in mind the earlier pressure applied due to THAAD deployment; and anticipating regional dynamics in case of a severe North Korean provocation. Nothing suggested a reversal of the ongoing tilt to the United States. With China warning against it and North Korea expected to be on the verge of a more serious provocation, Yoon was finding it challenging to stick to the course he had chosen.

*I am indebted to Hong Sanghwa, Jung Seyoon, and Shin Munkyoung for preparing the "Country Reports: South Korea" in *The Asan Forum* over this period. This chapter draws heavily on them.

Notes

1 See Won Byun, "Chinese Views of South Korea: Aligning Elite and Popular Debates," in Gilbert Rozman, ed., *Joint U.S.-Korea Academic Studies. East Asian Leaders' Political Frameworks, New National Identity Impact, and Rising Economic Concerns with China* (Washington, DC: KEI, 2020), p. 164.
2 Sanghwa Hong, "Country Report: South Korea," *The Asan Forum*, November 2020, citing Chosun Ilbo, September 26.
3 Dong Xiangrong, "Shared History, Divided Consciousness: The Origins of the Sino-ROK Cultural Clash," in Gilbert Rozman, ed., *Joint U.S.-Korea Academic Studies. Questioning the Pandemic's Impact on the Indo-Pacific: Geopolitical Gamechanger" Force for Deepening National Identity Clashes? Cause of Shifting Supply Chains?* (Washington, DC: KEI, 2021); Dong Xiangrong, "Perceptions and Misperceptions between China and South Korea Amid the COVID-19 Pandemic," *The Asan Forum*, January 11, 2021.
4 Woo Jong Yeop, "How COVID-19 Has Affected the Geopolitics of Korea," in *Questioning the Pandemic's Impact on the Indo-Pacific*, p. 95.
5 Sanghwa Hong, "Country Report: South Korea," *The Asan Forum*, September 2020, citing Xinhua News.
6 Gilbert Rozman, "China's Strategies Toward South Korea, Japan, and Australia in the Biden Era," *The Asan Forum*, March 2, 2021.
7 Eun A. Jo, "Double Allegiance: Moon Jae-in's Strategy Amid US-China Rivalry," *The Asan Forum*, August 27, 2021.

8 Scott A. Snyder, "The Pandemic and Its Impact on the South Korea-Japan Identity Clash," in *Questioning the Pandemic's Impact on the Indo-Pacific,* p. 71.
9 Cheol Hee Park, "South Korean Views of Japan: A Polarizing Split in Coverage," in *East Asian Leaders' Political Frameworks,* p. 174.
10 Sanghwa Hong, "Country Report: South Korea," *The Asan Forum,* March 2021.
11 *JoongAng Ilbo,* April 14, 2021.
12 *Donga Ilbo,* May 24, 2021.
13 Kim Tae Hwan, "Value Diplomacy Driving Global 'Blocization' of Values: Implications of Great Power Cases for Korea's Public Diplomacy," *Culture and Politics,* Vol. 6, No. 1 (2019), pp. 5–32.
14 *Hankyoreh,* October 10, 2021.
15 *Joongang Ilbo,* September 26, 2021.
16 Sanghwa Hong, "Country Report: South Korea," *The Asan Forum,* March 2021.
17 *Chosun Ilbo,* April 5, 2021.
18 *Asahi Shimbun,* April 11, 2021.
19 *Seoul Kyungjae,* July 1, 2021.
20 *JoongAng Ilbo,* July 14, 2021; *JoongAng Ilbo,* July 16, 2021; *Newsis,* July 16, 2021.
21 Ministry of Foreign Affairs of the People's Republic of China, "ROK's President Moon Jae-in Meets with Wang Yi," September 15, 2021; *Joongang Ilbo,* September 16, 2021.
22 *Donga Ilbo,* November 11, 2021.
23 Sanghwa Hong, "Country Report: South Korea," *The Asan Forum,* March 2021.
24 *Donga Ilbo,* November 18, 2021.
25 J. James Kim, "Alliance First and Mutual Respect: Yoon's Foreign Policy Approach on China and the United States," *The Asan Forum,* December 26, 2022.
26 J. James Kim, "Stepping Up to the Challenge and Embracing Pragmatism: Two Visions of Foreign Policy in the South Korean Presidential Election of 2022," *The Asan Forum,* March 2, 2022.
27 *Hankyoreh,* May 20, 23, 2022.
28 Jung Seyoon and Shin Munkyoung, "Country Report: South Korea," *The Asan Forum,* July 2022.
29 Ibid.
30 Yonhap News, February 24, 2022; *Hankyoreh,* February 24, 2022.
31 The Presidential Office of Ukraine, "Speech by the President of Ukraine in the National Assembly of the Republic of Korea," April 11, 2022.
32 Ministry of Foreign Affairs of the People's Republic of China, "Wang Yi Holds Virtual Meeting with ROK's New Foreign Minister Park Jin," May 16, 2022; *Segye Ilbo,* May 17, 2022.
33 Ministry of Foreign Affairs of the People's Republic of China, "Explanation of Vote by Ambassador Zhang Jun on the UN Security Council Draft Resolution on the DPRK," May 26, 2022.
34 *Yomiuri Shinbun,* November 13, 2022.
35 *Kukmin Ilbo,* May 23, 2022.
36 *Kyunghyang Shinmun,* May 20, 2022.
37 김예경, "수교 30주년 한중관계의 미래: 윤석열 정부 대중정책의 쟁점과 시사점," Issues and Perspectives. National Assembly Research Service, No. 1975, August 4, 2022; 정재흥, "윤석열 정부의 대중국 정책, 도전과 과제," No. 19, April 4, 2022; 박병광, "윤석열 대통령 당선인의 대중정책 방향과 새로운 한중관계," Issue Brief. INSS. No. 337, March 22, 2022.
38 Office of the President, Republic of Korea, "President Yoon Returns after 1st Summit with China in Bali," November 16, 2022.
39 Ministry of Foreign Affairs of the People's Republic of China, "President Xi Jinping Meets with ROK President Yoon Suk-yeol," November 15, 2022.
40 J. James Kim, "Alliance First and Mutual Respect," *The Asan Forum,* December 2022.

41 J. James Kim, "Stepping Up to the Challenge and Embracing Pragmatism: Two Visions of Foreign Policy in the South Korean Presidential Election of 2022," *The Asan Forum*, March 2, 2022.
42 The Genron NPO, September 12, 2022.
43 U.S. Department of State, "Secretary Anthony J. Blinken and Republic of Korea Foreign Minister Park Jin at a Joint Press Availability," June 13, 2022.
44 *Donga Ilbo*, June 8, 2022.
45 Park Cheol-hee, "The Adhesive for South Korea-Japan Cooperation," *Asia Sentinel*, January 3, 2023.

9
BATTLING PARTISAN NARRATIVES

Eun A Jo

The second half of Moon Jae-in's presidency was marred by diplomatic deadlock, as talks between North Korea and the United States collapsed, tensions between China and the United States deepened, and relations with Japan hit a new nadir. In this thorny climate, partisans debated South Korea's shifting role in the region as well as the scope of its foreign policy autonomy. Having inherited the THAAD crisis, Moon was especially attuned to Beijing's sensitivities regarding the regional reach of the US-South Korean alliance and the potential costs of Chinese retaliation. This awareness underlay his administration's reluctance to participate in the Free and Open Indo-Pacific (FOIP) agenda, which Beijing has time and again framed as US-led encirclement. Meanwhile, the worsening feud with Japan made its multilateral framework politically untenable for Moon, who had made a "victim-centered" approach to history issues with Japan the cornerstone of his progressive legacy. The onset of the global COVID-19 pandemic, however, obscured the slowdowns in Moon's foreign policy.

Partisan narratives continued to polarize as conservatives—emboldened by Moon's diplomatic failures—campaigned on promises of strategic clarity, based on a rehabilitated alliance relationship with the United States and partnership with Japan. Upon inauguration, Yoon Suk-yeol has sought to institutionalize this back-to-the-basics foreign policy agenda, though the details of his newly introduced Indo-Pacific Strategy suggest some continuity with the Moon-era ambiguity. The resulting partisan debates have thus concerned the substantive contours of strategic clarity and the necessity, desirability, and feasibility of such geostrategic alignment. The futures that conservatives and progressives imagine for South Korea's role in the Indo-Pacific appeared to diverge drastically from one another.

The Moon Presidency

The final two years of Moon's presidency were marked by four interrelated developments: (1) collapse of diplomacy with North Korea; (2) frictions in the alliance with the United States; (3) tensions in the relationship with China; and (4) hostilities in relations with Japan. Partisan narratives during this period continued to diverge over the prospects of peace—both inter-Korean and regional—and the right approach to pursue it.

North Korea

The collapse of diplomacy with North Korea was far from unexpected. Trump's diminished interest in the North Korean problem, rising US-China hostilities over trade and pandemic issues, as well as growing partisan divisions in South Korea—particularly in the lead up to the presidential elections—all boded ill for Moon's initiative. At home and abroad, he found himself increasingly isolated, with little recourse to jumpstart the deadlocked dialogue with Pyongyang.

By the end of 2019, North Korea's nuclear and missile provocations were growing in frequency and scale. Pyongyang began to test the bounds of its self-imposed moratoriums, conducting rocket engine tests in 2019, short-range ballistic missile firings in 2020, cyberattacks on South Korean defense industry in 2021, and finally, launches of intercontinental ballistic missiles in 2022. Initially, these activities accompanied curated messages, aimed at bringing Trump back to the negotiating table; in December 2019, Vice Foreign Minister Ri Thae-song offered a reminder in KCNA: "it is entirely up to the US what Christmas gift it will select to get." This calibrated rhetoric had little desired effect, however, and it would soon be replaced with the more typical warnings and bluster as signs of disinterest mounted in Washington.

In fact, Trump was increasingly occupied with China in his last year of tenure. The pandemic and the growing visibility of his populist base had made China a more natural target for his reelection bid. Even when Kim Jong-un renounced the nuclear and ICBM test moratorium and warned of a "shocking actual action"— the course of which, he claimed, would be determined by Washington's "future attitude" to North Korea—Trump paid minimal attention.[1] Instead, he deflected: "We have to do what we have to do… But he [Kim Jong-un] did sign an agreement talking about denuclearization."[2] Trump still emphasized that he maintained "a very good relationship with Kim Jong-un" and that he believed Kim to be "a man of his word." In stark contrast to this lukewarm response, the Trump administration adopted a "whole-of-government" strategy toward China: in 2020 alone, his administration took at least 210 public actions, spanning across 10 departments. These included 22 by the Justice Department (e.g., indictments and arrests), 66 by the State Department (e.g., visa restrictions), 27 by the White House (e.g., executive orders surrounding trade), and 23 by the Defense Department (e.g., freedom of navigation operations).³ The shift in focus from diplomacy with North Korea to competition with China was, by this point, glaring.

If progressive narratives around the breakdown of US-North Korean talks placed a familiar emphasis on inter-Korean cooperation, conservative narratives appeared to diverge into two streams. Along more traditional lines, some conservative editorials interpreted Washington's refusal to return to negotiations as a purposeful signal, not only to Pyongyang but to Seoul as well. A *Donga* editorial on February 13, for instance, suggested that the Moon administration had been operating too unilaterally, without coordination with and the trust of Washington. Specifically, it criticized Moon's initiative to develop inter-Korean economic projects (e.g., joint tourism), which could undermine the efficacy of the existing multilateral sanctions regime. Meanwhile, other more revisionist frames also appeared, expressing anxieties about what Washington's neglect might mean for denuclearization. A *Munwha* editorial on the same day argued that Washington's preference for the "status quo" on the Korean Peninsula would only embolden the North to advance its nuclear program. In these narratives, Washington was portrayed less as a trusted ally and more as a mounting liability.

Though these fractures in the traditional conservative narrative revealed the damage Trump had inflicted on US credibility, Biden's electoral victory helped reassure the South Korean conservative establishment of the importance and durability of the alliance. Rather than the "everything for everything" approach under Trump or "nothing for nothing" approach under Obama, Biden promised a "calibrated, practical approach to diplomacy with the North with the goal of eliminating the threat to the United States."⁴ Crucially, Biden rejected the "step by step" formulation, preferred by Moon, and reaffirmed denuclearization as the ultimate objective.⁵ This represented a major departure from Trump's more flexible strategy and, to the relief of many South Korean conservatives, a semblance of normalcy. For Moon, however, opportunities to upend the status quo on the Korean Peninsula appeared to be narrowing.

The growing domestic divergence between the two ideological camps over their preferred North Korea strategy manifested starkly around the 2020 anti-leaflet legislation. The progressive-majority national assembly had passed the "Development of Inter-Korean Relations Act," which barred any transfers of printed materials, money, and items across the border as well as loudspeaker broadcasts of anti-regime propaganda that had long been touted as a psychological warfare tactic. The controversy over the law's constitutionality reached its height when in April 2021, the Tom Lantos Human Rights Commission—a bipartisan caucus of the US House of Representatives—held a public hearing titled, "Civil and political rights in the Republic of Korea: Implications for human rights on the Peninsula." The hearing included five witnesses—including former South Korean ambassador to Russia Lee In-ho, two prominent human rights activists, and two policy commentators—who shared concerns about how criminalizing leaflet activities might excessively restrict freedom of speech in the South. Then

South Korean unification minister Cha Deok-cheol downplayed the impact of this event, noting that the commission has "no voting power," and that "the nature of its hearings is considered closer to a policy research panel."[6]

Partisan narratives in South Korea were divisive. Conservative media, including *Donga* and *Chosun*, portrayed the hearing as a broader indictment of Seoul. Their editorials argued that the Moon administration's concerns about offending North Korea had become excessive, outweighing the imperative to preserve and uphold freedom of expression in South Korea.[7] In particular, *Chosun* condemned Moon for legislating "on behalf of the Kims," asserting that the blueprints for an anti-leaflet law were "ordered" barely within four hours of complaints from Kim Yo-jong—North Korea's chief propagandist and Kim Jong-un's sister.[8] Progressive outlets, however, cast the hearing as both politically motivated and ideologically skewed. *Hankyoreh* urged the Moon administration to coordinate more actively with the US Congress to allow a more "balanced" discussion of human rights on the Korean Peninsula in the future.[9]

Conservative narratives around human rights abuses in North Korea—and correspondingly, their critique of Seoul's continued silence—gained broader resonance as Moon's tenure came to a close. On the tenth anniversary of Kim Jong-il's death, just as Kim Jong-un implored North Koreans to place "absolute trust" in him,[10] the UN General Assembly passed a resolution condemning North Korea for its human rights violations for the 17th consecutive year. In response, conservative outlet *Seoul Shinmun* called the Kim regime a "brutal fearocracy," linking the country's extreme poverty and diplomatic isolation to Kim's obsession with nuclear weapons.[11] Meanwhile, *Joongang Ilbo* argued that the failure of "byungjin" policy showed the inherent contradictions in simultaneously advancing the nuclear program and economic modernization; this delusion had been sustained and emboldened by the Moon administration's naivete.[12] In this vein, other conservative outlets such as *Segye* also urged Seoul to take a firmer and more coordinated stance on the issue, beginning by co-sponsoring multilateral resolutions on the North's misconduct.[13] Progressives, meanwhile, mostly echoed the administration's earlier talking points—namely, that condemning Pyongyang could harm diplomacy—but such narratives found little traction in the context of a long-deadlocked dialogue.

United States

While concerns about the health of the alliance accelerated during Trump's tenure, they also persisted under Biden. Trump's transactional worldview, combined with his general disregard for foreign policy institutions and norms, meant that the terms of the alliance were often put in doubt and derided as a "bad deal." Negotiations over defense cost-sharing and economic decoupling from China revealed that Trump prioritized short-term political gains from the alliance, more so than long-term strategic cooperation. And though Biden underscored the centrality of US allies to its grand strategic visions, his decisions on geoeconomics issues have sustained some tensions over the lingering "America First" subtext.

Trump's incessant demands for increased burden sharing and threats of unilateral action rattled the South Korean conservative foreign policy establishment. In April 2020, amid stalled negotiations over a new Special Measures Agreement (SMA), Seoul had proposed to fund the labor costs for Korean national employees in the US Forces Korea (USFK) who were placed on unpaid leave that month.[14] Though this proposal provided a welcome stop-gap measure, tensions continued to mount as Washington insisted on what many in Seoul believed were "excessive" demands, reaching as high as $5 billion.[15] (For reference, Seoul had to pay roughly $900 million for the year before.) Conservatives in South Korea questioned Trump's motives for threatening troop removal and reduction, despite intensifying rivalry with China and provocations from North Korea.[16] Some like *Donga* even warned of a potential breakdown in the alliance, and blamed Trump's isolationist, transactional approach for it.[17]

Meanwhile, Trump's pressure on allies to decouple from China also provoked partisan debates. While most conservatives continued to insist that the alliance must take precedence—or that there was "no alternative"[18]—some conservative commentators began to question the utility of total balancing against China, arguing that any "unreasonable demands" should be resisted. Some, for instance, asserted that joining the US strategy to contain China would pose too heavy a cost on South Korea. Rather than decoupling, it recommended a longer-term structural effort to diversify South Korea's economic ties to protect it from the broader competitive dynamics. This was more aligned with the mainstream progressive narrative, which underscored the importance of hedging and restraint in South Korean foreign policy.[19] For progressives, US efforts to forge an ideological economic bloc—as in Trump's proposal for an Economic Prosperity Network (EPN)—were anachronistic and unnecessarily hostile to China.[20] It was not in South Korea's national interest to support such ideological bifurcation of the global market.

Though Biden sought to restore confidence in the alliance, his pragmatism—and diminished appetite for interventionism by the United States in general—posed questions about its shifting boundaries. On the one hand, Biden promised to reinvigorate the alliance network in Asia and strengthen "integrated deterrence." This meant bolstering the production of and access to allied defense capabilities by minilateral or multilateral institutions (e.g., the AUKUS partnership, which was announced in September 2021). It also meant closer coordination of defense priorities by means of routine summitry and working-level dialogues, much of which had eroded under Trump's more callous approach to alliance management. On the other hand, Biden also promoted self-strengthening efforts of the allies and, to this end, tolerated greater strategic autonomy. For instance, he agreed to removing the 1979 US-Korea Ballistic Missile Guidelines, which would allow Seoul to develop advanced strike capabilities as well as pursue its space ambitions.[21]

Yet, the extent to which these two approaches were compatible was not always clear, and the tensions were visible when it came to the US Indo-Pacific Strategy and the roles that Washington expected its allies to play in countering China. Indeed, much like Trump, Biden explicitly named China as a challenge to the region's rules-based order.[22] Though some had criticized the strategy in its early stages of development for stoking a Cold-War-style confrontation with China,[23] it had since garnered bipartisan consensus in the United States. In February 2022, the Biden administration released an official document on the Indo-Pacific Strategy, emphasizing the role that "like-minded" partners played in its implementation.[24] Combined with his "Summit for Democracy," Biden's regional strategy appeared to take a more conspicuously ideological turn, foreshadowing a clash of worldviews against a rising, authoritarian China.[25]

This resulted in two sets of concerns, particularly among progressives, in South Korea. First, Trump's transactionalism and its underlying logic—"Americans before allies"—had become a mainstream foreign policy attitude of the American public. Given Biden's own, more domestic focus, the vestiges of "America First" suggested that more would be expected of allies abroad. Second, the ideological bent of Biden's grand strategy naturally squeezed the space for strategic autonomy in Seoul, even as Washington encouraged the self-strengthening of allies. This meant a tight balancing act for Moon, who sought to exercise greater autonomy in South Korea's foreign policy decisions but also preempt any charges—particularly from the conservative opposition—that he was undermining allied initiatives.

Debates over these broader concerns inflamed over two issues in particular. Bilaterally, the developments around the renegotiated SMA continued to generate friction. On March 9, the Ministry of Foreign Affairs announced that South Korea and the US agreed on a six-year 11th SMA. South Korea's contribution for 2020 would remain at the current level and from 2021 to 2025 would be increased in line with its annual defense budget rise. Conservative outlets welcomed the news, urging the two allies to focus on improving joint defense posture. *Joongang* also recommended using specific cost areas, rather than the overall stationing costs as a benchmark for making future cost-sharing decisions.[26] Meanwhile, progressive media and organizations criticized the agreement as "unacceptably expensive, humiliating, and harming national sovereignty in budgeting."[27] *Kyunghyang* described the deal as "not even remotely fair and balanced," citing the cost estimate for 2025 of 1.5 trillion won, which would be comparable to Trump's earlier demand of a 50% increase.[28] In these narratives, the contention lay in the perceived fairness of the deal, in particular the proportionality of the cost increases for Seoul over the years.

Multilaterally, partisans debated the Quad and South Korea's role in it. Since its reintroduction in 2017, the Quad had become increasingly institutionalized as a mechanism for regional governance, with a shared objective of building "a region that is free, open, inclusive, healthy, anchored by democratic values, and unconstrained by coercion."[29] The first summit on March 12, 2021, deepened what had been more speculative discussions about the Quad's implications for regional security. For many conservatives, South Korea's absence in the Quad was a true policy failure and its participation as a "Quad-Plus" partner, the next-best imperative. *Segye Ilbo* admonished: "Amid US worries about Korea's tilting toward China, there is no time to spare, but to join the grouping as a Quad-Plus partner"—a decision that would "strengthen not only the ROK-US alliance, but also security against North Korea."[30] Some, such as *Joongang,* acknowledged the constraints South Korea faced, given its trade dependencies on China.[31] But the overarching message remained uniform: Seoul needed to align more closely and clearly with Washington; otherwise, it risked being left out of critical discussions, including on North Korean denuclearization.[32] Unsurprisingly, the progressives were less enthused by the development of the Quad and even more ambivalent about the nature of Seoul's participation in it. *Hankyoreh* explicitly noted that the Quad was designed to "constrain China," and called on the Moon administration to act "prudently." None, however, specified what this entailed.[33]

In this divisive climate, the United States held the first Summit for Democracy in December 2021 with leaders from 110 countries, including South Korea. The virtual summit sought to establish and announce collective commitments by attendees to defend democracy against authoritarianism, fight corruption, and promote respect for human rights. Chinese Ambassador to South Korea Xing Haiming vehemently criticized the summit, stating "China resolutely opposes fake democracy that weaponizes democracy, interferes with internal affairs of other countries and suppresses development."[34] Sensing Beijing's discomfort, Moon refrained from any remarks that might implicate China but pointed to populism, extremism, and fake news as major threats against democracy.[35]

This event—and Seoul's ambivalent status—sustained narrative polarization among partisans. Conservatives such as *Chosun Ilbo* stressed that Moon's emphasis on fake news was not aligned with Washington's framing of authoritarian advances.[36] Similarly, *Seoul Kyungjae* opined that South Korea's "tightrope diplomacy," attempting to maintain a balance between two superpowers, would result in the loss of trust from both sides.[37] Choosing a side was better than losing both. On the other hand, progressive voices like *Hankyoreh* expressed concern over the summit's ideological bent, dividing the world into good and evil and depriving countries of opportunities to cooperate on imminent threats, including the COVID-19 pandemic and climate change, regardless of ideological differences.[38] In this way, partisan narratives about South Korean grand strategy appeared to veer further in opposing paths.

China

With the hardening of anti-Chinese attitudes in South Korea due to COVID-19 and the intensifying US-China competition, Moon's space for foreign policy autonomy was shrinking and relations with China tense. Washington pressed Seoul to play a larger role in the US-led regional architecture, while Beijing reminded Seoul, to varying degrees of intensity, of the harm it could incur for siding with Washington. Seoul needed to respond to this changing strategic environment, but the exact contours of its response stayed mostly vague.

In broader terms, partisan debates surrounded decisions about the shape and timeline of Seoul's realignment. Progressives preferred strategic ambiguity under the Moon administration as a guiding principle. *Hankyoreh* and *Kyunghyang* argued that South Korea must pursue "balanced" diplomacy between Washington and Beijing rather than picking sides, given China's essential role—whether constructive or destructive—for reviving inter-Korean diplomacy and the domestic economy. They voiced concern about joining a series of US-led initiatives in the region and the possibility that this could trigger another downward spiral in South Korea's relations with China (after a difficult recovery from the THAAD dispute). Progressives thus advised the Moon administration to seek balance and urged Biden to respect South Korea's "unique circumstances," which make the prospects of participating in Washington's "anti-China coalitions" untenable.[39]

By contrast, conservatives doubled down on the traditional frame of alliance centrality in South Korean foreign policy and promoted strategic clarity in Seoul. In the immediate aftermath of Biden's electoral victory, *Chosun*, *Joongang*, and *Donga* all asserted that the alliance provided a basis for strengthening cooperation with China. In a series of editorials, conservatives stressed that strategic ambiguity was no longer defensible and that a "values-based" foreign policy would best serve the country's national interests. In particular, they underlined the significance of repairing South Korea-US-Japan trilateral cooperation on broader shared challenges, including global pandemics, climate change, supply chains, and emerging technologies, as well as specific security aims that require better allied coordination such as nuclear deterrence against North Korea.

Domestic political dynamics favored the conservative narrative in at least two ways. First, most of the South Korean public blamed China for both the emergence of the COVID-19 pandemic and the subsequent global economic chaos. Anti-Chinese sentiments ran high, this meant that South Koreans were less likely to punish Seoul for crossing Beijing's lines. Second, the public saw little prospect of de-escalation in the US-China competition: an Asan survey showed that more than half the respondents (56.8%) saw their rivalry as hegemonic in nature, rather than tied to specific domains of competition such as trade. Importantly, the same survey showed that, when it came to choosing sides, South Koreans ultimately favored the US (73.2%) over China (15.7%).[40] These twin developments, if true, boded ill for strategic ambiguity: the public was increasingly anti-China and believed the competition was deeply entrenched. For them, the choice became clearer as it became more necessary: Seoul needed to side with the United States.

One area in which the US-China competition was felt sharply in South Korea concerned the global supply chain governance. In February 2021, Biden signed the executive order 14017 on America's Supply Chains.[41] Showing a chip in his hand, he underscored the potential impact of a semiconductor shortfall and the importance of securing the resilience of its supply chains. Subsequently, at a virtual CEO summit on semiconductor and supply chain resilience, he quoted from a letter from 23 senators that said, "the Chinese Communist Party aggressively plans to reorient and dominate the semiconductor supply chain," adding at last that "[it] is not waiting."[42]

Unsurprisingly, this generated anxieties in South Korea about the implications of supply chain restructuring for high-technology industries of which it is a leader, especially semiconductors. Major media outlets, whether conservative or progressive, expressed serious concern over the growing uncertainty in the semiconductor industry and the possibility that the US would restrict China by attracting major semiconductor-producing countries.

Conservative outlets criticized the Moon administration for lack of foresight and strategy. *Chosun*, in this light, urgently called for improving public-private partnership to cope with the impending US-China technology competition. It noted a recent US proposal to ban exports to China of semiconductor manufacturing equipment, which would damage existing operations by Samsung Electronics and SK Hynix in China.[43] Meanwhile, these companies may choose to establish production lines in the United States as opposed to domestically. Noting that Samsung Electronics was one of the participants at the virtual CEO summit held at the White House on April 12, *Joongang* urged the Moon government to develop a survival strategy by mobilizing all diplomatic resources rather than leaving the responsibility solely to private companies.[44]

Progressives, by contrast, proposed greater domestic investment. *Hankyoreh* editorialized over the pros and cons of Biden's approach to expanding the semiconductor supply chain. It pointed out that the expansion of tax benefits could be seen as an opportunity for Samsung Electronics, which was considering the establishment of additional factories in the United States. Yet, it also warned of negative effects of the competition such as reduction in domestic investment and loss of job opportunities.[45] *Kyunghyang* similarly argued that the effective countermeasure in this context is to secure the best technology. South Korea needed to invest more in the research and development of semiconductors as well as the localization of their production.[46]

Tensions with China seemed to subside in November 2021—after months of escalation—when Biden and Xi held their first virtual summit.[47] While, overall, positively assessed in Seoul, the summit left no impressions of a meaningful rapprochement, but foreshadowed a continued challenge for South Korea.[48] This helped to deepen the partisan rift over policy prescriptions, as some conservatives began to push for strategic clarity and progressives doubled down on strategic ambiguity.

Conservatives made the case for a values-based reorientation of South Korean foreign policy. For too long, South Korea had played the role of a balancer, trying to walk the diplomatic tightrope between the United States and China. Now that their competition was entering a new phase of escalation, it was time that South Korea finally made a choice. In this line of argument, *Segye Ilbo* asserted that a realignment based on values of democracy, market economy, and human rights would necessitate curbing South Korea's reliance on China.[49] Other conservative voices were tamer, recognizing the difficulty this poses for Seoul. *Joongang* and *Donga* thus supported a more "sophisticated diplomatic strategy," which would allow South Korea to navigate the protracted US-China competition even as it made difficult choices.[50]

Progressives were, meanwhile, on the defensive, with no clear guidelines for how to maintain or advance strategic ambiguity. Instead, they emphasized the positive outcomes of the summit.[51] *Kyunghyang* noted that, despite their standoff on many issues—including human rights in Hong Kong and Xinjiang, freedom of navigation in the South China Sea, and trade practices—the two leaders were able to agree on a shared need for crisis and risk management.[52] The progressive *Hankyoreh* similarly posited that cooperation between the US, China, and the international community was required to maintain peace in Taiwan and Northeast Asia.[53] Progressives thus urged the two great powers to engage in better communication and mutually responsible conduct, which would help prevent unintended escalation and an accidental clash.

Japan

If Moon had been anxious to work out the differences with North Korea, the United States, and China, he showed little interest in mending ties with Japan. Since 2019 when Japan removed South Korea from its "whitelist" of favored trading partners for disputes over "history issues"—in this case, South Korean court rulings over Japanese wartime forced labor—the two had been locked in tit-for-tat reprisals over trade and military arrangements. Though more overtures were made in the wake of Biden's election and leadership transitions in Japan, they remained largely tepid and bilateral relations did not recover.

There were some efforts to improve ties following the transition in Japanese leadership to Suga Yoshihide. In a press briefing, presidential spokesperson Kang Minseok said that the president is ready to sit down anytime with the government of Japan.[54] On September 24, 2020, Moon and Suga had their first official phone call. This was the first conversation between the leaders of the two countries since the Korea-Japan-China trilateral summit held in Chengdu in December 2019. Moon proposed that the two countries work together to find an "optimum" solution to the wartime forced labor issue. Suga also noted various pending issues between the two countries, including historical issues, and expressed hope for establishing bilateral relations in a forward-looking way.[55]

But talks made little progress. During the working-level dialogue in Seoul, the two sides mostly repeated their original positions on the issue of forced labor. Kim Jung-han, director-general for Asian and Pacific affairs of the foreign ministry, emphasized that the "Japanese government and the defendant companies need to show a sincerer attitude in order to resolve the issue." Kim also called for the Japanese government to withdraw its "unjust" export restrictions, and stressed the need for Tokyo to "respond actively" to Seoul's efforts to host the Korea-Japan-China trilateral summit within this year.[56] In response, Takizaki Shigeki, director-general of the Asian and Oceanic Affairs Bureau of Japan's foreign ministry, strongly urged Seoul to find a solution for the forced labor issue in a way that does not liquidate the seized assets of Japanese firms.[57]

If conservatives mainly repeated the need for cooperation between the two, progressives questioned its prospects. Indeed, some urged both leaders not to be chained to past issues and emotions and stressed the importance of cooperation in addressing COVID-19, nuclear-armed North Korea, and the intense US-China strategic rivalry. *Donga* also recalled Suga's earlier remarks that "Ignoring a neighboring country and denying its history will not serve any strategic interest for either of the countries" and expressed hopes that he will open up a "new horizon" of ROK-Japan relations.[58] But *Kyunghyang* expressed skepticism that Japan was in fact invested in mending ties. Citing a Kyodo News report that the Japanese government threatened to boycott the trilateral summit unless South Korea prevents the liquidation of Japanese corporate assets in South Korea, *Kyunghayng* argued that Tokyo would not be making such an "unreasonable argument" if it took reconciliation seriously.[59]

Meanwhile, controversies continued to arise. On January 8, the Seoul Central District Court ruled that the Japanese government must pay KRW 100 million to each of the 12 plaintiffs who were victims of wartime sexual slavery during the Japanese colonial period. This is the first court ruling in South Korea that recognizes the Japanese government's responsibility for the victimization of the "comfort women." The Japanese side did not appear in court, citing sovereign immunity. However, the verdict stated that the "theory of 'state immunity' was not established for states that violate international peremptory norms and cause grave harm to individuals in another country to be provided with an opportunity to hide behind a theory and avoid providing compensation and indemnification."[60] The next day, Kang Kyung-wha and her Japanese counterpart Motegi Toshimitsu had a telephone exchange for about 20 minutes to discuss the court ruling, during which Motegi refused to acknowledge the ruling.[61] Tensions appeared to be reaching new heights.

Partisan narratives framed the issue in different ways. Progressives saw the issues over court rulings as a matter of international legal responsibility. *Hankyoreh* wrote that the South Korean government had no choice but to respect the judiciary's ruling and that the Japanese government must acknowledge its historical and legal responsibility for its inhumane past.[62] Conservatives, meanwhile, focused on the strategic implications of the frayed ties. Though *Donga* criticized Suga for his "irresponsibility," it also argued that the Moon administration had failed to propose an alternative to the bilateral agreement on "comfort women" victims in 2015.[63] The onus, thus, fell on Seoul to initiate dialogue.

The tit-for-tat disputes persisted even as Japan underwent another leadership change, this time to the former foreign minister Kishida Fumio. Just as in his congratulatory call to Suga, Moon reminded Kishida of the differing interpretations of the scope of the 1965 Basic Treaty and suggested accelerating the search for a diplomatic solution to the forced labor and "comfort women" issues. Controversies continued to emerge from both sides, as Kishida deliberately left out mentioning South Korea in his first press conference[64] and sent his first ritual offering to the Yasukuni Shrine,[65] and a South Korean official made a public visit to the disputed territory, Dokdo (known in Japan as Takeshima).[66] Still, the balance of blame in South Korean media coverage fell predominantly on Japan, whose continued historical revisionism—in listing Dokdo as its own territory in the Defense White Paper, for example—was increasingly blatant.[67] In what are commonly polarizing partisan narratives, Japan proved to be an enduring source of consensus for South Koreans.[68]

The Yoon Presidency

In March 2022, the conservative candidate—and political novice—Yoon Suk-yeol was elected president. Speculation of a radical reversal of "strategic ambiguity" abounded, given Yoon's electoral promises, including "clarity and boldness" as well as a "commitment to principles."[69] More specifically, Yoon argued that South Korea must "rise to the challenge of being [...] a 'global pivotal state,' one that advances freedom, peace, and prosperity through liberal democratic values and substantial cooperation."[70] Many expected a closer realignment of South Korean foreign policy with the Indo-Pacific framework of the United States, and with it, a diminished priority given to diplomacy with North Korea and engagement with China. This also meant more concerted efforts to reconcile with Japan, with whom strained ties over history issues had impeded cooperation.

Four developments, in particular, sustained and intensified South Korean debates surrounding South Korea's evolving role in international and regional security, and especially the scope of its integration into the US-led regional framework: (1) the Ukraine war, (2) Abe's assassination, (3) Biden's foreign economic policy, and (4) Yoon's nuclear ambitions. Assessments of Yoon's performance were mixed in each respect, further driving partisan rifts in South Korea over its preferred grand strategy.

The first major development was the war in Ukraine. Indeed, though criticisms of Putin abounded in South Korean media, partisans remained divided over South Korea's obligations. This became particularly salient in April 2022, when Ukrainian President Volodymyr Zelensky implored South Korean national assemblymen to send weapons, analogizing Ukraine's plight to the Korean War.[71] But the Ministry of National Defense decided against it, citing the security situation on the Korean Peninsula.[72] This, for conservatives, was yet another strategic blunder. According to *Kukmin Ilbo*, Seoul was taking few proactive measures to protect the democratic order and national sovereignty, as evidenced by its late participation in the multilateral sanctions regime against Russia.[73] Progressives, meanwhile, found the decision to limit military support to Ukraine prudent. *Hankook Ilbo* argued that such involvement would only raise the risks of escalation on the Korean Peninsula, given North Korea's support of Russia.[74] These partisan narratives highlighted the inevitability of viewing international and regional security through the lens of the inter-Korean conflict.

The second source of shock was the assassination of Abe and its implications for Japan's "normalization." While South Koreans, across partisan lines, condemned the act of political terrorism, much coverage was swift to note the momentum Abe's death might provide the right-wing movement in Japan to amend the pacifist constitution. This was a double-edged sword for South Korea, for whom Japan's more active role in the region could help counter North Korean threats but also rekindle memories of Japanese aggression—much of which Japan had begun to deny and distort.[75] For the South Korean progressives in particular, Japan's trajectory toward "normalization" boded ill for diplomacy on both "history problems" and regional security issues, including inter-Korean peace.[76] In these narratives, the prospects of cooperation with Japan—whether bilateral or trilateral—appeared dim, despite Seoul's ambitions to deepen it.

The third source of friction was the Inflation Reduction Act (IRA). Under the act, new tax credits for adopting electric vehicles (EV) did not apply to those assembled outside the United States. It was highly likely that this would negatively impact South Korea's major automakers, including Hyundai and Kia Motors, which recorded the second-highest market share in the EV market in the United States during the first half of 2022. The law was heavily criticized in South Korea—across partisan lines—for its discriminatory nature,[77] violation of the KORUS free trade agreement,[78] and unilateral approach to international trade.[79] As the centrist *Hankook Ilbo* put it, the IRA did not only violate the principles of a free-market economy but also undermined solidarity between allies.[80] Implicit in these narratives was a need for Seoul to remain vigilant against the lingering "America First" impulses of the Biden administration.

The final source of contention was the South Korean pursuit of tactical nuclear weapons. In October 2022, amid the increasing North Korean provocations, South Korea's president and some members of the ruling People Power Party (PPP) raised the possibility and importance of redeploying US tactical nuclear weapons to South Korea.[81] The US reaction was mostly dismissive. US Ambassador to South Korea Philip Goldberg said during a public forum that "all this talk about tactical nuclear weapons […] is irresponsible and dangerous."[82] Amid visible fissures over the issue, South Korean newspapers called for greater caution and coordination with Washington. Underscoring the enormous repercussions that could follow, *Joongang Ilbo* asserted that this was a decision South Korea cannot make independently. Instead, it advocated for strengthening US extended deterrence by preparing and reviewing detailed, joint response scenarios.[83] The centrist *Hankook*

Ilbo similarly warned that any irresponsible decisions in this regard would only worsen South Korea's security.[84]

South Korea's indecision became particularly noticeable when, in mid-December 2022, Japan's Kishida administration released its revised defense papers: the New Security Strategy, the National Defense Strategy, and the Defense Buildup Program. Together, the papers signaled "great transformation" in Japan's posture from pacifism to activism, in lock step with the United States' evolving regional security framework.[85] This entailed pursuing counterstrike capabilities, including a long-range strike capability; doubling the country's defense budget from 1 percent of its GDP to 2 percent within five years; creating a combined forces command within the Japan Self-Defense Forces; and deepening its military cooperation with the United States. There was no doubt Japan intended to side with the United States.

Amid growing tensions on the Korean Peninsula, Japan's military ambitions posed a dilemma for South Korea. On the conservative side, Japan's "normalization" was a boon for regional security. In this line, *Kukmin Ilbo* argued that cooperation with Japan was now "inevitable," even if it undermined South's efforts to improve inter-Korean relations.[86] *Joongang Ilbo* similarly asserted that stepping up cooperation with the US and Japan was a top priority to prepare for the worst security environment since the Korean War.[87] Crucially, in these narratives, China and North Korea were the culprits.[88] Thus, while acknowledging the anxieties around Japan's "old intentions," conservatives criticized China for its failure to play a constructive role in the North Korean denuclearization agenda, providing Japan the rationale—if not pretext—to rearm.[89]

On the progressive side, Japan's rearmament only helped to trigger an arms race in Northeast Asia. *Hankook Ilbo* argued that Japan's "aggressive" security strategy, combined with North Korea's missile threat, would bring a tectonic change in the region.[90] Likewise, *Seoul Shinmun* admonished that Japan's new military ambitions foreshadowed its unsolicited intervention in the event of war on the Korean Peninsula.[91] Meanwhile, progressives also picked up on Japan's sovereignty claims over Dokdo (known as Takeshima in Japan) in the documents.[92] *Hankook Ilbo* noted that Japan's repeated territorial claims were not only unfair but also provocative and counterproductive for the recovery of South Korea-Japan relations.[93] Calling it "deplorable," *Hankyoreh* also demanded Japanese genuine contrition for its colonial aggression.[94] In these narratives, Japan's reorientation signaled not a reaction to the worsening threat environment but a dangerous misrecognition of its history.

It was in this climate of heightening tension that the Yoon administration introduced its own, much-anticipated Indo-Pacific Strategy. The document established key tasks for safeguarding a rule-based international order and promoting regional cooperation in areas of non-proliferation, counter-terrorism, cybersecurity, public health, and supply chain resilience.[95] While broadly appreciated, many also noticed that it characterized China as "a key partner" with which South Korea will seek a sounder and more mature relationship. That was in stark contrast with Japan's identically named report, which called China an "unprecedented strategic challenge."

Partisan narratives remained contentious but for different reasons. For the conservatives, the report did not go far enough to address the threats to values posed by China and North Korea. *Segye Ilbo*, for instance, asserted that Seoul cannot remain muted about their human rights violations. This indecision could render Seoul's commitment to values mere rhetoric.[96] Meanwhile, the progressives questioned what the new strategy meant for South Korea's ties with China. *Hankyoreh* found some reassurance in this regard, noting that Seoul's portrayal of China indicated a continuity in balancing values and interests.[97] Even the more centrist *Hankook Ilbo* similarly remarked that the wordings of the report reflected the indispensable need of cooperating with China on pressing issues, from North Korea's provocations to a looming economic recession.[98] Though widely perceived as timely, the specificities surrounding Seoul's commitment to values and its implications for relations with China remained somewhat open-ended.

Indeed, South Korea's emphasis on inclusivity as the foundation of its strategy—and promises that it "neither targets nor excludes any specific nation"—raised doubts about its implementation. This principle of inclusivity reflected South Korea's unchanged reality of trade dependency, both in general and more specifically in relation to China, and peninsular threats that precluded diplomatically alienating China.[99] Yet, it also challenged Yoon's values-based approach, which sought to maintain and strengthen the rules-based order that—according to its like-minded ally and partners—China was actively undermining. These contradictions were shaped by the lack of domestic consensus around South Korea's grand strategy and the appropriate scope of realignment.[100] Overall, the ongoing ideological bifurcation of regional security and economy boded ill for Yoon's ambitions to simultaneously pursue inclusivity and clarity.

Conclusion

The years 2020–2022 revealed both the changing ambitions and lingering limitations of South Korean foreign policy. If the transition from Moon-era "strategic ambiguity" to Yoon-era "strategic clarity" illustrated Seoul's desire to play a more active role in regional and international security, Yoon's continued reluctance to estrange China exposed Seoul's unresolved vulnerabilities. Indeed, there were long-standing, structural impediments to a more decisive realignment under Yoon, including North Korean security issues and South Korean economic demands—both of which commanded China's cooperation—as well as the unsettled "history problems" with Japan that compromised trilateral initiatives. Meanwhile, newer developments, such as the insular turn in American trade and technology policy and growing public support for indigenous nuclear weapons in South Korea, also complicated Seoul's Indo-Pacific strategy. Together, these issues sustained partisan debates around the specific configurations of strategic clarity under Yoon and the appropriate nature and scope of South Korea's realignment—between an enduring progressive vision of a critical balancer in the region and an emerging conservative one of a "pivotal state" in the maintenance of the liberal international order.

Notes

1. "N.K. Leader Says No Reason to Keep Moratorium on ICBM Tests, Warns of 'New Strategic Weapon'," Yonhap, January 1, 2020, https://en.yna.co.kr/view/AEN20200101001452325?section=nk/nk.
2. "Trump Voices Confidence in N.K. Leader Despite New Threat," Yonhap, January 1, 2020. https://en.yna.co.kr/view/AEN20200101003252325?section=nk/nk.
3. Bethany Allen-Ebrahimian, "Special Report: Trump's U.S.-China Transformation," Axios, January 19, 2021, https://www.axios.com/2021/01/19/trump-china-policy-special-report.
4. John Hudson and Ellen Nakashima, "Biden Administration Forges New Path on North Korea Crisis in Wake of Trump and Obama Failures," *Washington Post*, April 30, 2021, https://www.washingtonpost.com/national-security/biden-administration-forges-new-path-on-north-korea-crisis-in-wake-of-trump-and-obama-failures/2021/04/30/c8bef4f2-a9a9-11eb-b166-174b63ea6007_story.html.
5. Robert Einhorn, "The Rollout of the Biden Administration's North Korea Policy Review Leaves Unanswered Questions," *Brookings*, May 4, 2021, https://www.brookings.edu/blog/order-from-chaos/2021/05/04/the-rollout-of-the-biden-administrations-north-korea-policy-review-leaves-unanswered-questions/.
6. "Unification Ministry Downplays US Congressional Hearing on Leaflet Ban," KBS, April 9, 2021, https://world.kbs.co.kr/service/news_view.htm?lang=e&Seq_Code=160733.
7. *Donga Ilbo*, April 12, 2021.
8. *Chosun Ilbo*, April 10, 2021.
9. *The Hankyoreh*, April 14, 2021.
10. "Kim's Decade of Rule," *The Korea Times*, December 19, 2021, https://www.koreatimes.co.kr/www/opinion/2021/12/202_320815.html.
11. *Seoul Shinmun*, December 18, 2021.
12. *Joongang Ilbo*, December 18, 2021.
13. *Segye Ilbo*, December 19, 2021.
14. *Donga Ilbo*, April 26, 2020.
15. "Exclusive: Inside Trump's Standoff with South Korea Over Defense Costs," Reuters, April 10, 2020, https://www.reuters.com/article/us-usa-southkorea-trump-defense-exclusiv/exclusive-inside-trumps-standoff-with-south-korea-over-defense-costs-idUSKCN21S1W7.
16. *Hankook Ilbo*, June 16, 2020.
17. *Donga Ilbo*, June 24, 2020.
18. *Chosun Ilbo*, June 10, 2020.
19. *Hankyoreh*, May 18, 2020.
20. *Kyunghyang Shinmun*, May 18, 2020.
21. Tom Corben and Peter K. Lee, "Fancy Footwork: Biden's Two-Step Approach to Indo-Pacific Allies," *The Diplomat*, March 16, 2022, https://thediplomat.com/2022/03/fancy-footwork-bidens-two-step-approach-to-indo-pacific-allies/.
22. The 2017 U.S. National Security Strategy labeled China a revisionist state and a strategic competitor. White House, "National Security Strategy," December 2017, https://trumpwhitehouse.archives.gov/wp-content/uploads/2017/12/NSS-Final-12-18-2017-0905.pdf.

23 Michael Swaine, "A Counterproductive Cold War with China," *Foreign Affairs*, March 2, 2018, https://www.foreignaffairs.com/articles/china/2018-03-02/counter-productive-cold-war-china.
24 White House, "Fact Sheet: Indo-Pacific Strategy of the United States," February 11, 2022, https://www.whitehouse.gov/briefing-room/speeches-remarks/2022/02/11/fact-sheet-indo-pacific-strategy-of-the-united-states/.
25 U.S. Department of State, "The Summit for Democracy," November 2022, https://www.state.gov/summit-for-democracy/.
26 *Joongang Ilbo*, March 9, 2021.
27 *Hankook Kyungjae*, March 16, 2021.
28 *Kyunghyang Shinmun*, March 11, 2021.
29 White House, "Quad Leaders' Joint Statement: 'The Spirit of the Quad'," March 12, 2021, https://www.whitehouse.gov/briefing-room/statements-releases/2021/03/12/quad-leaders-joint-statement-the-spirit-of-the-quad/.
30 *Segye Ilbo*, March 10, 2021.
31 *Joongang Ilbo*, March 11, 2021.
32 *Joongang Ilbo*, March 15, 2021.
33 *Hankyoreh*, March 14, 2021.
34 *Maeil Kyungjae*, December 8, 2021.
35 "Remarks by President Moon Jae-in at Virtual Summit for Democracy," 대한민국 정책브리핑, December 11, 2021, https://english1.president.go.kr/BriefingSpeeches/Speeches/1118.
36 *Chosun Ilbo*, December 11, 2021.
37 *Sedaily*, December 10, 2021.
38 *Hankyoreh*, December 10, 2021.
39 *Hankyoreh*, May 18, 2020; *Kyunghyang Shinmun*, November 5, 2020.
40 J. James Kim and Kang Chungku, "The U.S.-China Competition in South Korean Public Eyes," Asan Institute, August 25, 2020, http://en.asaninst.org/contents/the-u-s-china-competition-in-south-korean-public-eyes/.
41 Country Report: South Korea (May 2021), *The Asan Forum,* April 27, 2021.
42 White House, "Remarks by President Biden at a Virtual CEO Summit on Semiconductor and Supply Chain Resilience," April 12, 2021, https://www.whitehouse.gov/briefing-room/speeches-remarks/2021/04/12/remarks-by-president-biden-at-a-virtual-ceo-summit-on-semiconductor-and-supply-chain-resilience/.
43 *Chosun Ilbo*, April 14, 2021.
44 *Joongang Ilbo*, April 14, 2021.
45 *Hankyoreh*, April 13, 2021.
46 *Kyunghyang Shinmun*, April 13, 2021.
47 White House, "Readout of President Biden's Virtual Meeting with President Xi Jinping of the People's Republic of China," November 16, 2021, https://www.whitehouse.gov/briefing-room/statements-releases/2021/11/16/readout-of-president-bidens-virtual-meeting-with-president-xi-jinping-of-the-peoples-republic-of-china/.
48 *Yonhap News*, November 16, 2021.
49 *Seoul Kyungjae*, November 17, 2021.
50 *Joongang Ilbo*, November 17, 2021; *Donga Ilbo*, November 17, 2021.
51 *Hankook Ilbo*, November 17, 2021.
52 *Kyunghyang Shinmun*, November 16, 2021.
53 *Hankyoreh*, November 17, 2021.
54 *Maeil Kyungjae*, September 16, 2020.
55 *Hankyung*, September 24, 2020.
56 Ministry of Foreign Affairs, "Outcome of ROK-Japan Director-General-Level Consultation (Oct. 29)," October 30, 2020, https://www.mofa.go.kr/eng/brd/m_5676/view.do?seq=321319&srchFr=&srchTo=&srchWord=&srchTp=&amp

;multi_itm_seq=0&itm_seq_1=0&itm_seq_2=0&company_cd=&company_nm=&page=1&titleNm=.
57 *Chosun Ilbo*, October 30, 2020.
58 *Donga Ilbo*, September 15, 2020.
59 *Kyunghyang Shinmun,* October 13, 2020; *Kyunghyang Shinmun,* October 14, 2020.
60 *Hankyoreh*, January 11, 2021.
61 *Chosun Ilbo,* February 3, 2023.
62 *Hankyoreh,* January 11, 2021.
63 *Donga Ilbo,* January 9, 2021.
64 *Kyunghyang Shinmun*, October 5, 2021.
65 *Segye Ilbo*, October 17, 2021.
66 *Hankook Ilbo*, November 19, 2021.
67 *Hankook Ilbo*, November 18, 2021.
68 *Donga Ilbo*, November 18, 2021.
69 Yoon Suk-yeol, "South Korea Needs to Step Up," *Foreign Affairs*, February 8, 2022, https://www.foreignaffairs.com/articles/south-korea/2022-02-08/south-korea-needs-step.
70 Ibid.
71 The Presidential Office of Ukraine, "Speech by the President of Ukraine in the National Assembly of the Republic of Korea," April 11, 2022, https://www.president.gov.ua/en/news/promova-prezidenta-ukrayini-v-nacionalnij-asambleyi-respubli-74257.
72 *Hankyoreh*, April 11, 2022.
73 *Kukmin Ilbo*, April 12, 2022.
74 *Hankook Ilbo*, April 12, 2022.
75 *Donga Ilbo*, July 11, 2022.
76 *Kyunghyang Shinmun*, July 10, 2022.
77 *Segye Ilbo,* September 6, 2022.
78 *Joongang Ilbo*, September 2, 2022.
79 *Hankyoreh*, September 8, 2022.
80 *Hankook Ilbo*, September 7, 2022.
81 "김기현 '국회의원도 전쟁터 나가야…육십 넘었지만 총 들고 나올 것'," KBS, October 19, 2022, https://news.kbs.co.kr/news/view.do?ncd=5581824.
82 "Talk of Tactical Nuke Redeployment 'Irresponsible': US Ambassador," *Korea Herald*, October 18, 2022, https://www.koreaherald.com/view.php?ud=20221018000650; "(LEAD) U.S. Remains Open to Dialogue with N. Korea Despite Kim Remarks: NSC Spokesperson," *Yonhap News Agency*, October 12, 2022, https://en.yna.co.kr/view/AEN20221012000251325.
83 *Joongang Ilbo*, October 14, 2022.
84 *Hankook Ilbo*, October 13, 2022.
85 "日, '반격 능력' 보유 결정…안보정책 대전환," Yonhap, December 16, 2022, https://www.yna.co.kr/view/AKR20221216063751073?site=mapping_related.
86 *Kookmin Ilbo,* December 19, 2022.
87 *Joongang Ilbo*, December 19, 2022.
88 *Hankook Kyungjae*, December 18, 2022.
89 *Maeil Kyungjae*, December 18, 2022.
90 *Hankook Ilbo*, December 19, 2022.
91 *Seoul Shinmun*, December 18, 2022.
92 Ministry of Foreign Affairs, "일본 국가안보전략(NSS)의 독도 기술에 대한 외교부 대변인 논평," December 16, 2022, https://www.mofa.go.kr/www/brd/m_4080/view.do?seq=373173.
93 *Hankook Ilbo*, December 17, 2022.
94 *Hankyoreh*, December 16, 2022.

95 "윤 대통령 '자유·평화·번영 3대 비전으로 인도-태평양 전략 이행'," 대한민국 정책브리핑, November 11, 2022, https://www.korea.kr/news/policyNewsView.do?newsId=148908196.
96 *Segye Ilbo*, December 28, 2022.
97 *Hankyoreh*, December 28, 2022.
98 *Hankook Ilbo*, December 29, 2022.
99 "What South Korea's Indo-Pacific Strategy Says About the Development of a 'Yoon Doctrine'," Council on Foreign Relations, December 29, 2022, https://www.cfr.org/blog/what-south-koreas-indo-pacific-strategy-says-about-development-yoon-doctrine?amp.
100 Clint Work, "The Tensions Within South Korea's Indo-Pacific Strategy," US-Korea Economic Institute, December 7, 2022, https://keia.org/the-peninsula/the-tensions-within-south-koreas-indo-pacific-strategy/.

INDEX

Abe Shinzo, death of 151, 166–67; proactive policy 8, 28; revisionism 34–35, 38, 40, 42, 49–52; seventieth anniversary speech 38
ASEAN 86, 136
Asian Infrastructure Investment Bank (AIIB) 39, 50, 75
AUKUS 137, 159
Australia 80, 144

balancer 1–2, 12–13, 29, 34, 42, 78; and Yoon 143, 162–63, 170
Ban Ki-moon 18
Belt and Road Initiative (BRI) 29, 149
Biden, Joe, summits with Asian leaders 118, 129, 135–36, 142–46
bipolarity 13, 37, 40, 128–30, 136–37, 141
Bolton, John 5, 61–62, 82
Bush, George W. 40, 47, 107

candlelight movement 12, 70, 73, 90, 98, 109
chaebol 3, 141
China, mutual respect with 10, 144, 148–49, 152, trust-building with 7, 29
China-Japan-Korea (CJK) summit 85, 164
"comfort women" 38–39, 51, 96–98, 140, 150; agreement 11–12, 53, 70, 72, 79–80, 90; backtracking on agreement 9, 73–74, 81, 86, 101–3
COVID-19 113–17, 122, 129–35, 142–43, 156, 161–62

democratization 7, 13, 70, 136
diplomatic diversification 13, 40, 71, 145
Dokdo (Takeshima) 42, 51–52, 140, 166, 168
Dresden Declaration 20–21, 35

East China Sea 130
Eastern Economic Forum 78–79, 86
economic security 10, 13, 129–30, 140–48, 152
"end of war" declaration 5, 10, 83, 86, 105, 131
Eurasian diplomacy 7–8, 28, 33, 36, 75, 79, 87, 96
extended deterrence 6, 37, 45, 118, 123; credibility of 46, 141

family reunions 19–21, 24, 45, 64, 103, 105
forced labor issue 9, 86, 101–3, 134; and Yoon 140, 150–52, 164–65
"Free and Open Indo-Pacific" (FOIP) 12, 83, 129, 150
"freedom of navigation" 38, 129, 144, 164

General Security of Military Information Agreement (GSOMIA) 71–72, 81, 86–87, 90–93, 97–98, 132; and Yoon 150
global pivotal state 13, 140

Hanoi Summit 3, 5, 9, 56–57, 61, 83–84; failure of 64–65, 84–85, 108, 111, 122
high-tech decoupling 128–30, 136, 146

Hong Kong 132, 138, 142, 147, 164
human rights 10, 22, 74–75, 81, 94, 129, 132–35; and trade 141; and Yoon 144–47, 157–58, 164, 169
humanitarian assistance 16–17, 19–20, 38, 44, 65, 116, 118

impeachment 3–4, 57–59, 70–73, 77, 90, 98
India 80, 86, 140, 144
Indo-Pacific Economic Framework (IPEF) 129, 142–43, 146–48
Indo-Pacific regionalism 10, 12, 75, 77, 135–38; and Yoon 141, 146–47, 152, 160
Indo-Pacific Strategy of Korea 142, 144, 148, 168–69
Inflation Reduction Act 166

Jang Song-taek 19, 32, 42–44
Japan, export controls of 86–87, 101, 134, 150, 164–65; militarism of 32, 94
Joint Comprehensive Plan of Action (JCPOA) 47

Kaesong Industrial Complex (KIC) 16–19, 25, 44, 83, 105, 108, 112; closing of 4, 8, 45, 57–58, 70, 92–93, 114
Kaesong (inter-Korean) liaison office 5, 63–64, 83, 114
Kim Dae-jung 16, 18, 40
Kim Jong-un, first-use nuclear doctrine 6, 119–20
Kishida Fumio, defense spending 6, 121, 168
Korean War 24, 64, 138; end of 15, 17, 133
Korean Wave 133
KORUS FTA 74, 82, 167

Lee Myung-bak 2, 15–16, 18, 30, 40, 48, 52, 91, 98

middle power, potential of 6, 30, 36; significance of 2, 50, 135, 137
Mount Geumgang 19, 64, 105, 112

New Northern Policy 9, 74, 79, 87, 137, 146
New Southern Policy 86, 140, 146
Non-Proliferation Treaty (NPT) 46
North Korea, attacks by 15–16, 23–24, 40, 113; cyberattacks of 17

Northeast Asia Peace and Cooperation Initiative (NAPCI) 8, 10, 28, 30, 34–37, 44, 75, 96
Northern Limit Line (NLL) 62

Obama, Barack, rebalance (pivot) to Asia 8, 10, 28–30, 33–39
OPCON transfer 46–48, 53
Osaka G20 summit 83, 85, 87

Panmunjom Declaration 6, 62–63, 82, 105, 116, 147
Putin, Vladimir, "Turn to the East" 8, 28, 79; summits with 19, 29, 65
Pyeongchang Winter Olympics 4–5, 60–61, 81–82, 102–7
Pyongyang Declaration 105–6

Quad 10, 132, 135–38; and Yoon 142–43, 147, 160–61

reunification, as central task 2, 7, 13, 40; as jackpot 4, 20, 32, 38
Roh Moo-hyun 1, 16, 18, 31, 47–48
Russia, peripheral role of 7, 83, 86

semiconductors 128–29, 135–36, 143, 148–49, 163
Senkaku Islands 38
Seoul Olympics 13, 70
Singapore Joint Declaration 6, 64, 82, 108, 116, 147
Singapore Summit 56, 61, 63, 83, 105, 108, 112
Sino-Russian relations 40, 69–70, 86, 129, 141, 145
Six-Party Talks 30, 33–37, 40, 47, 50, 76
South China Sea 10, 38, 70, 77, 130, 136, 144; court ruling on 71
South Korea, nuclear option 12–13, 46–47, 53, 93–95, 104–6, 109, 121, 167
Southeast Asia 34, 86, 140
Summit for Democracy 137, 160–61
Sunshine Policy 6, 11, 42, 66, 111
supply chains 3, 132–35, 139, 146–49; and Yoon 10, 142, 144, 150, 162–63, 168

Taiwan 10, 129–30, 136, 142–51
Terminal High-Altitude Area Defense (THAAD) 50, 109, 141, 147; additional

launchers 118; deployment of 4, 8, 29, 34–39, 57–60, 66, 90–91, 96–101; pressure over 2, 9, 12, 70–72, 75–77, 82, 100, 133, 139
three no's 2, 4, 9, 12, 57, 77–78, 99–101, 107–09, 130, 148
trade war 72, 82, 84–85, 87, 128, 130, 136
Trans-Pacific Partnership (TPP) 33, 39, 75, 142
trilateral security 38, 71–72, 79–80, 91, 93, 129, 132; and Yoon 142–43, 150
Trump, Donald, "America First" 12, 93, 96, 106–9, 167; "fire and fury" 4–5, 56–57, 60, 65–66, 70, 74–75, 90, 104; illusions of 9, 73, 94–95; squeezing Seoul 9, 75, 78, 81, 84, 131, 159
trustpolitik 42–43, 75, 90; aim of 8, 11, 15–20, 28–29; failure of 12, 57, 66, 92–94; launch of 4, 44–45

Ukraine War 3, 10, 122, 150–52; impact on South Korea 6, 111, 128, 130, 140, 143–46
United Nations Security Council resolutions 17, 57–58, 70, 75, 79–80, 145, 147
Uyghurs (Xinjiang) 132, 138–39, 147, 164

values-based alliance 10, 13, 34–35, 38, 45, 129, 132; and Yoon 143–44, 147, 150, 162–64, 169
Vietnam 65

"wolf warrior" belligerence 70, 73, 77, 138
World War II Victory Day commemoration 24–26, 29, 33, 37, 48–50, 57, 75, 91, 96

Xi Jinping, honeymoon with 2, 18, 22, 28, 57, 75, 87

Yasukuni Shrine 11, 35, 42, 51–53, 166

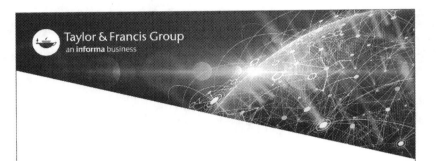

Printed in the United States
by Baker & Taylor Publisher Services